IMAGES
of America

ALONG THE KANAWHA RIVER

On the Cover: As a project being administered under the National Industrial Recovery Administration Act, the construction of the Winfield Locks and Dam was extensively documented by photographers sent to Putnam County. Shown here are PWA workers guiding the concrete bucket into place for pouring into fabricated molds on top of one of the roller gate piers. (Courtesy of Army Corps of Engineers.)

IMAGES
of America

ALONG THE KANAWHA RIVER

Joseph M. Phillips

ARCADIA
PUBLISHING

ISBN 978-0-7385-9945-8

Published by Arcadia Publishing
Charleston, South Carolina

Printed in the United States of America

Library of Congress Control Number: 2013930466

For all general information, please contact Arcadia Publishing:
Telephone 843-853-2070
Fax 843-853-0044
E-mail sales@arcadiapublishing.com
For customer service and orders:
Toll-Free 1-888-313-2665

Visit us on the Internet at www.arcadiapublishing.com

To William A. Frassanito, who taught me to study photographs, and to the residents of Putnam County, West Virginia, for sharing their history

Contents

ACKNOWLEDGMENTS

I must extend my appreciation to everyone who aided me in the completion of this book, whether it was through the contribution of time, photographs, historical background, or family stories. Compiling a pictorial history of a county in West Virginia was at times daunting for a boy born north of the Mason-Dixon Line, but several individuals and organizations helped to bridge the difficulties, with the results found in the following pages.

My deepest thanks go to my coworkers and colleagues in Rivers to Ridges Heritage Trail. Lowell Wilks provided invaluable motivation, assistance, and even entertainment during the long process of bringing together the various sources in this book. Chris Gress provided needed expertise on Winfield Locks and Dam, while Rich Hively likewise shared his extensive knowledge of Nitro's history. Leah Higgenbotham, Jim Caruthers, Freeda Young, and Mark Harris were kind enough to share with me their photographs and knowledge of the area's past. Community members such as Richard Savilla, Dr. Sam Sentelle, and Ronnie Matthews graciously shared books and journals on Putnam County's history. This book would have been impossible had it not been for the decades of historical research and compilation of sources by William D. Wintz and the Upper Vandalia Historical Society, whose members have been willing to "talk history" with me when needed.

Finally, I must thank Tom Grubbs for being a constant source of inspiration and Jamie Blake for always being there, even when I didn't quite know why.

Introduction

It is difficult to imagine Putnam County, West Virginia, without the Kanawha River. The waterway descends from Fayette County, West Virginia, flows through Charleston, West Virginia, and eventually empties into the Ohio River at Point Pleasant, West Virginia. On its way to the Ohio, it cuts a defining route through Putnam County. Man has constructed several towns along the river's course through the county, some of which predate even the formation of Putnam County and the independence of the state of West Virginia. For hundreds of years, man has called the shores of the Kanawha home. Of these many towns and villages that border the water's edge, no two share identical characteristics or histories. Though their details are diverse, they share a common geographic trait; they are *Along the Kanawha.*

Prior to European settlement of the region, a succession of prehistoric American peoples inhabited the Kanawha River Valley. Around A.D. 1300, inhabitants in the region established large villages along the river, such as a settlement near present-day Buffalo. By the end of the 17th century, it is likely that these communities had been displaced from the region due to military excursions into the area by the Iroquois Confederated Nations. The origin of the name "Kanawha" is itself shrouded in uncertainty. Many theories have been advanced, but the name appears to have most likely come from the Algonquian language family. *Keninshekacepe*, being a Delaware word for the river, and *kenhawie*, being a Shawnee word for "long," point toward a possible origin. Two other early names for the river, Chinodaista and Mondongachate, may have their origins in the Iroquoian language family.

European settlers traversed the Kanawha River Valley sporadically throughout the 17th and 18th centuries. However, it was not until 1837 that Putnam County's oldest chartered town came into existence. Most likely named after the nearby Big Buffalo Creek, the town of Buffalo was from its beginnings inextricably tied to the river. A large portion of the town's inhabitants earned a living as captains and crewmen aboard river vessels that plied the length of the Kanawha and Ohio Rivers. Subsequent growth from river trade allowed for the founding of the Buffalo Academy in 1849. Offering a liberal education that was unrivaled in the region, the school thrived until the Civil War, when occupation by both Federal and Confederate armies resulted in extensive damage that closed the building and led to its transfer of ownership to the county board of education.

Buffalo was not alone in its 19th-century development along the Kanawha. Around 1818, a man named Charles Brown began operating a ferry along the Kanawha, just over 25 miles downstream of Charleston. In the years that followed, a hamlet began to grow on the south side of the river near the ferry crossing, so that in 1848, when Putnam County was created from portions of Cabell, Mason, and Kanawha Counties, the first county court was established nearby due to the area's central location within the county and its proximity to the river. The town took on the name Winfield, in honor of the popular American military general Winfield Scott, who had filled newspaper headlines during the Mexican-American War of 1846–1848. Officially incorporated in 1868, the town is to this day the county seat.

Upon the dawn of the 20th century, settlement along the Kanawha had yet to cease. Upon the United States' entrance into World War I in 1917, it became obvious to the War Department that the nation sorely lacked crucial production capacity of critical war supplies, such as gunpowder. In October 1917, Congress authorized the creation of three large explosives plants, the first of which was constructed along the Kanawha River, 15 miles outside of Charleston. Construction began in 1918, with the new settlement taking the name Nitro, after nitrocellulose—a key ingredient in explosives. The site for the new industrial city was chosen largely due to its location along the Kanawha, where barges and riverboats could readily deliver and pick up supplies at hastily constructed docks. In 11 months, nearly 2,000 acres of farm fields turned into a bustling ordnance-supply town. Upon the close of the war in 1918, plans began for the "industrial city" to be sold off to private entities. In the coming years and decades, corporations such as Nitro Pencil Company, American Viscose Company, and Monsanta Chemical came to utilize the town's manufacturing capacities.

The economic growth of Nitro in the 1920s segued into conversely harsh economic conditions a decade later with the beginning of the Great Depression in October 1929. Five years later, with Franklin D. Roosevelt in the White House, plans went into motion to create three subsistence homestead communities in West Virginia. One was to be located along the Kanawha River in Putnam County with the name Red House Farms. The first lady, Eleanor Roosevelt, was a vocal supporter of these three New Deal settlements; consequently, as a show of appreciation, sometime around 1935 the name of the town was changed to Eleanor. Originally, around 150 families settled upon over 2,000 acres of land that had once belonged to George Washington. Residents of the town farmed the fertile fields of the Kanawha River Valley, labored in dairy farming, and engaged in various other wage-labor tasks, such as rock quarrying. In the mid-1940s, the residents who remained in the homestead project were given the opportunity to purchase their homes and property, which ensured the longevity and permanence of the town of Eleanor along the Kanawha.

While Eleanor found its beginnings in the 1930s, the nearby town of Winfield also witnessed great changes. In 1933, plans were initiated to begin construction of a large locks and dam project on the Kanawha just a short distance outside of town. Implemented in conjunction with two other locks and dams farther up the river, as well as a site on the Ohio River, the construction of Winfield Locks and Dam provided much-welcomed labor to Depression-era residents of the surrounding region.

These river towns located along the Kanawha continue to grow and to evolve. In the life of Putnam County, this work stands merely as an early childhood photo album—chronicling the area's early years of life while the area continues to move into a future of change.

One

BUFFALO
THE FIRST RIVER TOWN

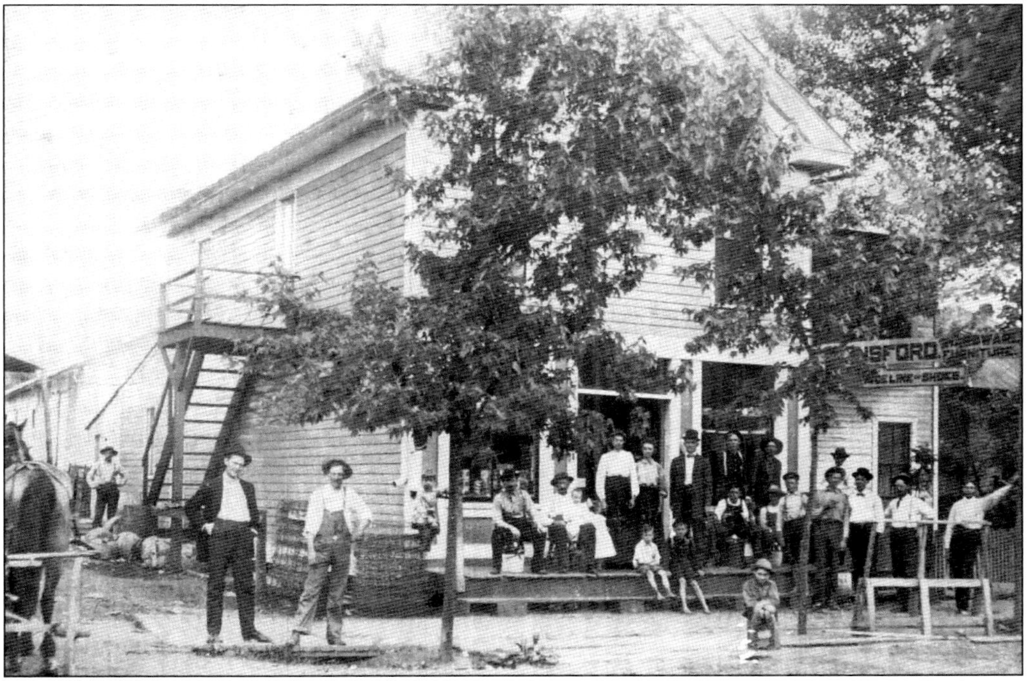

Around 1900, the Lundsford General Store in Buffalo sold hardware and furniture as well as a "nice line of shoes." Items for sale were sold both within the store and on the front porch—the rolls of fencing wire being very prominent to the left of the porch. This photograph was probably taken to mark the grand opening of the store. (Courtesy of Putnam County Historic Landmark Commission.)

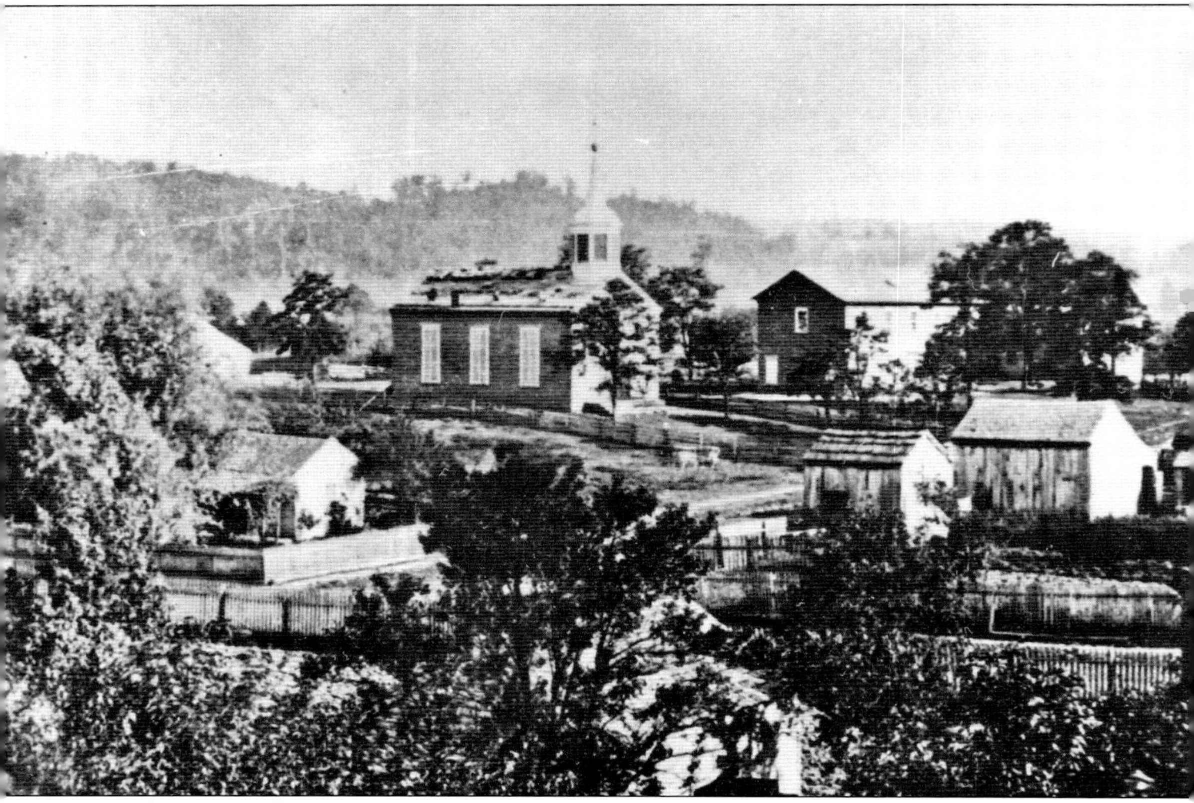

In the 1840s and 1850s, a growing number amongst the Presbyterians in the area of Buffalo petitioned the denomination's governing body in Greenbrier for permission to form a congregation and erect a church. Permission was granted in 1856, and the new church building was dedicated in 1857. The building required a new roof roughly 15 years later, as evidenced in this view. The structure still contains the slave gallery from its pre–Civil War days. Note that the Buffalo Academy is clearly visible directly to the right of the church. (Courtesy of West Virginia State Archives.)

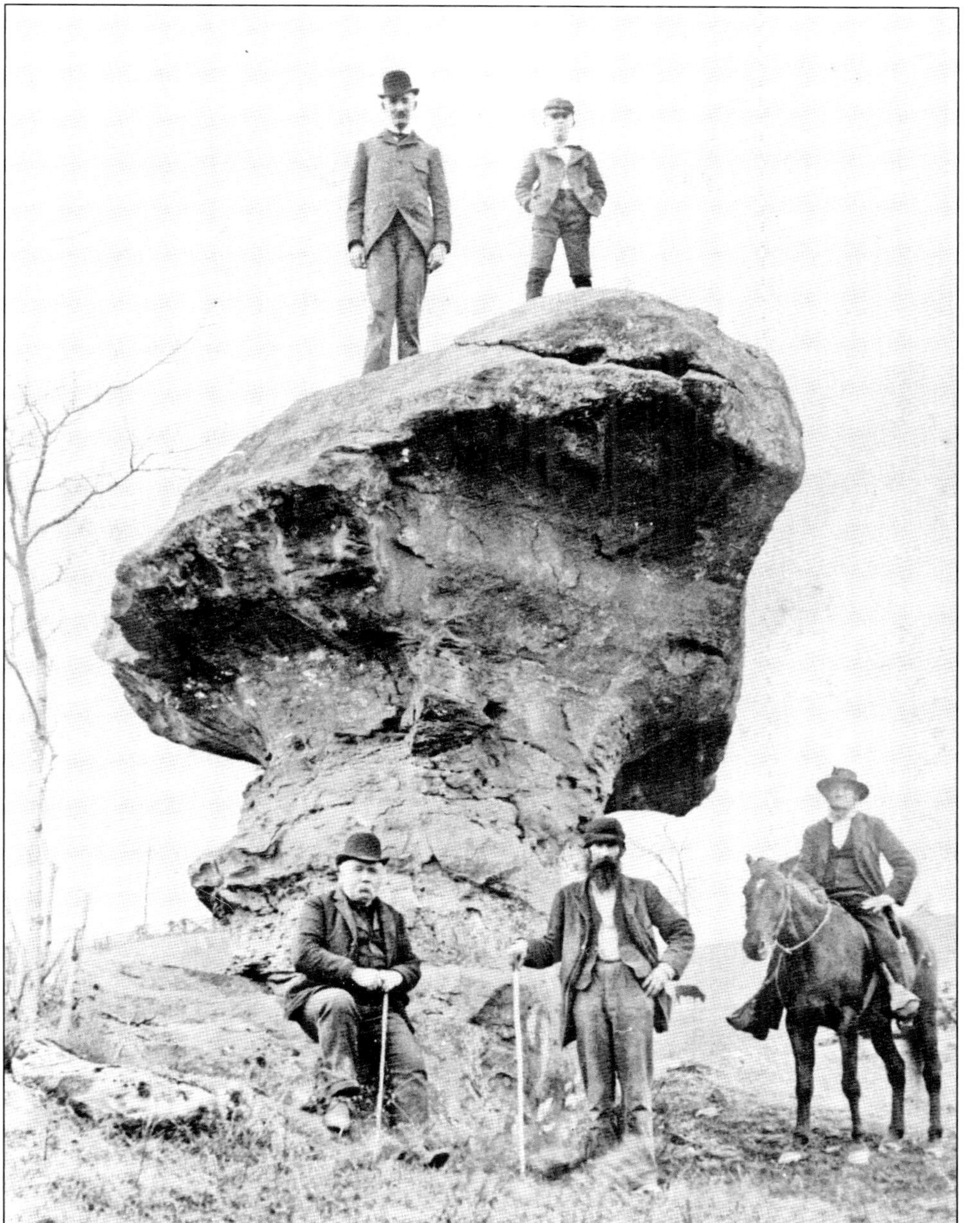

Located several miles east of Buffalo on a large, rocky ridge stands a huge geologic formation that has captured the attention of area residents for hundreds of years. Often referred to by locals as the "Devil's Tea Table," this gigantic, mushroom shaped example of erosive power has often been the subject of photographs by curious visitors. This view is one of the earliest known images of the rock structure. Seated and holding the walking cane with both hands is Squire J.H. Collins of Buffalo in the late 1800s. During the Civil War, Collins was a member of the Union 12th Ohio Volunteer Infantry Regiment, and he saw action at the Battle of Scary Creek, just 20 miles up the Kanawha River near present-day Nitro. After the war, Collins became a justice of the peace and was a board member of local Grange organizations. (Courtesy of Mark Harris.)

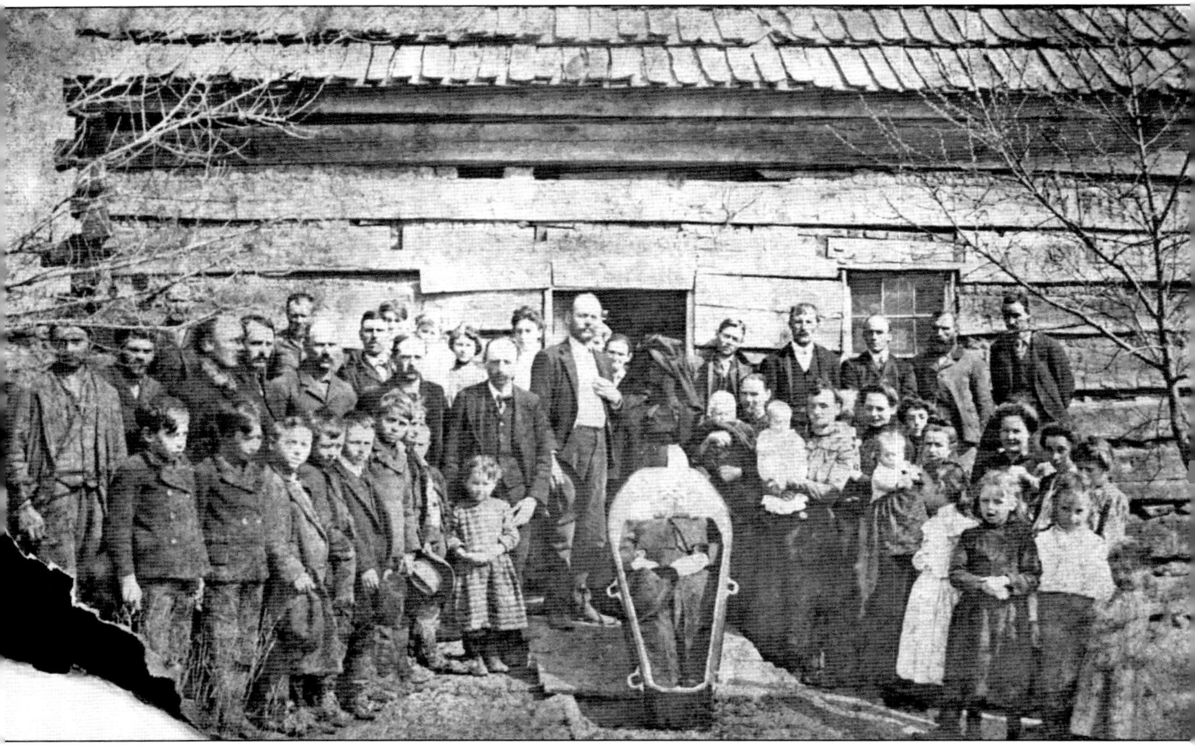

Born probably around 1835, Hezekiah Young lived much of his early life in Wetzel County, West Virginia. It was there that he married his wife and his first son was born. In the 1870s, Young moved with his wife and family down the Ohio River into Mason County. In 1885, he bought land near Fraziers Bottom in Putnam County and later expanded his real estate holdings into land surrounding Buffalo, including tracts on the hills above the town. In many ways, Hezekiah Young represented many of the area's residents for the time period, in that he was a farmer for all of his adult life. On April 4, 1904, he passed away as a result of heart disease. Members of the community, friends, and family members gathered for this photograph around the casket of Hezekiah. He was then buried near Fraziers Bottom in Evergreen Cemetery. (Courtesy of West Virginia State Archives.)

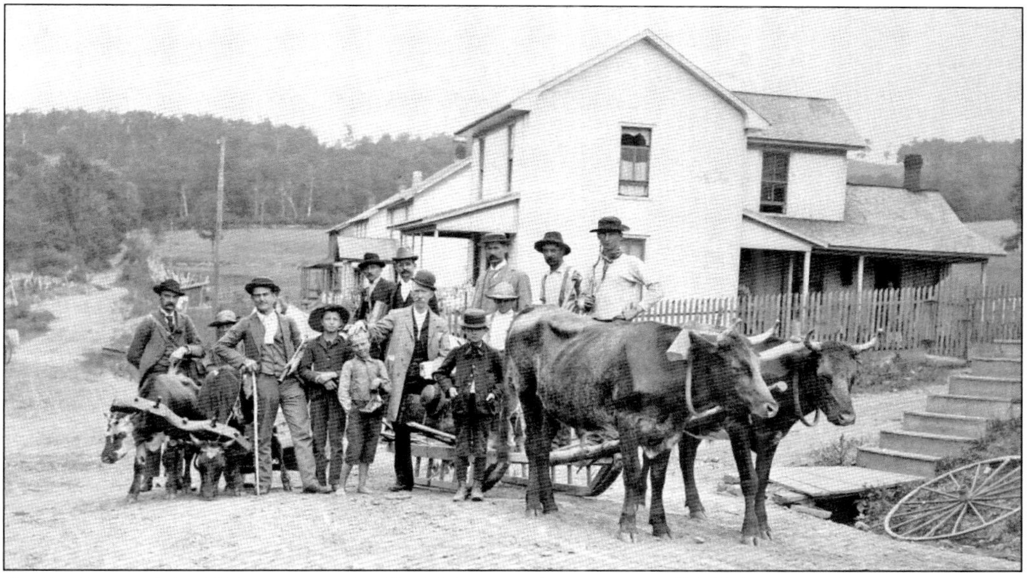

At the dawn of the 20th century, the Nash Farm, in the vicinity of Buffalo, was rather representative of one aspect of the economy of the surrounding region. While the state of West Virginia is best known for its mountains and rugged terrain, the Kanawha River Valley provides fertile, gently sloping ground on which farming has long been well adapted. Farmers in this region, though always producing at least enough food for subsistence, would have relied upon the Kanawha River to transport some of their produce to larger markets, either on the Ohio River or farther up the Kanawha in Charleston. By the 1900s, the railroad, which had come to the region, offered an even faster mode of transporting farm goods. Shown here are members of the farming family and farm workers gathering around some of the farm's livestock and wagons around 1905. (Courtesy of West Virginia State Archives.)

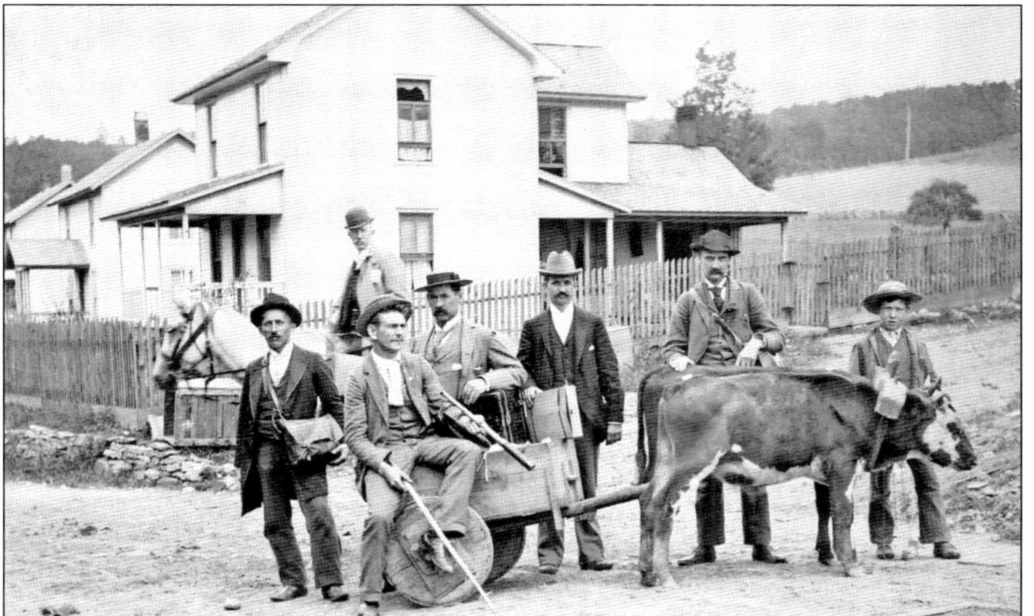

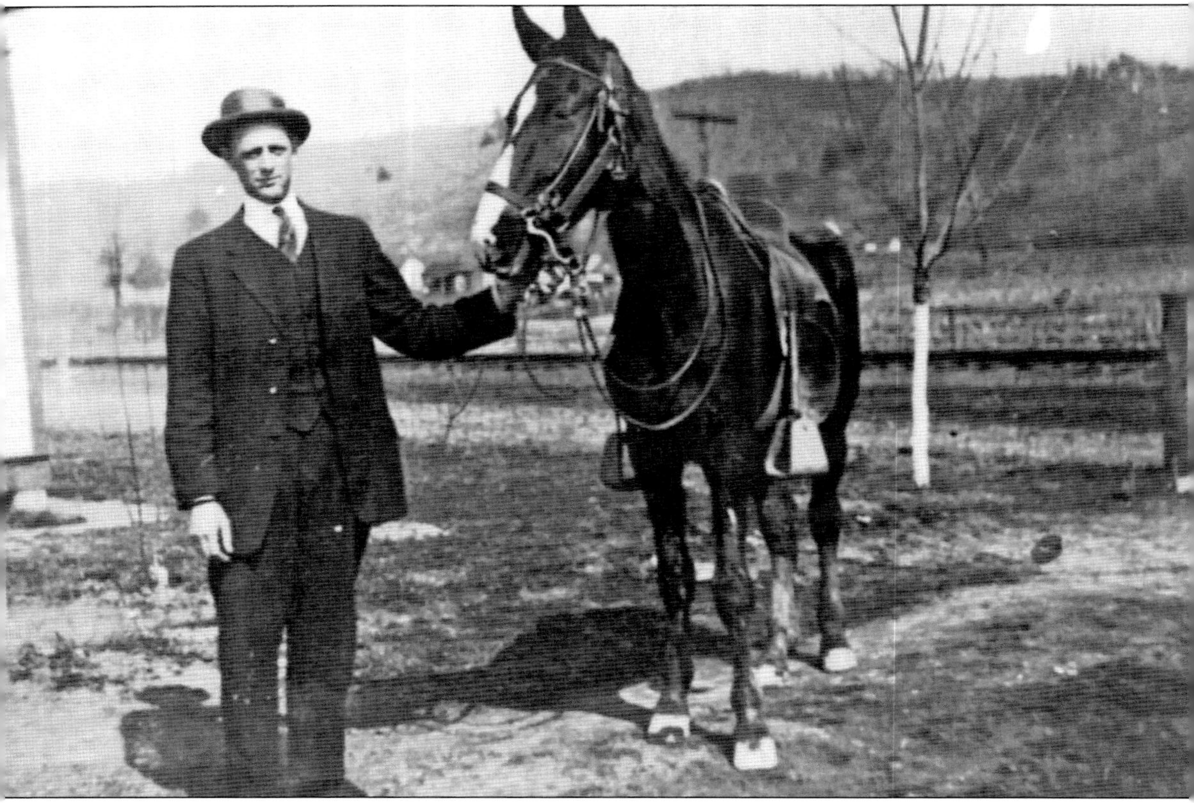

Dentist J.E. McComb stands with his horse at the Buffalo Depot around the year 1900. Being a sizable river town, Buffalo contained enough residents to allow for a multitude of businesses and services. In its heyday, Buffalo was truly a workingman's town that contained much of the many amenities expected of small towns at the time. For years, G.L. Hulbert's store on Route 35 provided Buffalo and the entire surrounding region with an expansive range of goods and merchandise. Additionally, hardware and general merchandise stores were staples of the town's services. By the late 20th century, however, economic demands for such localized businesses began to wane, with residents able to travel by automobile to larger locations in surrounding towns and cities. Interestingly, J.E. McComb was one of the first residents in Buffalo to be able to afford the purchase of an early automobile. In 1910, he bought a Maxwell Roadster. (Courtesy of Mark Harris.)

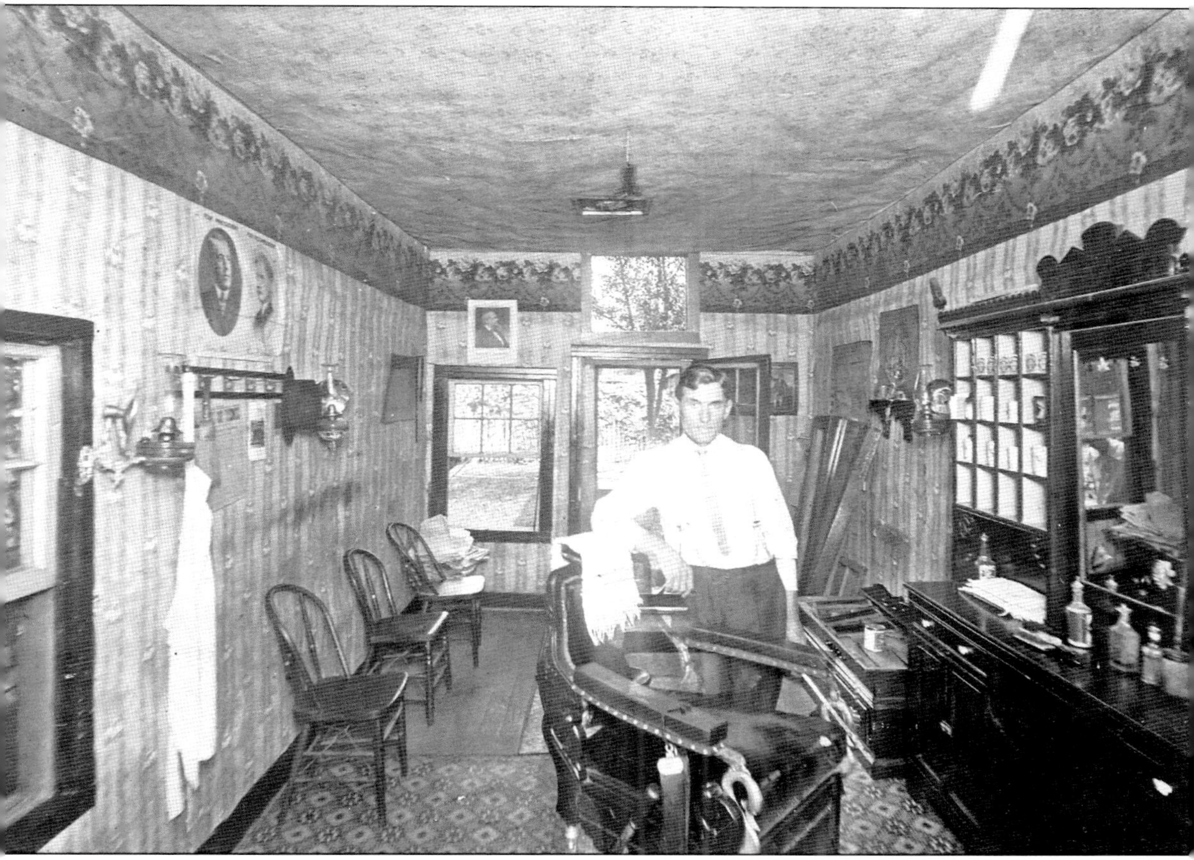

Male residents of town no doubt would have been quite familiar with the view of barber Charlie Holstein in his shop south of the modern-day Buffalo historic district. The barbershop served its obvious purpose of providing area men with hairdressing services, but the business was also a local hub of information. As male residents visited Holstein's shop every couple of weeks, the news and stories of the times were shared amongst those present. Though no exact date for this image is known, clues are available, such as the poster on the left-hand wall that says "For President" with a portrait of Woodrow Wilson, which points towards a date of either 1912 or 1916—both years in which Wilson was campaigning for president. In the 1912 election, Wilson ultimately won Republican West Virginia's eight electoral votes with 42 percent of the vote. (Courtesy of Leah Higginbotham.)

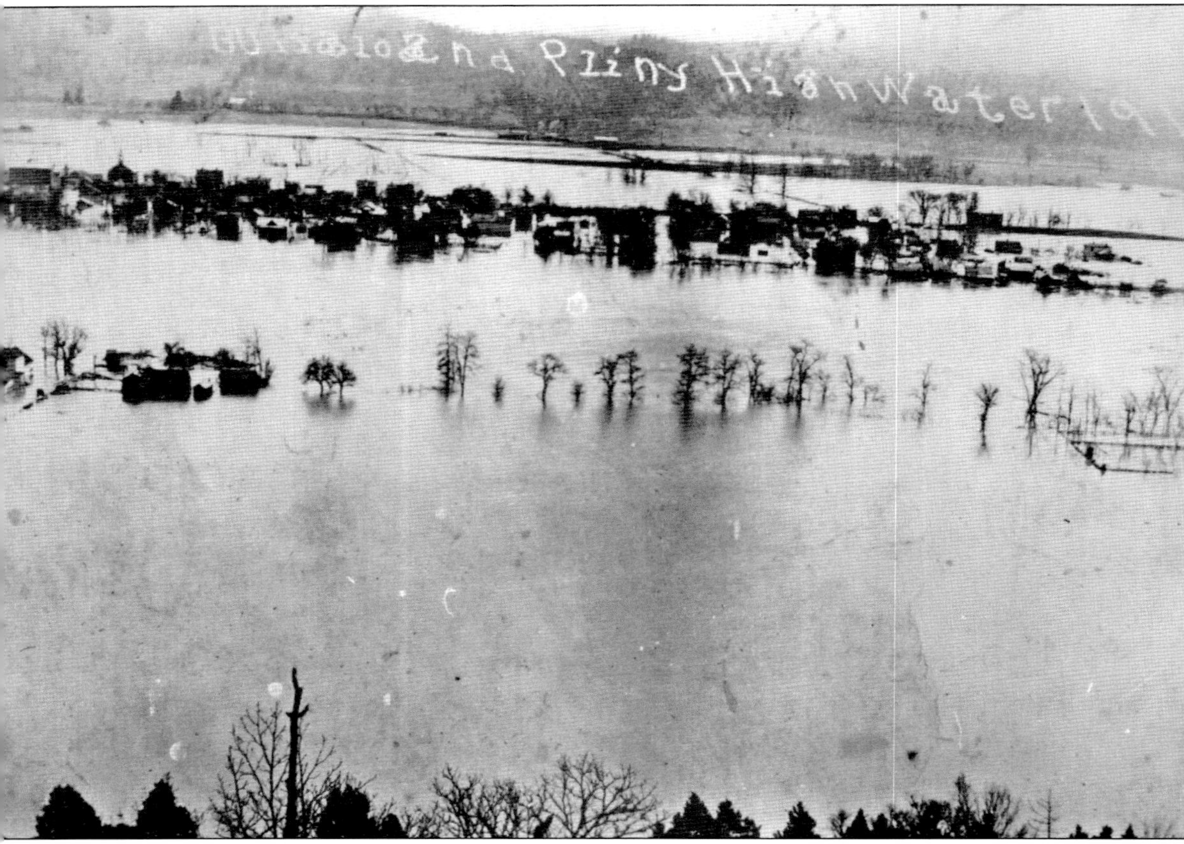

The first few months of the year 1913 brought instances of horrific natural disasters to Putnam County and the entire Kanawha River Valley, from Point Pleasant in Mason County to Charleston in Kanawha County. Two devastating floods occurred in a rather short period of time—first in January, then in March. Warmer temperatures in early March led to rapid melting of snow and ice in the region, which drained into the Ohio and Kanawha Rivers. As a result, when a heavy rainstorm settled over the area and dropped between 10 and 15 inches of rain on Easter Sunday, March 23, 1913, the ground, already saturated by snowmelt, could not handle these extreme precipitation totals, and the banks of the Ohio and Kanawha quickly overflowed their banks. This photograph, taken from the small town of Pliny, shows the floodwater engulfing the town of Buffalo. (Courtesy of Mark Harris.)

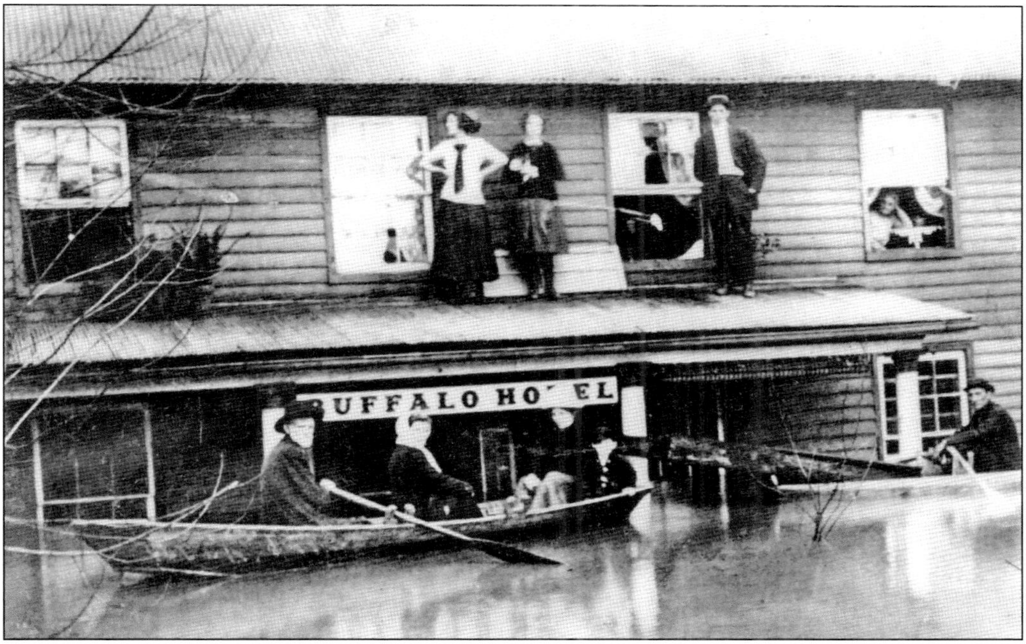

Shown above, residents of Buffalo huddled atop the front porch of the Buffalo Hotel to await rescue by boat during the height of the 1913 flood. The 1913 storm was surpassed almost a quarter-century later when another winter storm wreaked havoc on the Kanawha River Valley and nearby Ohio River. For over two weeks, daily precipitation and warmer weather led to a record-setting flood near the end of January along the Kanawha River. By January 24, 1913, the Ohio River flow had become stationary, which further contributed to high levels back up the Kanawha. At places along the waterway, water reached anywhere from 10 to 20 feet over flood levels. Floodwaters were notably high along US Route 35 (modern day Route 62) through the center of town (below). The round Esso station sign near the Buffalo Academy is visible in the distance. (Both, courtesy of Mark Harris.)

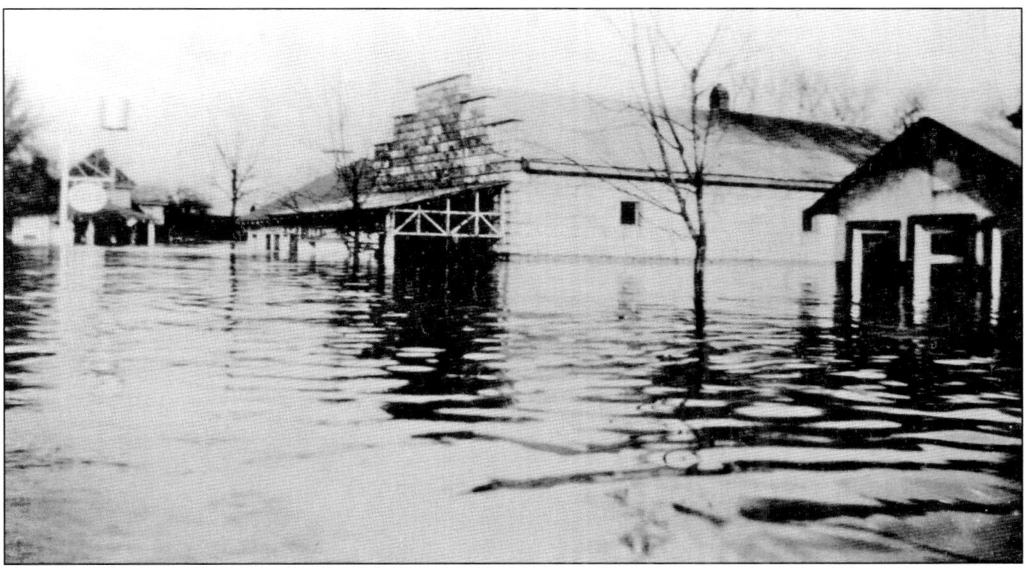

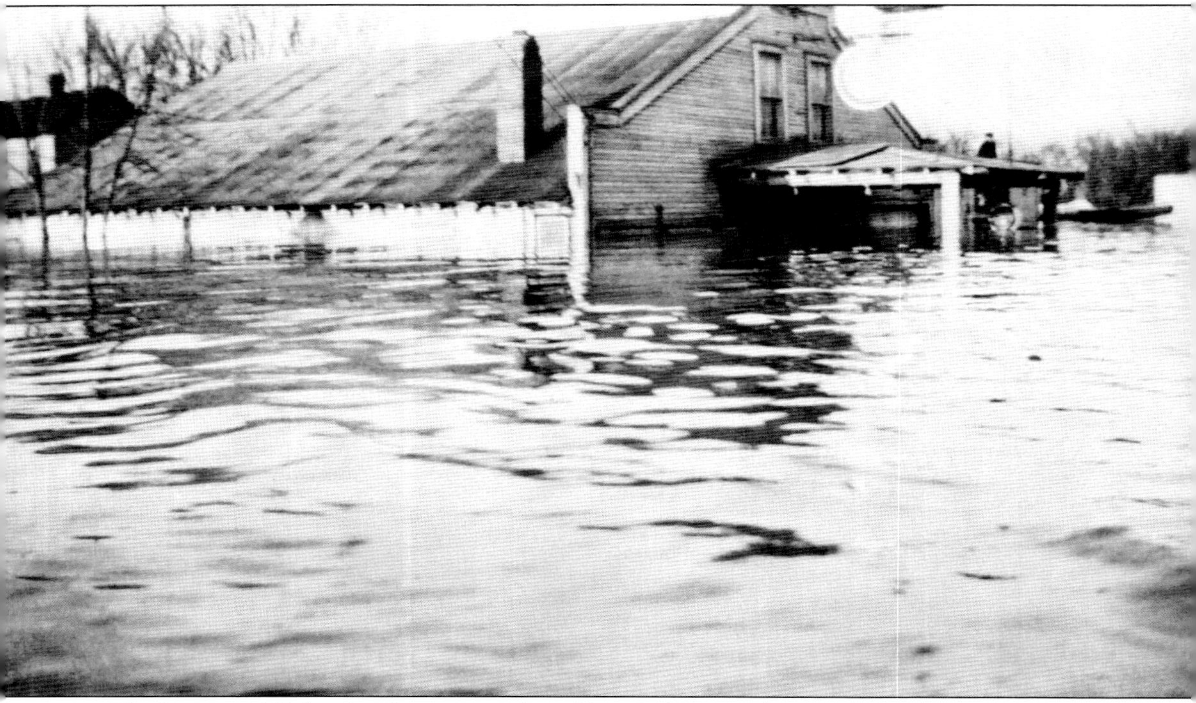

The January 1937 flooding hit states such as Ohio, Indiana, and Kentucky much more significantly than the interior of West Virginia along the Kanawha River. Perhaps the deadliest aspect of the natural event was that the prolonged rainstorms that began inundating the region in early January created a sense of complacency amongst residents, who were later surprised when floodwaters suddenly began cresting later in the month. These structures, located along US Route 35 in Buffalo, were visibly submerged through the entirety of the first floor, if not even higher. The height of the water, as well as the long duration of time before it receded, guaranteed severe damages to personal and commercial property as well as to lost productivity. Many of the buildings along the floodplain were built mostly of wood and were almost completely destroyed by the waters and by the impact of flood debris cascading down the river. (Courtesy of West Virginia State Archives.)

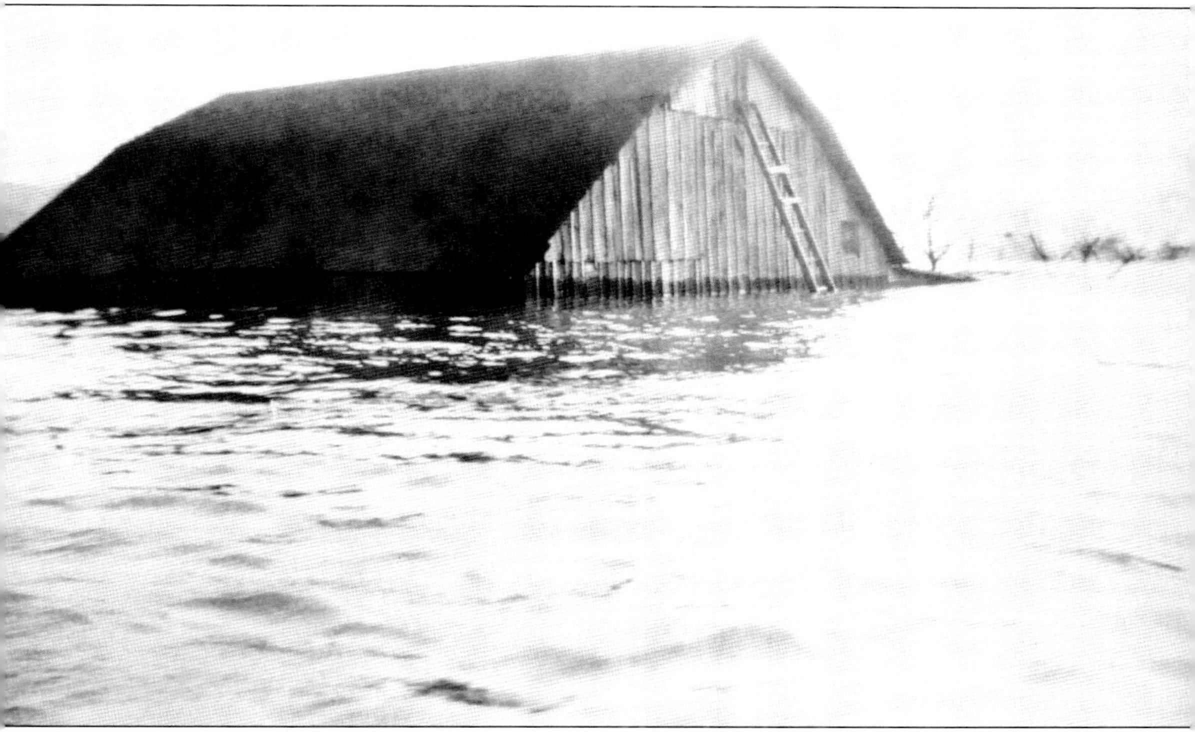

Flooding in the Ohio and Kanawha River Valleys had always been an immediate problem, and sometimes a deadly nuisance, dating all the way back to the earliest settlers to the region. The nearby town of Hurricane, West Virginia, probably got its name from the remnants of flood and wind-strewn trees that were discovered in the area when early travelers passed through. During much of the year, the Kanawha River was not especially deep—during especially dry times it could be traversed on foot in some places. However, when sudden rainstorms engulfed the valley, the Kanawha, along with its Ohio River neighbor, could suddenly become a raging torrent. When the flooding ended in 1937, over $20 million worth of damage had been done, or as high as $800 million in today's dollar. Official water levels recorded at nearby Huntington showed a peak of almost 70 feet, nearly 20 feet over the flood stage. (Courtesy of West Virginia State Archives.)

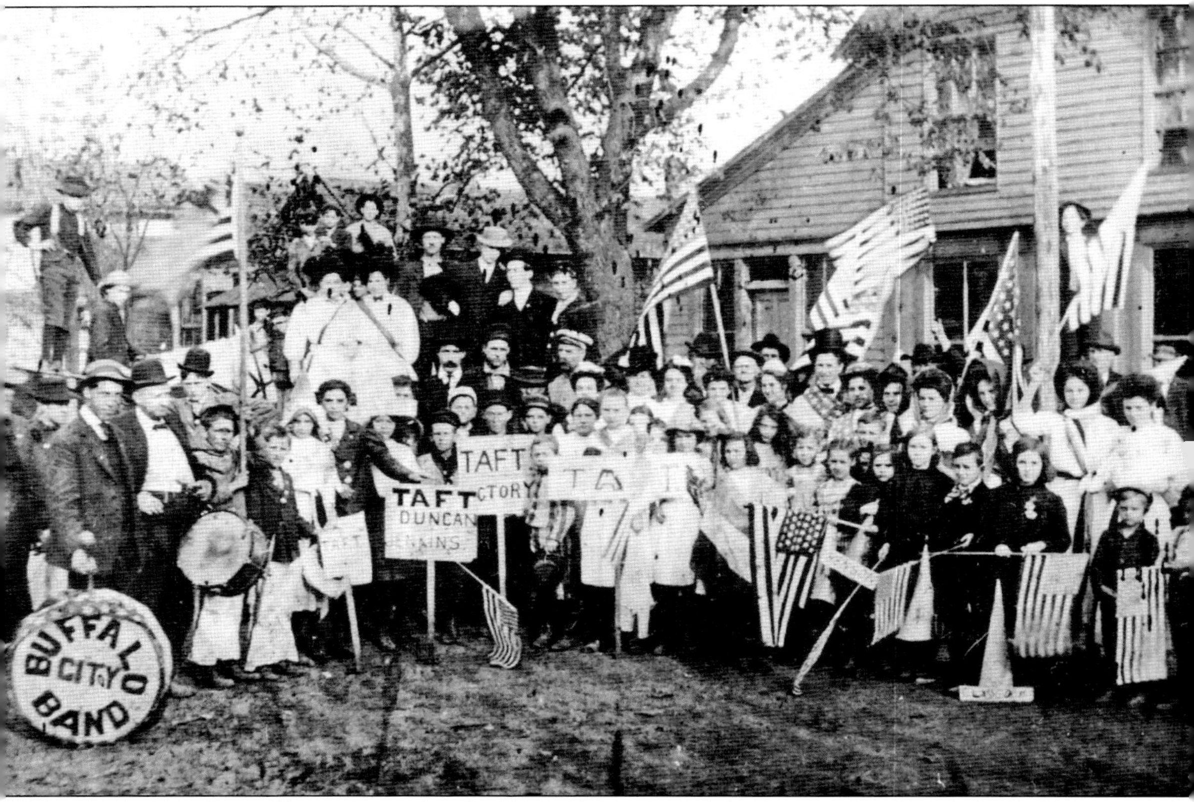

Support for William Howard Taft during the 1912 presidential campaign was quite prevalent in Buffalo, West Virginia. Sometime during late summer or early fall of that year, the Buffalo City Band and local supporters of the Republican candidate gathered for a rally to show their enthusiasm for Taft. Taft was running for his second term on a rather progressive, labor-friendly platform. Four years earlier, the majority of Putnam County's and of West Virginia's voters supported Taft; however, in 1912, former president Teddy Roosevelt entered the race and fragmented the Republican vote. As a result, West Virginia's electoral votes went to Democrat Woodrow Wilson. (Courtesy of Buffalo Historical Society.)

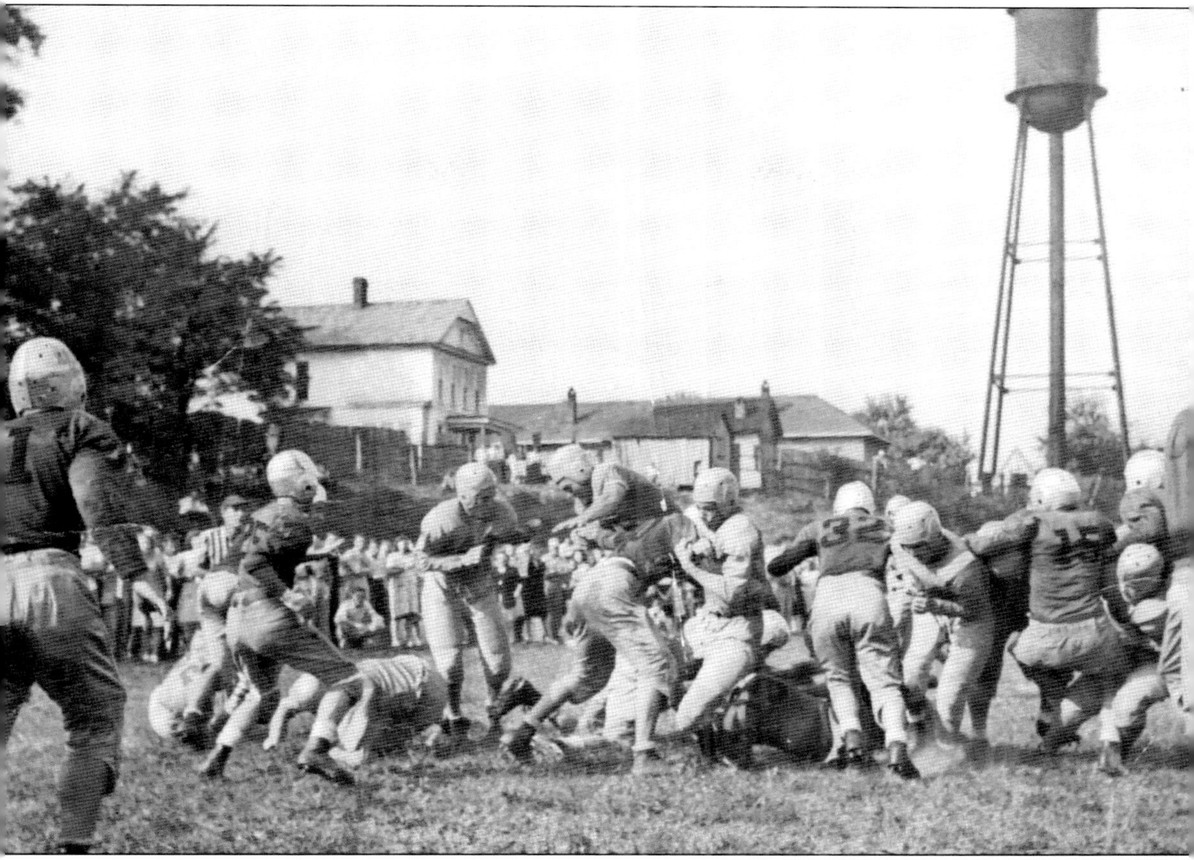

Shown here is a Buffalo High School football game played in 1946 on an athletic field that occupied ground behind the Buffalo Academy in the center of town. The opposing team was Nitro High School. With the growth of towns up and down the Kanawha River in Putnam, Mason, and Kanawha Counties, it was not uncommon by the 1940s and 1950s to have school sports teams from that wide of a region traveling to different schools for sporting events. This particular game ended with a Buffalo victory of 14 points over Nitro's 0, after most of the hard-fought game unfolded with no points on the scoreboard. Sports teams in Buffalo extended beyond the prominent high school organizations and included teams for elementary and middle school aged youth in football, baseball, and basketball as well as marching bands and parade organizations for all ages. (Courtesy of Freeda Young.)

HIGH SCHOOL

BUFFALONIAN

To What Height May We Attain When We Learn To See Clearly

BHS WINS THREE OUT OF FIVE FOR HIGHEST COUNTY

V. F. W. Organizes First Putnam County Post At Buffalo

Buffalo was the scene of the organization of the first post in Putnam county of the Veterans of Foreign Wars. The ceremony took place on September 16.

The VFW Post, The Shelton-Dunn Post No. 8369—was named in honor of two local boys—Haymond Shelton and Kearney Dunn—who gave their lives in the service of their country while serving overseas.

The following officers were elected: Commander, A. Harold Cobb; Sr. Vice Commander, S. F. Smith; Jr. Vice Commander, Lewis Rossi; Adjutant, Dale Curtis; Quartermaster, John Frazier; Officer of the Day, Hobert Crump; Guard, Harold H. Cochran; Trustee, Clyde Sergent; Trustee, L. A. Stokes; Trustee, Samuel J. Dunn.

The Veterans of Foreign Wars is an organization for those veterans only who served outside the limits of the continental United States in time of war or emergency and who earned a campaign medal for their service.

The many plans of the veterans include a clubhouse and a membership drive to enroll every Putnam county veteran, who served overseas, as a member.

THE BUFFALO FOOTBALL SQUAD

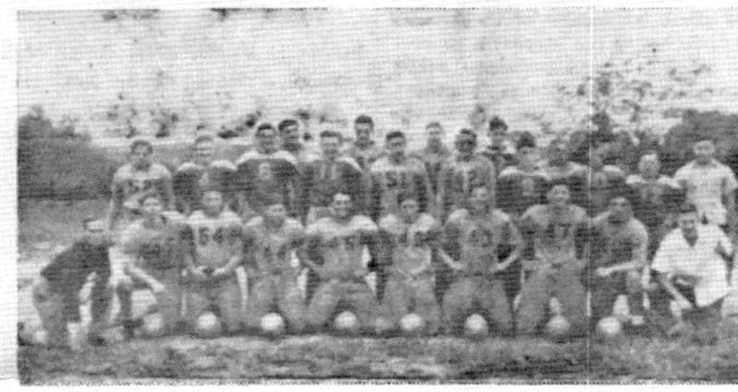

Left to Right, First Row: Coach William Hickman, Robert Rader, Paul Keeling, Blair Young, Harold Cochran, Don Johns, Roma Garrison, Jack Davis, Robert Henson, Frank Davis, Manager. Second Row: Carol Curtis, Kenneth Martin, William Garrison, Cecil Taylor, Edwin Clendenin, Jack Taylor, Donald Marshall, William Tucker, Herman Davis, Leonard Cash, Manager. Third Row: Laurence Davis, Gene Lewis, Joe Hager, William Allender and Jass Taylor.

Ninth Grade Girls Honor Senior Class With Tea On Oct. 9th

Members of the senior class, the faculty, and members of the football team were honored at an afternoon tea given on October 9, by the ninth grade girls.

Approximately sixty people were entertained between the hours of two and four.

The tea is simply another example of the fine progress our students are making as they pursue their studies and their preparation for the functions of life.

Home Economics Students Surprise Faculty With Dinner

The faculty of Buffalo high school was agreeably surprised on October 8 when they were invited to a surprise chicken dinner by home economics students Helen Bays, Joann Davis, Ann Bush, and Betty Wallace.

The table literally groaned with food which was excellently prepared and which rapidly disappeared before the attack by the faculty.

Mrs. Christian is the teacher of the home economics department and if you can judge from the opinions of the male teachers after such a fine dinner, she and her girls are certainly doing a fine job.

BHS SUPPORTS USO DRIVE; SKINNER, SCHOOL CHAIRMAN

Mr. Forrest Skinner, teacher in BHS, has been appointed chairman of the USO Drive to secure funds through the school and its patrons. He would appreciate a

H. D. Knapp Begins 2nd Term as Principal Of High School

Mr. H. D. Knapp, principal of Buffalo high school, is beginning his second term in that position and, as such, he is truly the keynote behind the success of our school. Although a man of many interests, Mr. Knapp is never too busy to help the members of our student body in their many enterprises.

Members of the football team have often expressed their praise of this fine man because of his constant aid in helping to make their many undertakings successful.

If any organization, class, pupil or teacher fails to get due consideration and full cooperation it is probably due to the fact that their plans have not been discussed in detail with Mr. Knapp or that its aims and objectives are not clearly defined. We have always found our principal ready to listen to our

School spirit and district news were conveyed in printed form through the monthly editions of the Buffalo High School newspaper—the *Buffalonian*. The issue shown here is from October 1946 and, not surprisingly, highlights the season's football team on the front page as well as other beginning of the school year news about school events, policies, and announcements and town news. The publication allowed generations of Buffalo High School students to develop and test their journalism talents—publishing stories that went beyond simply area news. This same October issue of the *Buffalonian* includes an article written about American foreign policy in post–World War II Europe amidst the Truman administration's attempts to rebuild the devastated countries. In a town the size of Buffalo, the *Buffalonian* newspaper was, in many ways, on par with area newspapers, including the local newspapers printed by residents of Buffalo itself. (Courtesy of Freeda Young.)

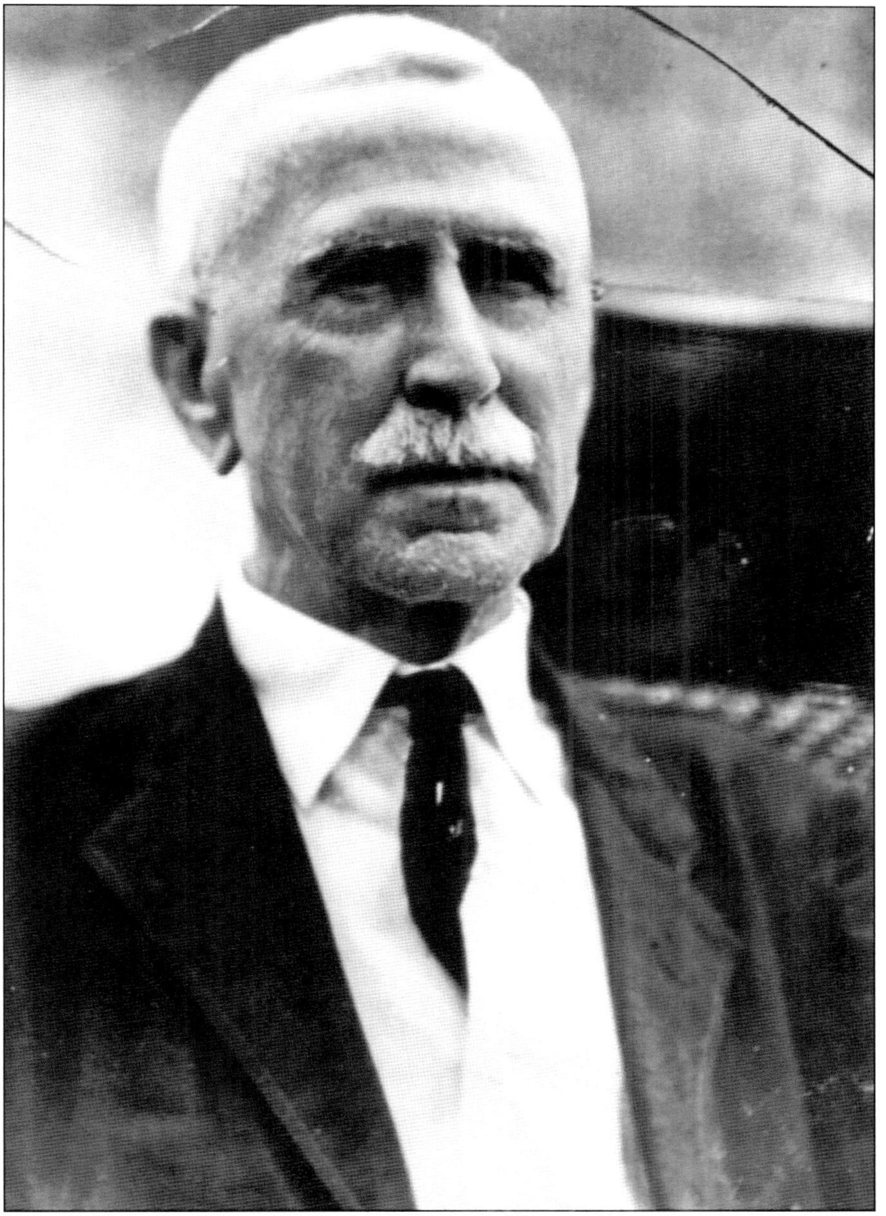

Born on a farm near Buffalo on August 16, 1851, William Hope Harvey attended the Buffalo Academy at the age of 14 before going on to briefly study law at Marshall University in nearby Cabell County, West Virginia. In the 1890s, a series of economic downturns and periods of hardship led to a political and economic movement known as "Free Silver," which argued for abandonment of the gold standard and for the coinage of silver. On a national level, prominent politicians such as William Jennings Bryan took up the flag of promoting Free Silver during various elections. However, Harvey earned fame in 1894 when he published *Coin's Financial School.* He also acquired the nickname "Coin" Harvey and became a national spokesman for Free Silver. In 1931, he founded the Liberty Party and ran as its presidential candidate, receiving 51,000 votes in the national election. (Courtesy of Library of Congress.)

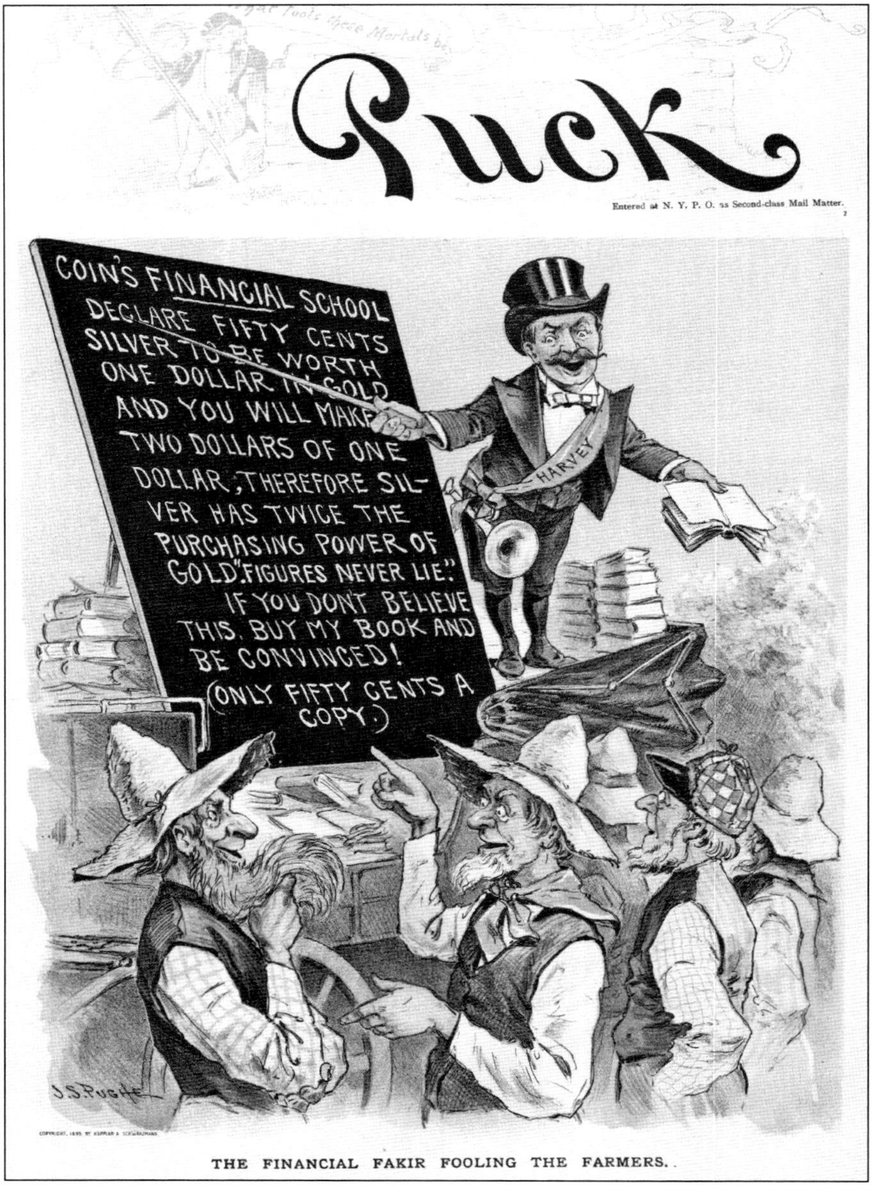

Shown here is one of numerous political cartoons from Harvey's lifetime that lampooned the alleged absurdity of Harvey's monetary proposals. Bankers and businessmen on the East Coast of the United States especially despised politicians and theoreticians like Harvey because of the fear that basing the US currency on both silver and gold would weaken the strength of the dollar and could lead to further economic downturns and bank panics. Hence, in this cartoon Harvey is portrayed as a slick salesman trying to defy basic logic by saying that a lesser amount of silver can be worth the same as a larger amount of gold. To the skeptic, the caricature Harvey says to simply, "Buy my book and be convinced!" Democratic president Grover Cleveland, in the White House in the 1890s during the height of the Free Silver movement, was vehemently against allowing proponents of silver, such as Harvey, to push for pro-silver legislation. (Courtesy of Library of Congress.)

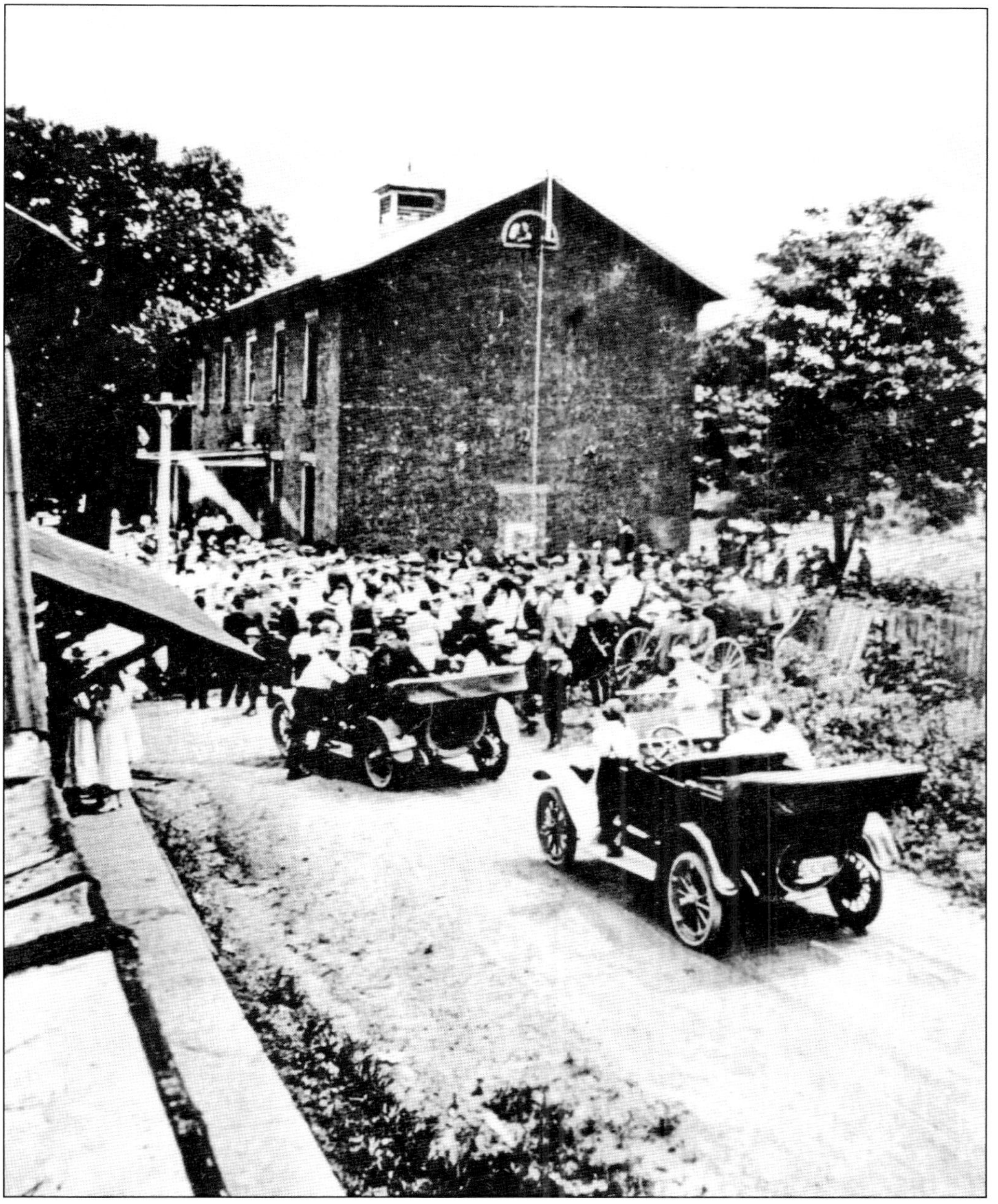

Upon the outbreak of World War I in Europe in 1914, the American public at first supported neutrality. However, by 1917, public support turned decidedly toward war and became anti-German. Shown here in early 1918, residents of Buffalo and the surrounding area gathered in the shadow of the Buffalo Academy for a patriotic rally in support of the new national war effort. All told, West Virginia supplied over 57,000 soldiers, of which around 5,000 became casualties. The war ended less than 18 months after American entry into the conflict, so a large proportion of US troops saw no combat. However, many of those killed died as a result of the great influenza epidemic of 1918 and 1919, such as Pvt. Carl L. Collier of nearby Pliny, who succumbed to the disease before Armistice Day and is buried at Pliny Presbyterian Church. (Courtesy of Mark Harris.)

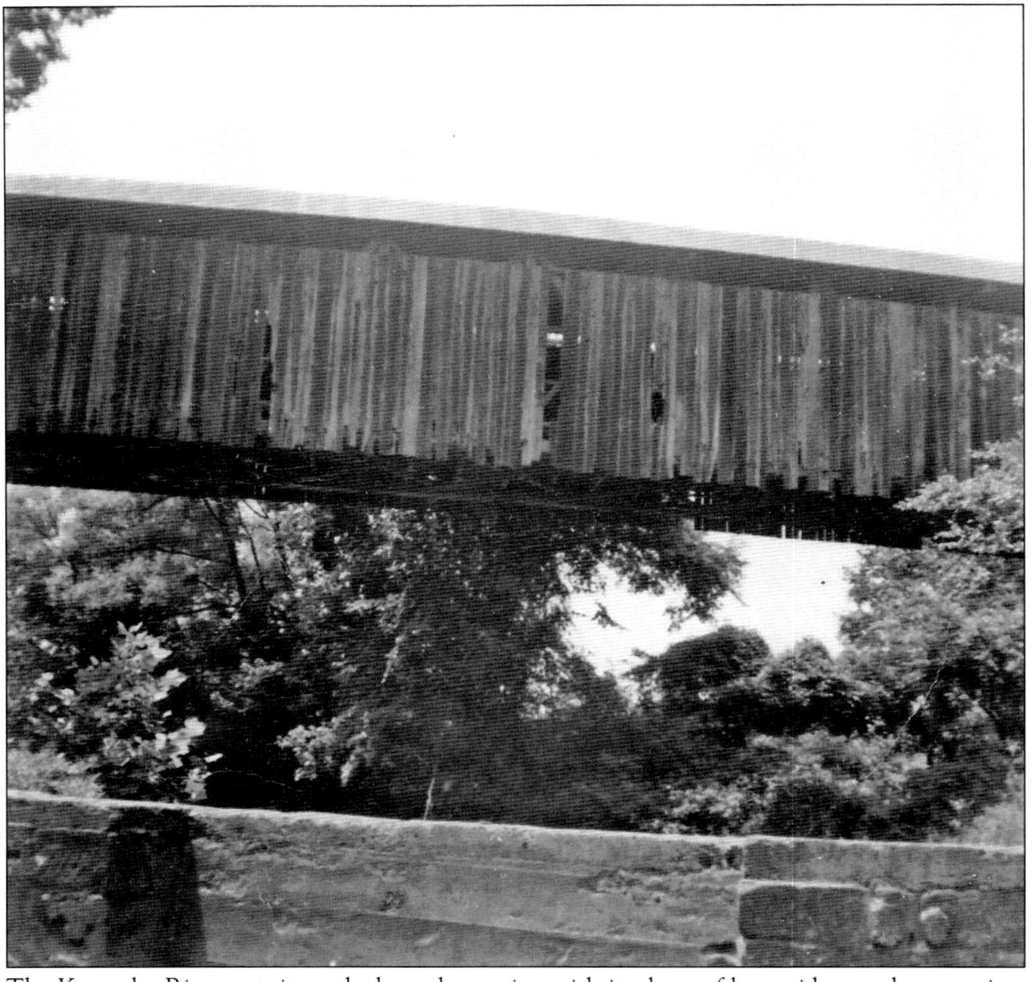

The Kanawha River cuts its path through a region with its share of large ridges and mountains, resulting in scores of small streams and creeks that empty from the highlands into the Kanawha River basin. As a result, bridges over these small streams have long been a common sight throughout Putnam County. Photographed here is the wooden covered bridge that spanned nearly 100 feet over Eighteen Mile Creek outside of the town of Buffalo. The bridge carried vehicular traffic westward away from the town of Buffalo on County Route 10. The wooden bridge dates back to the late 19th century and was in use well into the 20th century until around 1950, when a new concrete bridge was erected in 1953 to accommodate larger, heavier vehicles as well as to update maintenance procedures. (Courtesy of Freeda Young.)

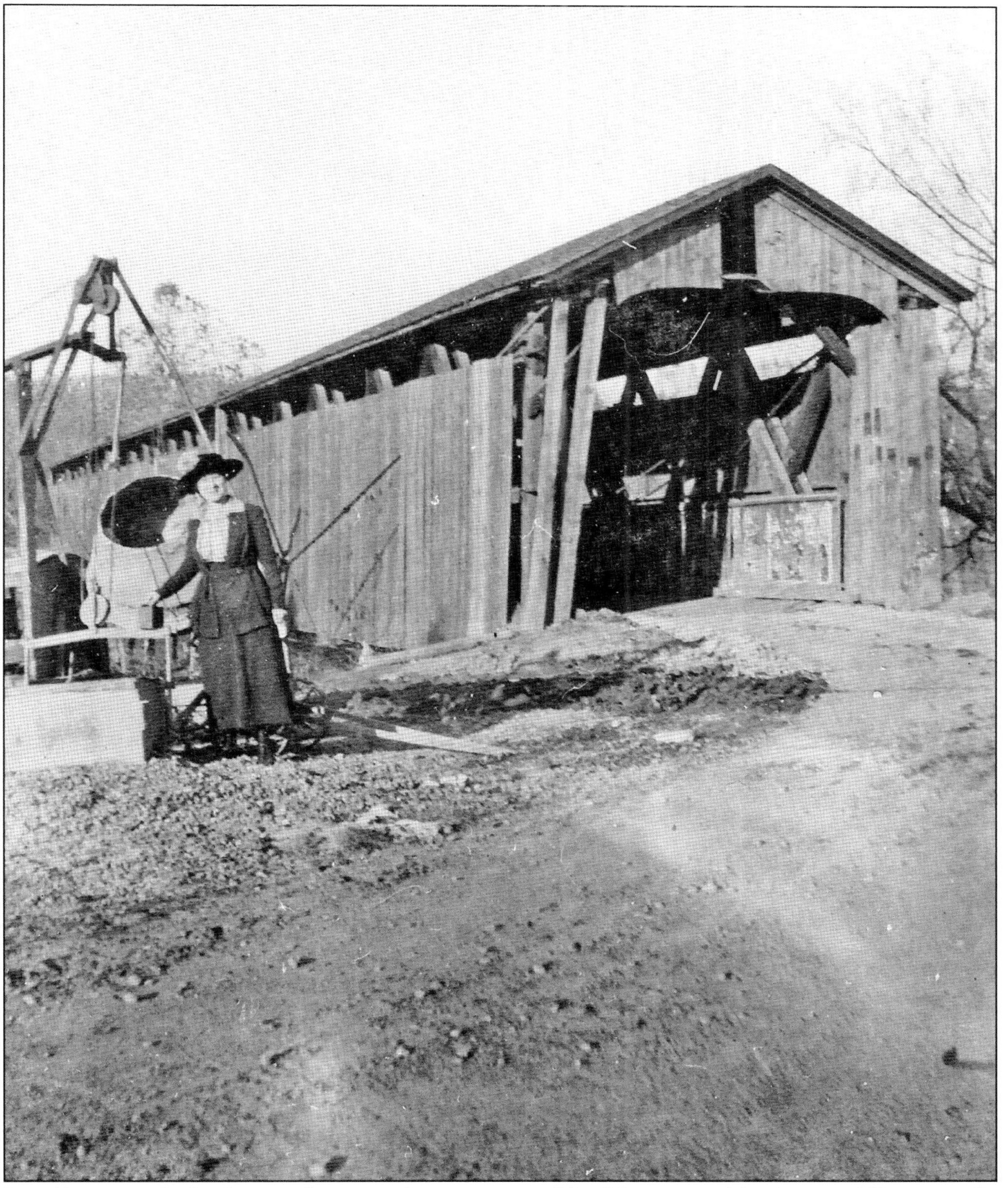

In addition to the bridges in the immediate vicinity of Buffalo, covered bridges could historically be found on the winding roads that radiated out into the countryside surrounding the town. At Cross Creek, a covered bridge was located in the center of present-day Buffalo, but historically it divided two sections of the town—Buffalo and Harveytown. Another covered bridge, Oldacker Bridge, was located only a matter of feet away from Oldacker Mill. Both bridges have been replaced by modern concrete spans. Pictured here, a sizable wooden covered bridge once stood in the vicinity of Poca, about 15 miles away from Buffalo. As is the case with the bridge that once stood over Cross Creek, the curious investigator can still find along the opposing shores of the stream traces of the stone foundations that once held up the massive wooden timbers and support trusses of the covered bridge in Poca. (Courtesy of Jim Caruthers.)

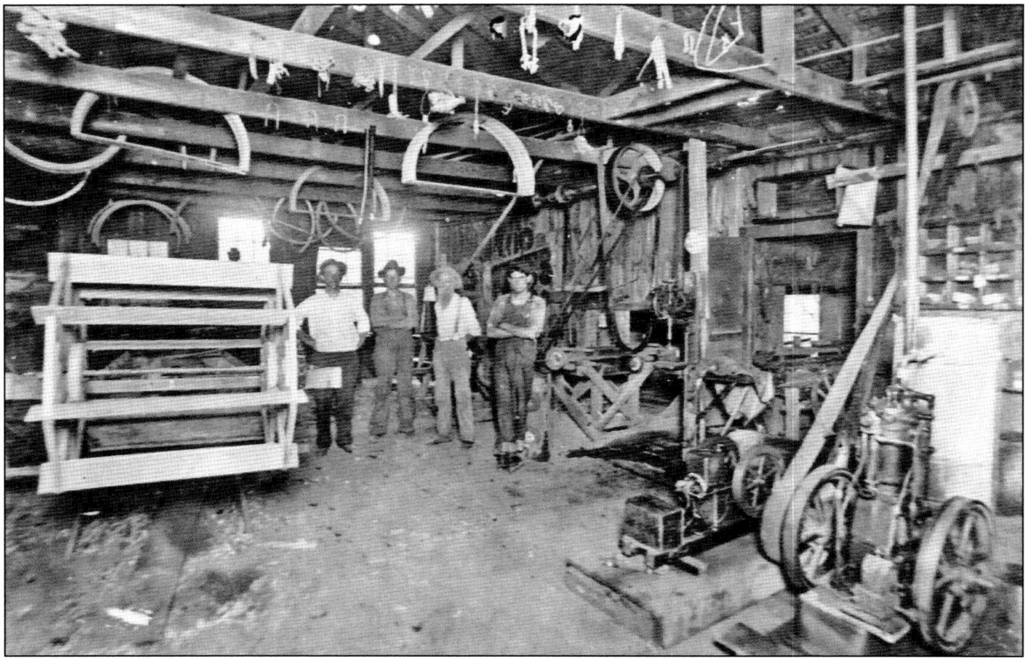

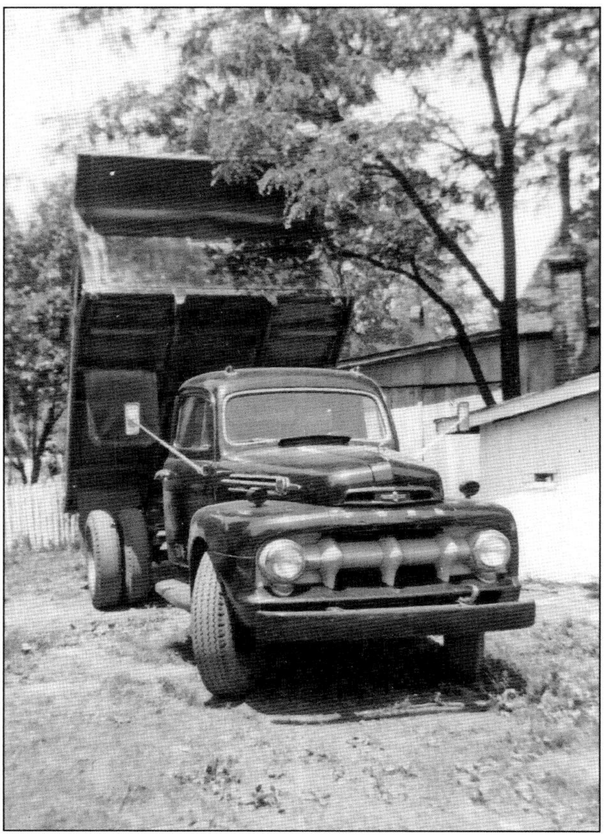

In addition to occupations related directly to the river or to agriculture, Buffalo residents engaged in craft trades such as woodworking, often crafting furniture. The above photograph captures the expansive interior of a furniture factory that was located on the northern side of Buffalo. The use of horses and other domestic animals for hauling large vehicles in the 1800s and early 1900s gave way to motorized alternatives. This 1950s Ford dump truck (left) was used for years by Buffalo resident Lewis Harris to move loads of coal and wood as needed. (Both, courtesy of Leah Higgenbotham.)

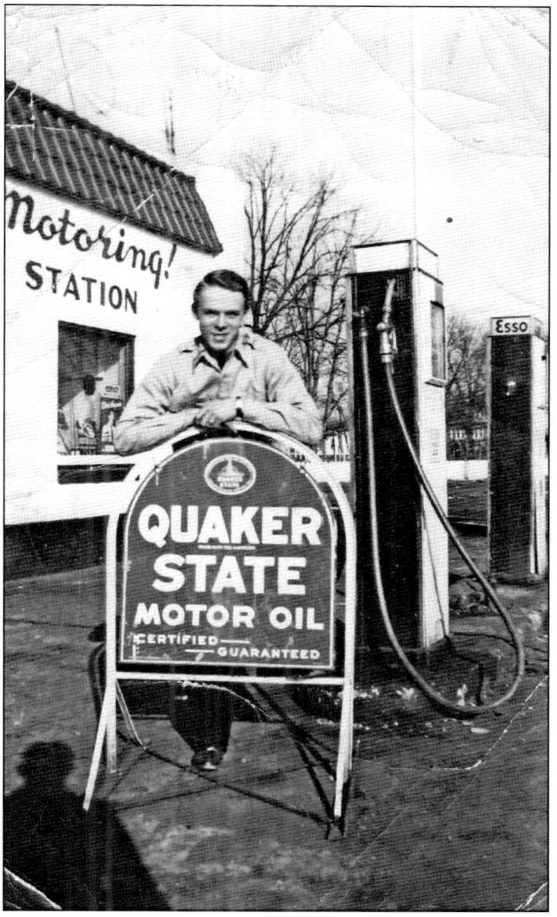

In the early 1900s, Standard Oil was broken up into a dozen and a half smaller, independent companies after a Supreme Court decision upheld charges that the company was a monopoly. In several states on the East Coast, the smaller companies retained the rights to the Standard Oil name, or its initials S.O., which was shortened to Esso. Hence, from the 1920s through the 1960s, Esso stations were prevalent all over West Virginia. Buffalo was home to one such station, located around a curve in Route 35 from the Buffalo Academy and owned by the Nease family. Photographed at right is Buffalo resident Tom Martin around 1930 in front of the Esso station. Below is Peter Nease, son of Clyde Nease, posing by his car around 1930. (Both, courtesy of Leah Higgenbotham.)

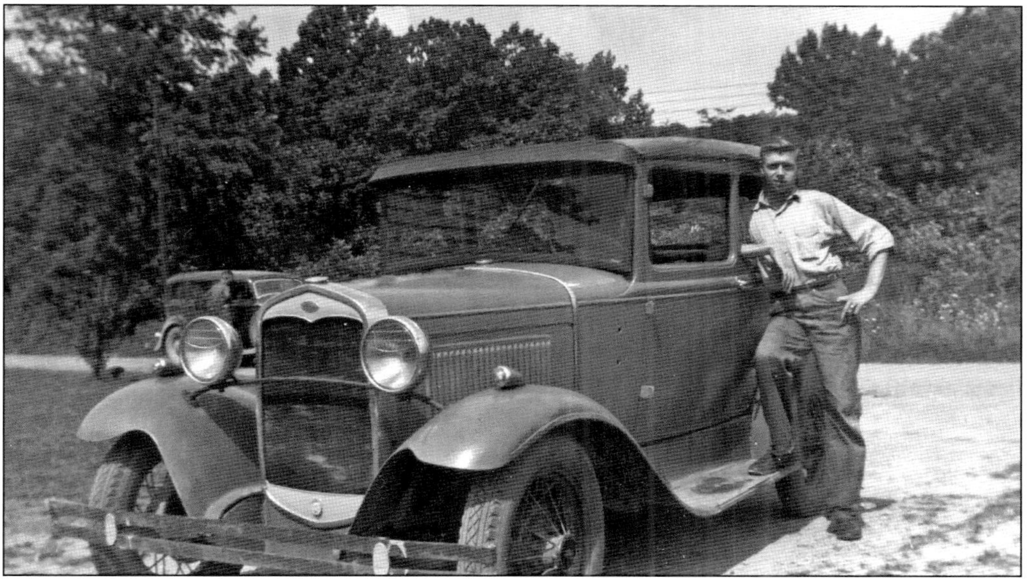

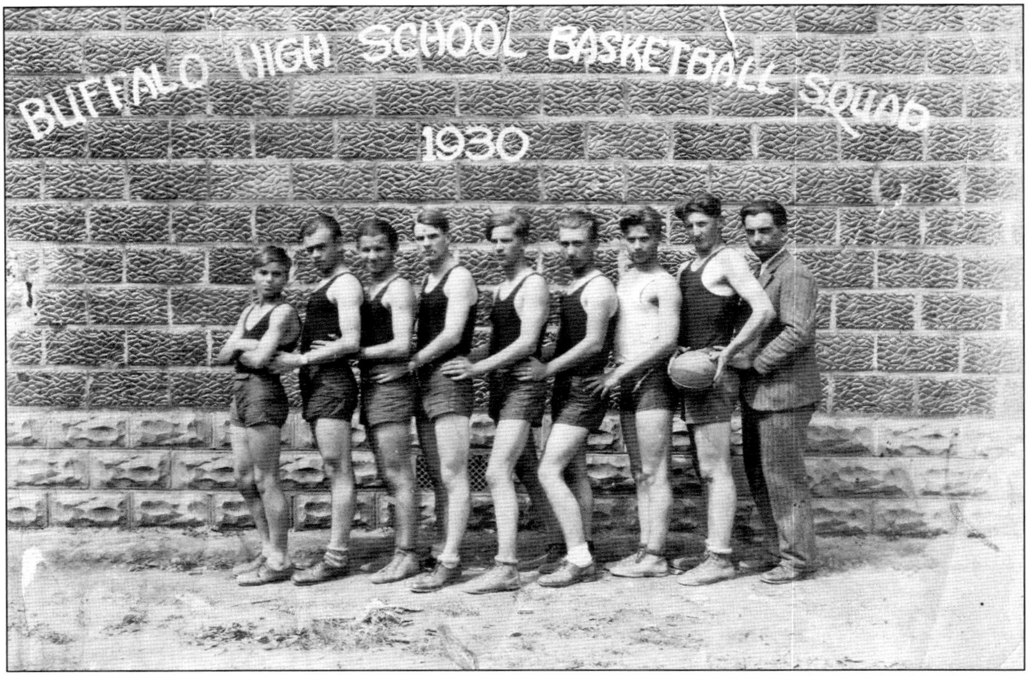

Buffalo High School during the 20th century was like most any other similarly sized school in the United States in regards to extracurricular sports programs that were offered for students. Shown above are the team members of the 1930 Buffalo High School basketball squad, along with their coach on the far right. Shown below is the Buffalo High School baseball team in the mid- to late 1950s. In addition to baseball and basketball, the high school in Buffalo fielded football, track and field, and wrestling teams as well as a band and cheerleading teams. (Above, courtesy of Leah Higgenbotham; below, courtesy of Freeda Young.)

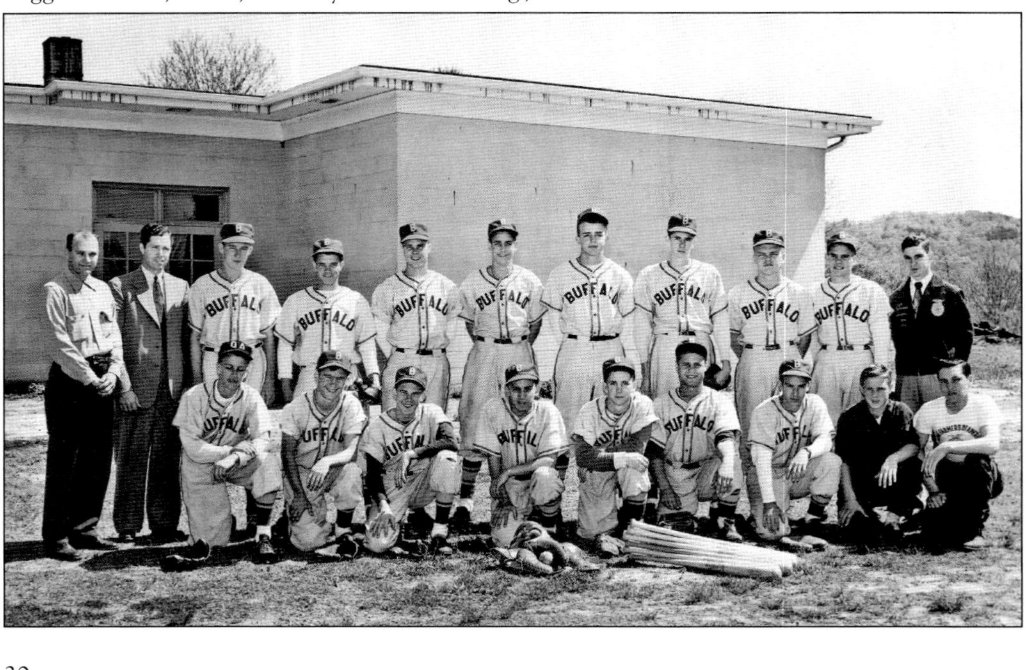

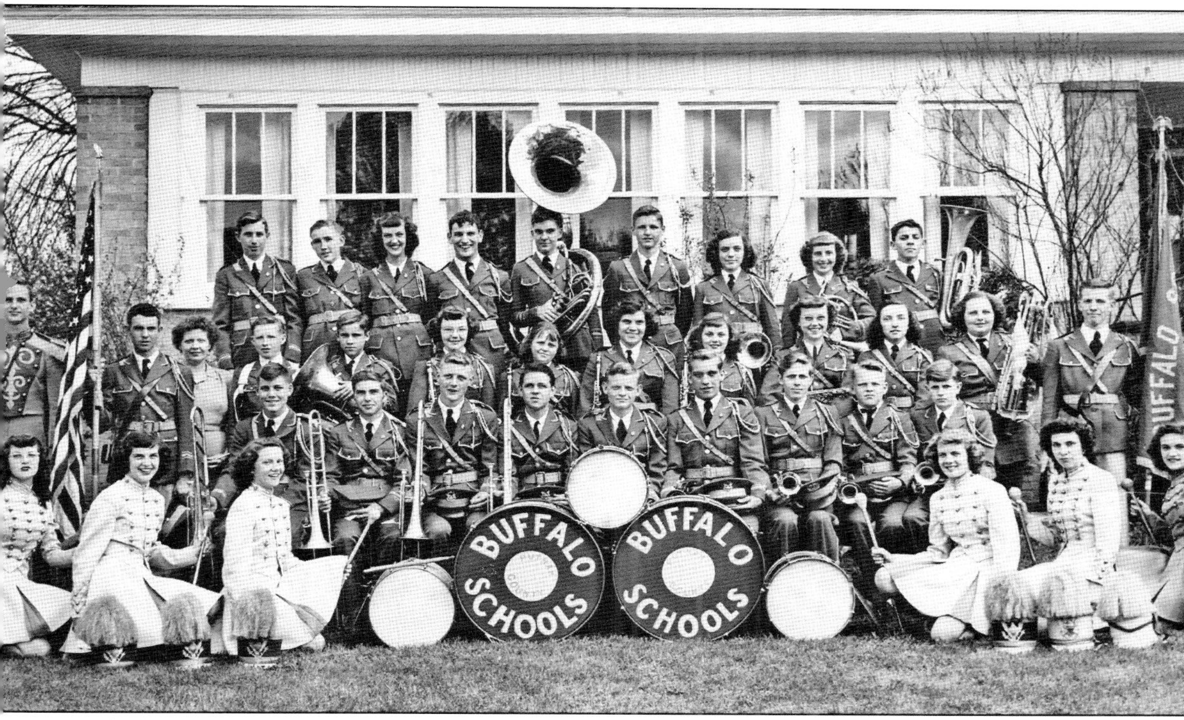

On the large expansive lawn situated next to the high school building, generations of citizens posed for photographs every year to commemorate group organizations—ranging from booster clubs to sports teams to civic and fraternal societies. The Buffalo High School marching band in the 1930s purchased new uniforms for the upcoming sports season and then posed for this photograph next to the high school. The arrival of the new garb attracted quite a lot of attention throughout the town, amongst not only the band members, but also students in the elementary and middle schools. Buffalo native Freeda Young recalls being quite awed and impressed by the new uniforms, which were distributed to all of the members of the marching band, including elaborate white dresses for the female color guards. She was not yet in high school at the time and remembers wishing she had been older like the students in the band. (Courtesy of Freeda Young.)

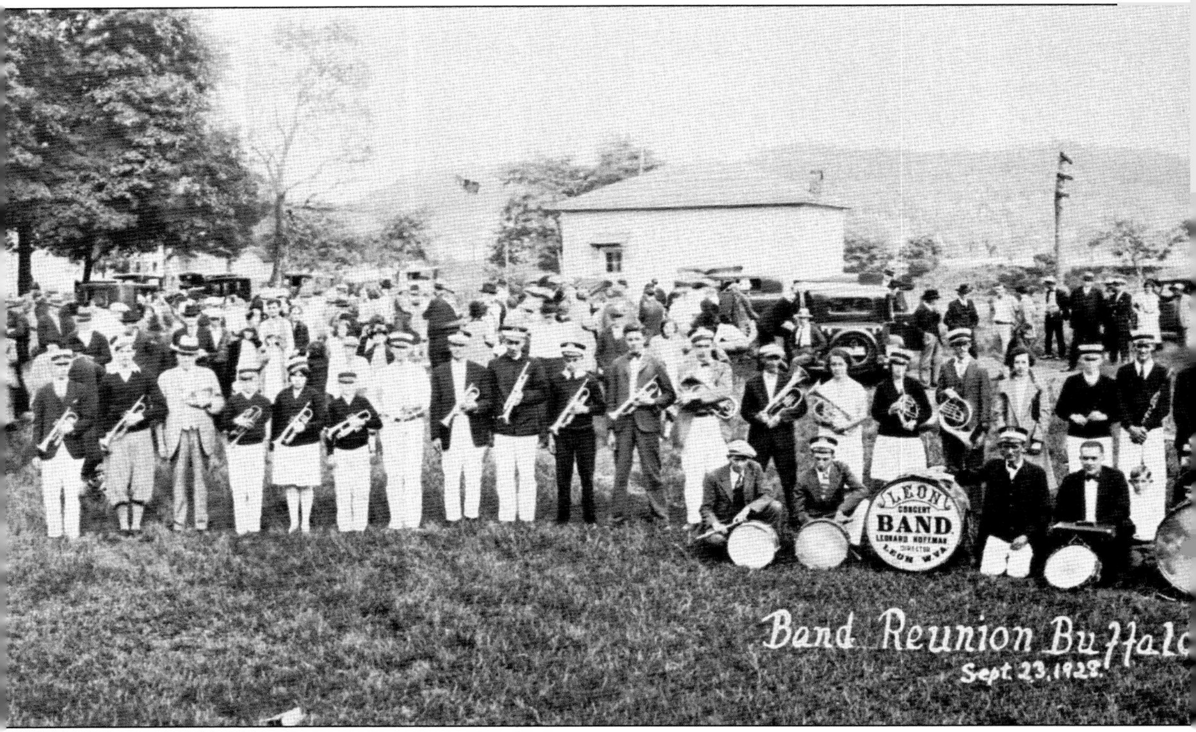

Like many towns of similar size and composition across the country, Buffalo has always had its large share of social clubs and organizations. The Knights of Pythias band reunion is shown here during a September 23, 1928, members' reunion on the outskirts of Buffalo. This particular lodge of the Knights of Pythias was based in the nearby town of Leon, about nine miles to the north of Buffalo in Mason County. The Knights of Pythias, though one of the lesser known of fraternal

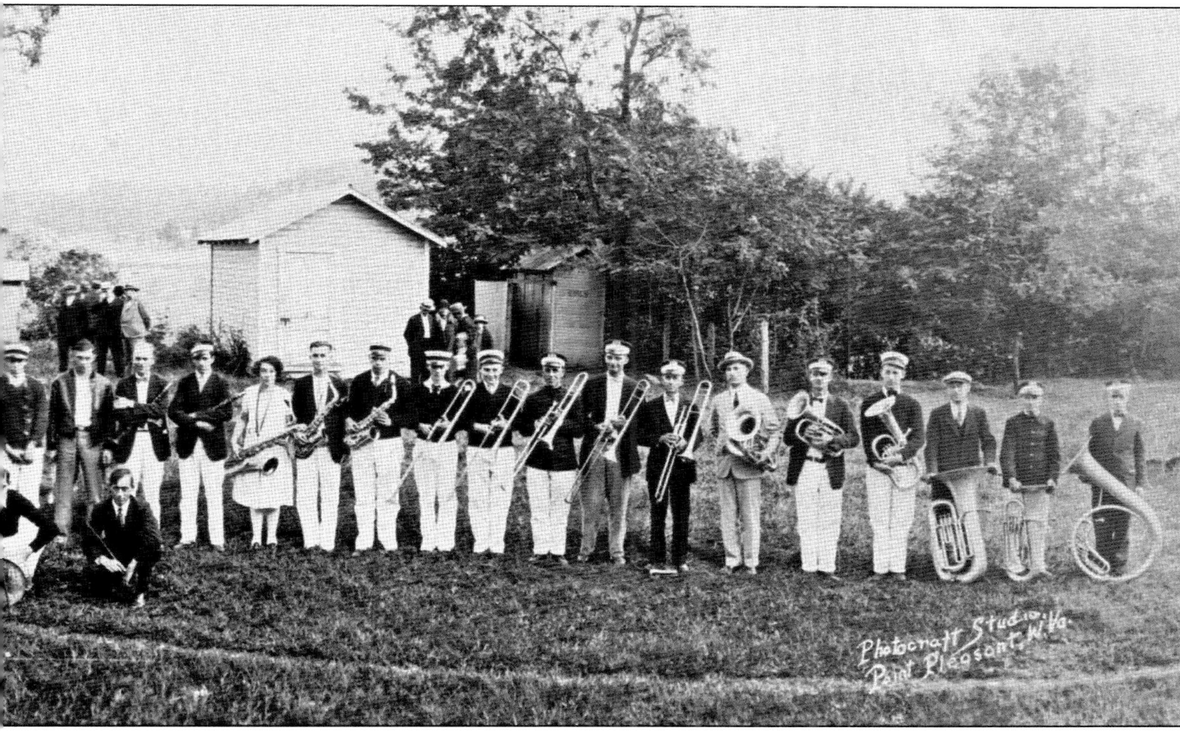

societies, was the first such fraternal order to be chartered by an act of Congress in the 1860s. The Leon lodge was established around 1918 and attracted members from the surrounding region, in both Putnam and Mason Counties. Many of the early members were World War I veterans shortly after returning home from the European conflict. The order's defining principles are friendship, charity, and benevolence. (Courtesy of West Virginia State Archives.)

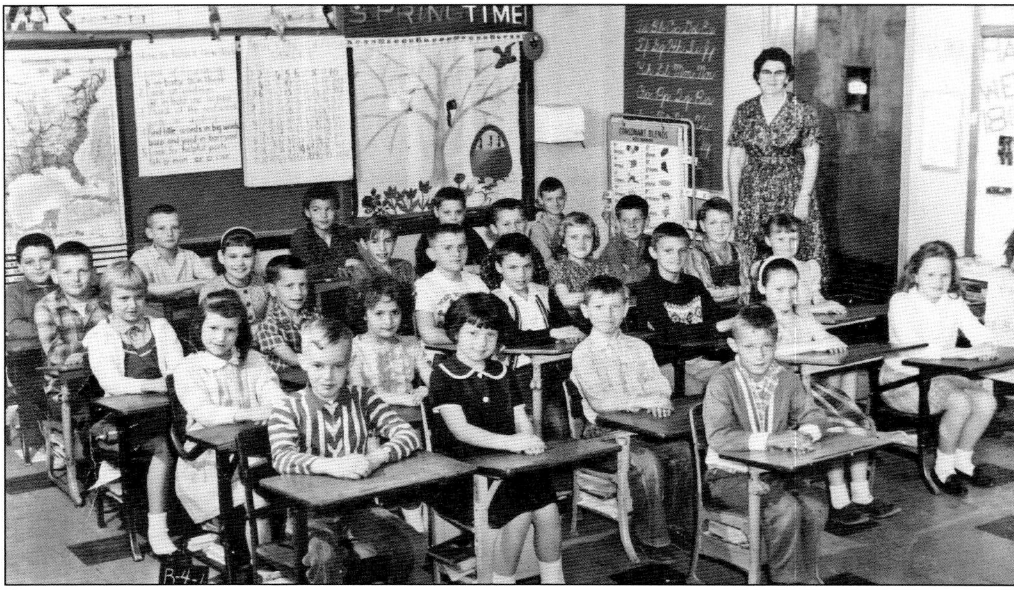

Following its time as a liberal arts institute, the Buffalo Academy was at various times used by the county's board of education as part of the larger public education system. First used as the high school for Buffalo, it subsequently became the grade school until a new elementary school building was constructed in 1951. Shown above is a class photograph of teacher Ada Knapp's class for the 1962–1963 school year. Buffalo High School occupied the Buffalo Academy for one year in 1921. Shown below is the Buffalo High School band around 1940, when the high school was located in a building on Franklin Street. (Above, courtesy of Leah Higgenbotham; below, courtesy of Mark Harris.)

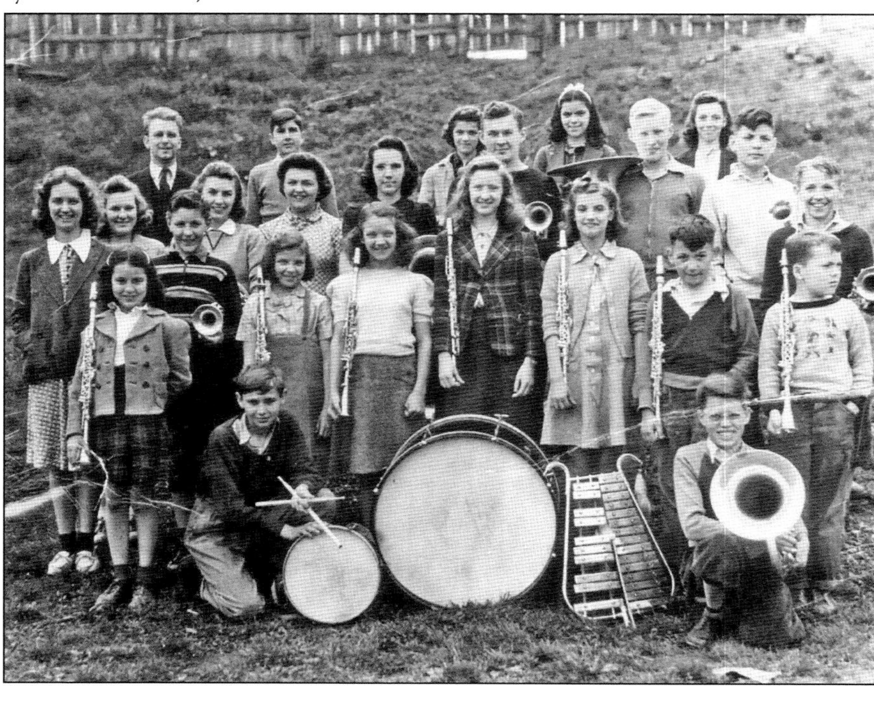

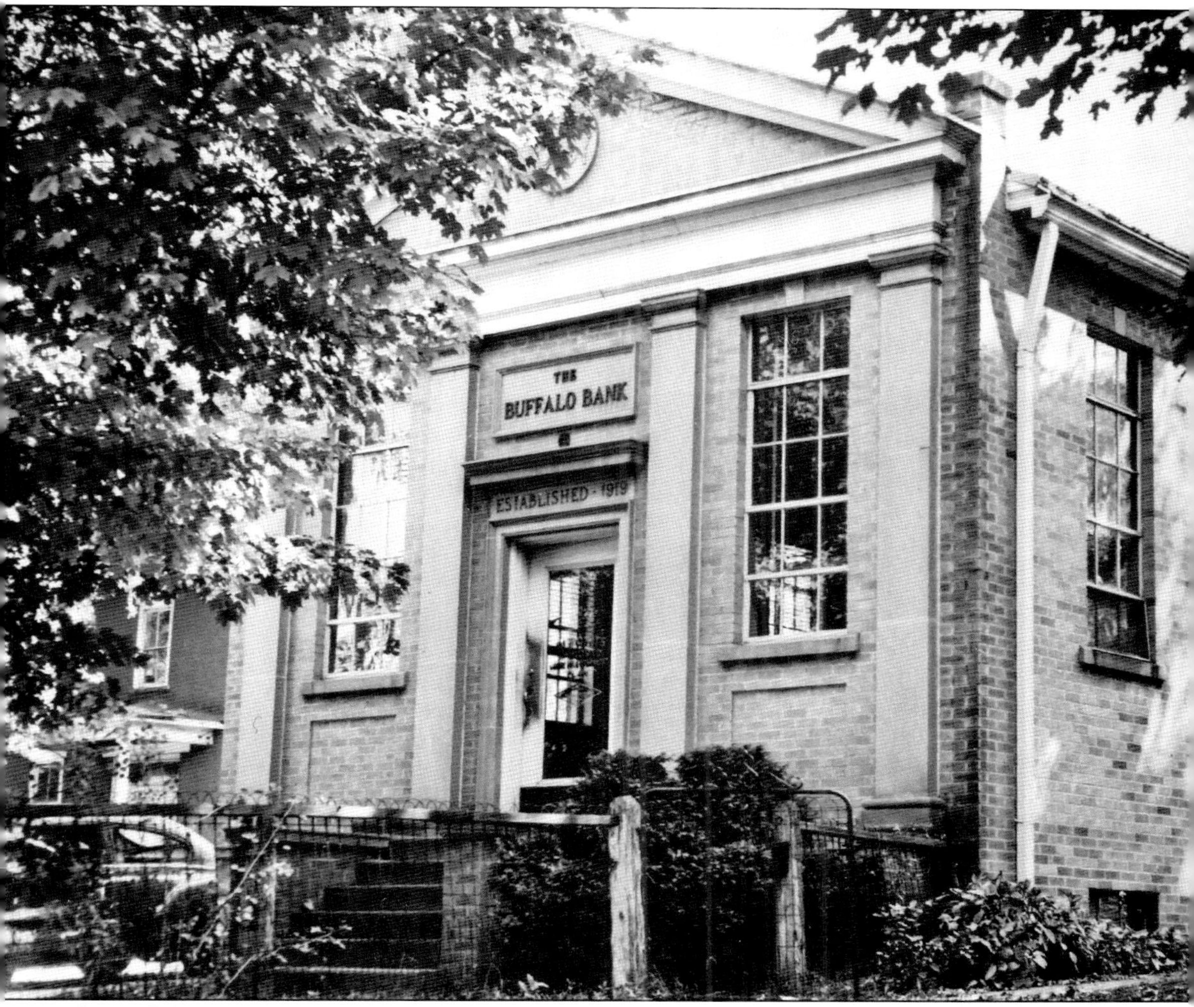

The Buffalo Bank building, photographed here, stands a few feet from the "S" curve that runs through the center of town. In 1919, several enterprising residents of Buffalo and Putnam County conferred on the possibility of founding a bank in Buffalo. Several potential stockholders were quickly consulted and the necessary number agreed to invest in the venture—those being John L. Dickinson, H.P. Blake, J.A. Cochran, M.V. Brown, and Thomas C. Atkeson, of state agricultural fame. In March 1919, with $25,000 in capital on hand, the Buffalo Bank opened its doors, though it did not operate in its brick building shown here; instead, it rented a structure across the street from Cochran's General Store in town. In 1929, the bank had done well enough financially to allow for the brick building to be constructed; it opened to the public in 1930 and operated until 1963. (Courtesy of Ann Murphy.)

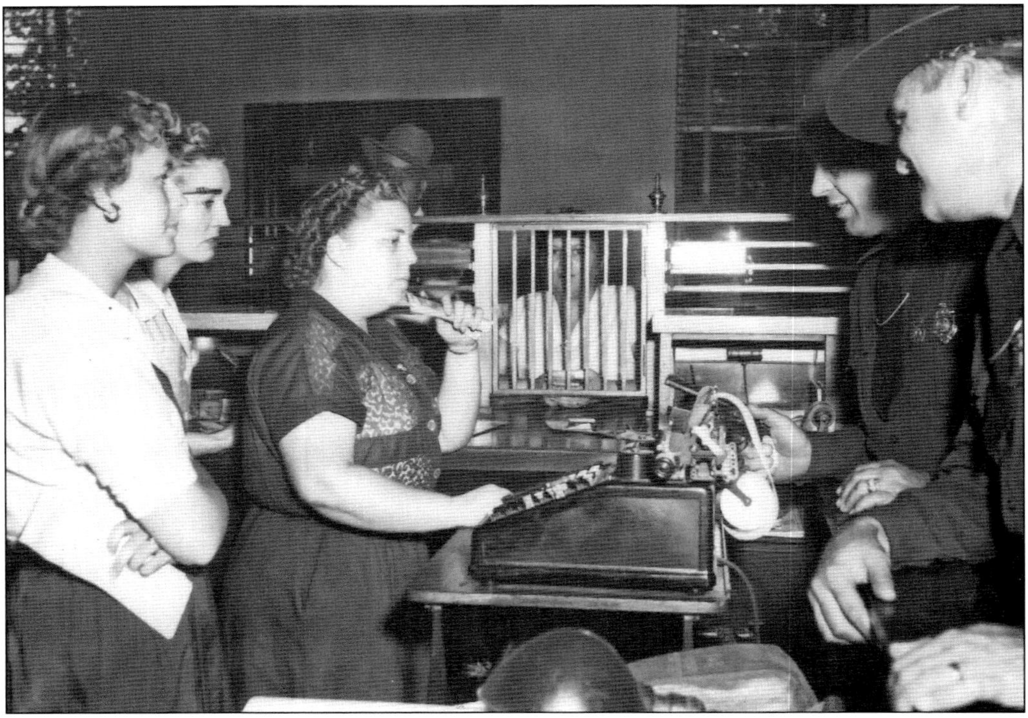

On October 1, 1953, three armed men robbed the Buffalo Bank in broad daylight, around 10:30 a.m. Shown above, bank employees Rose Haer, Jackie Cain, and Maxine Mitchell crunched the numbers on the bank adding machine after the robbery and after the perpetrators and money had been apprehended. With the currency returned, two police officers, Cecil Stewart and Dan Carlson, worked with the bank employees to make sure that all of the stolen money had been accounted for. Photographed below, residents from nearby, police officers, and newspaper reporters gathered on the bank property to discuss the events of the morning. (Both, courtesy of Ann Murphy.)

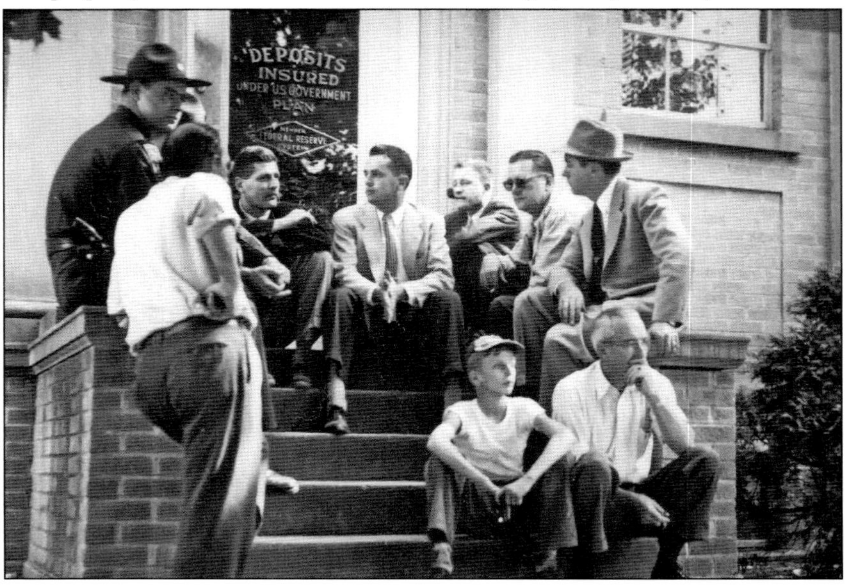

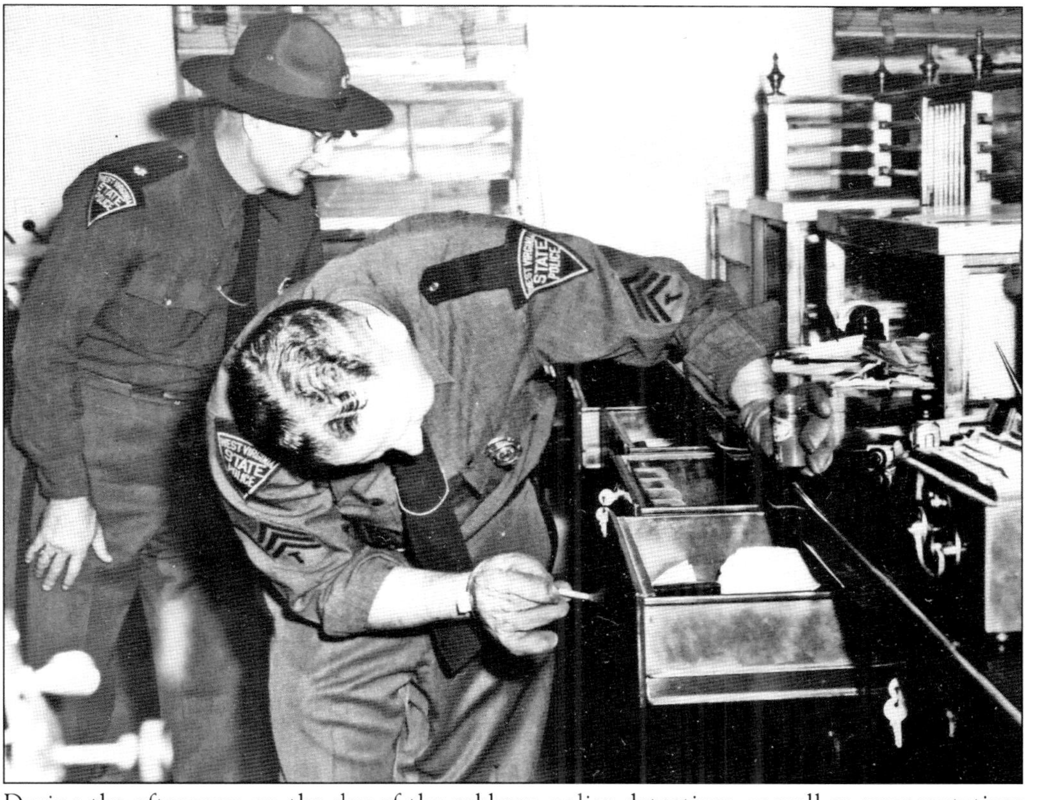

During the afternoon on the day of the robbery, police detectives, as well as representatives from the Federal Bureau of Investigation, collected evidence from the scene of that morning's crime. Shown above, police officer Lawrence Kraft dusts the money drawers behind the teller counter in the main room of the bank for fingerprints. In total, the bank robbers had stolen $9,544.76 from the bank in a large burlap bag. When apprehended, the money was pulled from the suspects' pockets and car along the side of the road (below). One of the robbers, seated with his head facing the ground, can be seen behind the police officer counting the money. (Both, courtesy of Ann Murphy.)

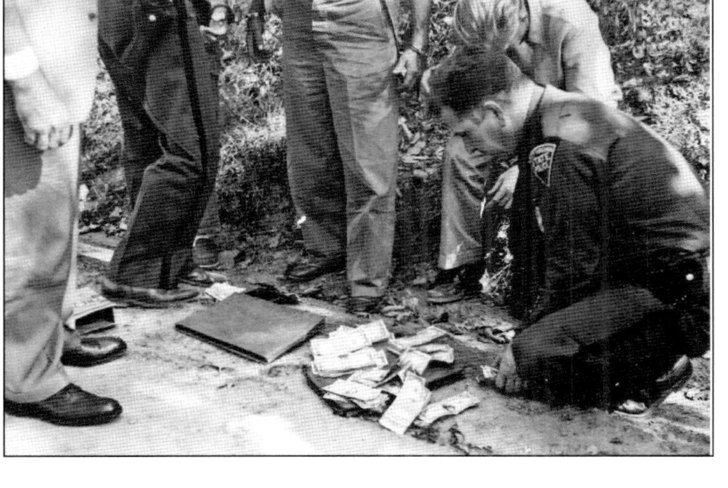

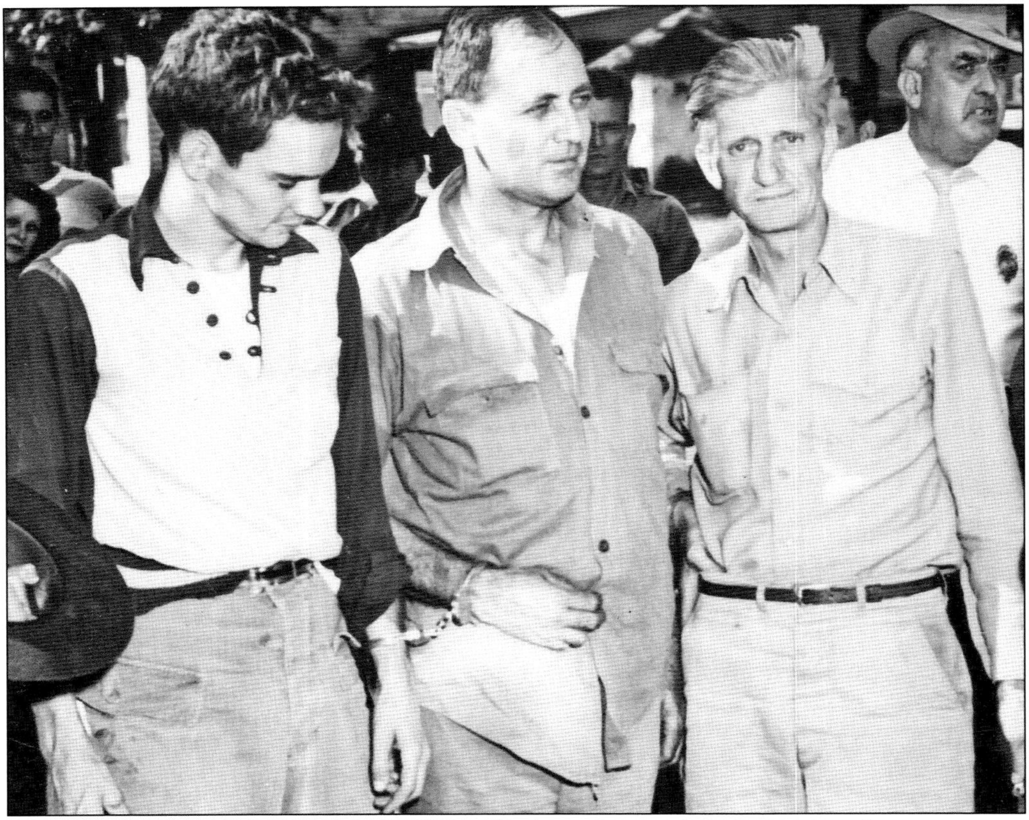

The three bank robbers were handcuffed and taken to the police department for questioning (above). They are, from left to right, Robert E. Combs, Clair C. Starcher, and Harold L. Page—all from the Charleston, West Virginia, area. In the photograph below, state troopers M.A. Murphy, left, and John Maciejczyk, right, pose with their hats stuffed full of the confiscated robbery money and the three apprehended fugitives standing between them. All three of the robbers had previous criminal records, including forgery, fraudulent checks, and parole violation. (Both, courtesy of Ann Murphy.)

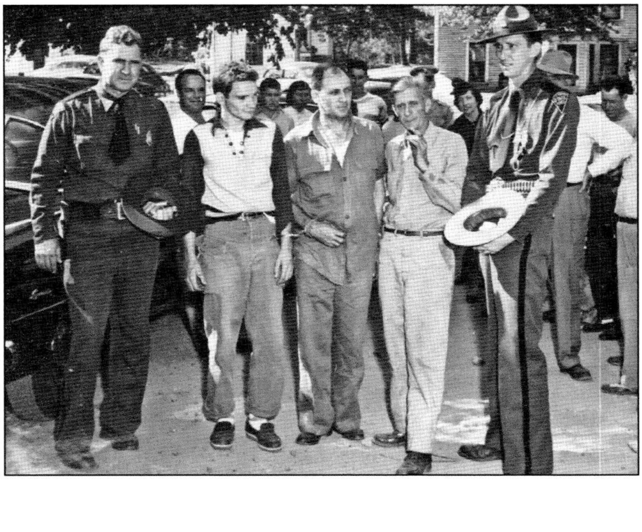

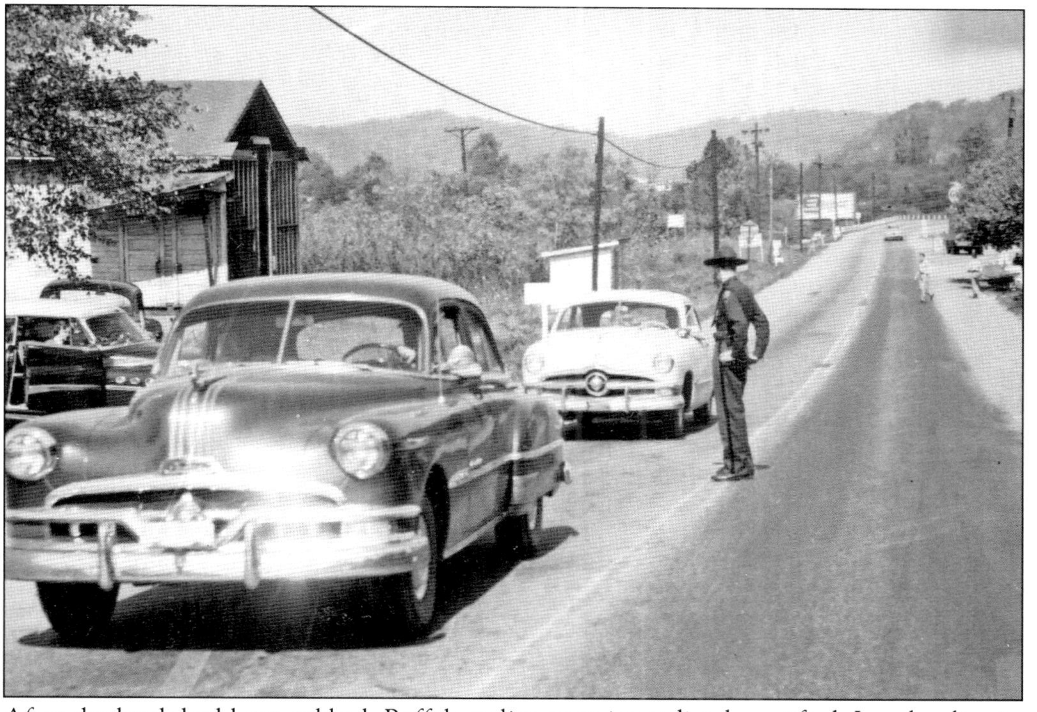

After the bank had been robbed, Buffalo police were immediately notified. Local police in turn radioed a description of the suspects' car to police in Point Pleasant, Barboursville, Nitro, Charleston, and Ripley. In a short amount of time, roadblocks were thrown up along all of the main transportation routes out of the area. Photographed above is one of the roadblocks on Route 35 and Route 25. The bank tellers all looked out of the window of the building as the bank robbers got into a blue, late-model Hudson (below) and casually backed out of a parking space to drive away. The *Charleston Gazette* reporter at the scene said that bystanders outside of the bank who saw the car drive away had no idea that a robbery had occurred. (Both, courtesy of Ann Murphy.)

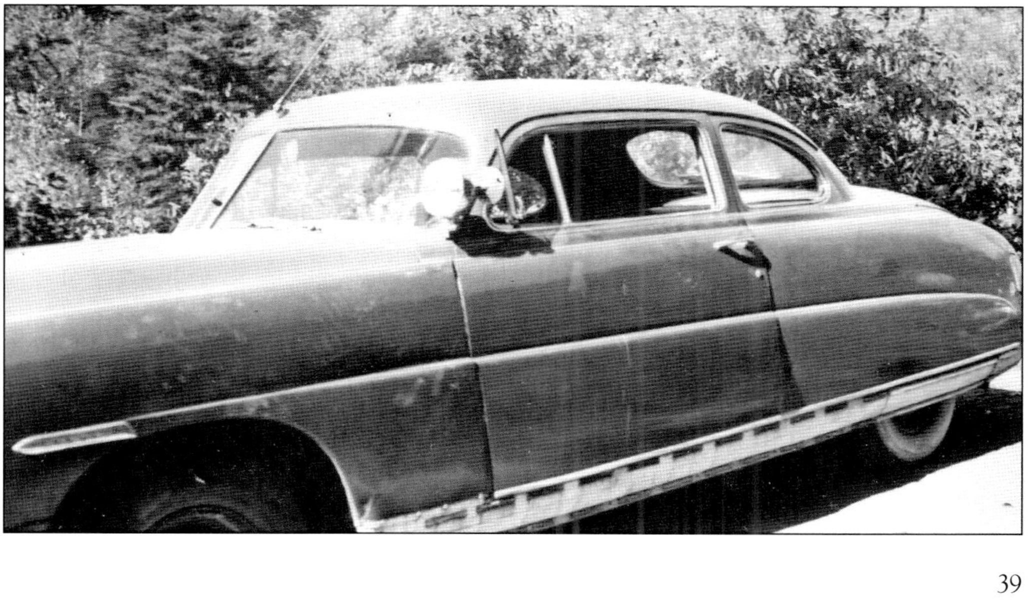

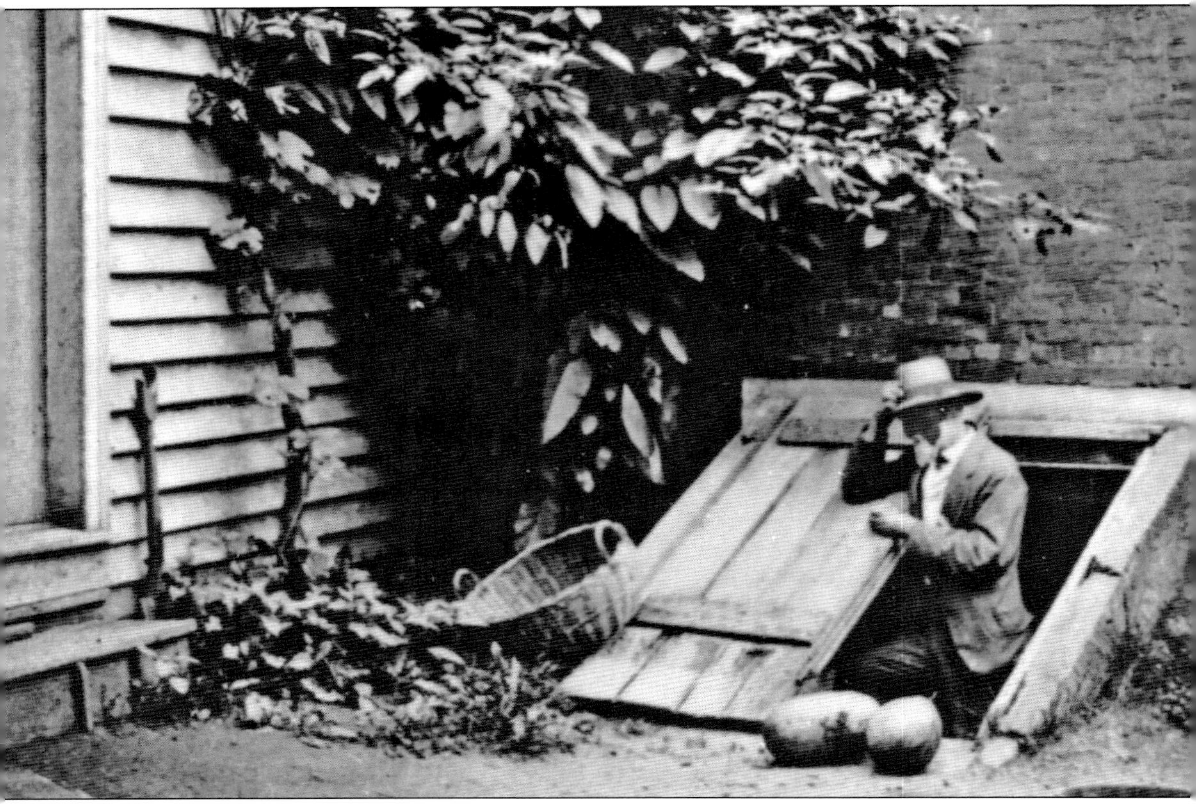

Shown here is a rare photograph from the early years of the 20th century, possibly depicting Confederate general John McCausland in the later years of his life. McCausland had been a Confederate officer in Tennessee, Mississippi, and Virginia during the Civil War. He earned much notoriety as one of the southern officers who carried out the burning of the town of Chambersburg in Pennsylvania on July 30, 1864, during Confederate lieutenant general Jubal Early's 1864 military raid into Maryland and Pennsylvania. Several years after the war, McCausland moved to the area around Pliny, opposite Buffalo, where he also constructed an impressive estate just over the county line in Mason County. He assumed the life of a farmer for over a half a century, until his death in 1927, at which time he was said to be the last surviving Confederate general. Even into his old age, he reportedly feared retaliation from angry citizens north of the Mason-Dixon because of his role in the destruction of Chambersburg. (Courtesy of Leah Higgenbotham.)

Two

Winfield
Crossroads and County Seat

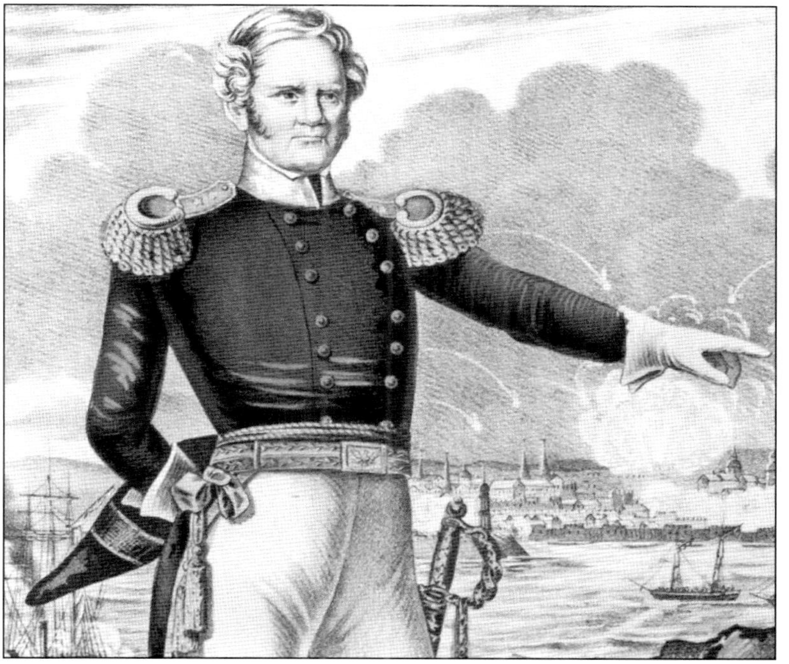

For residents of the United States in the late 1840s, few contemporary names would have been better known than Winfield Scott. His fame, resulting from his command of the victorious United States Army during the two year war with Mexico, led the residents of a small, rapidly growing town in newly created Putnam County to adopt the use of his name. (Courtesy of Library of Congress.)

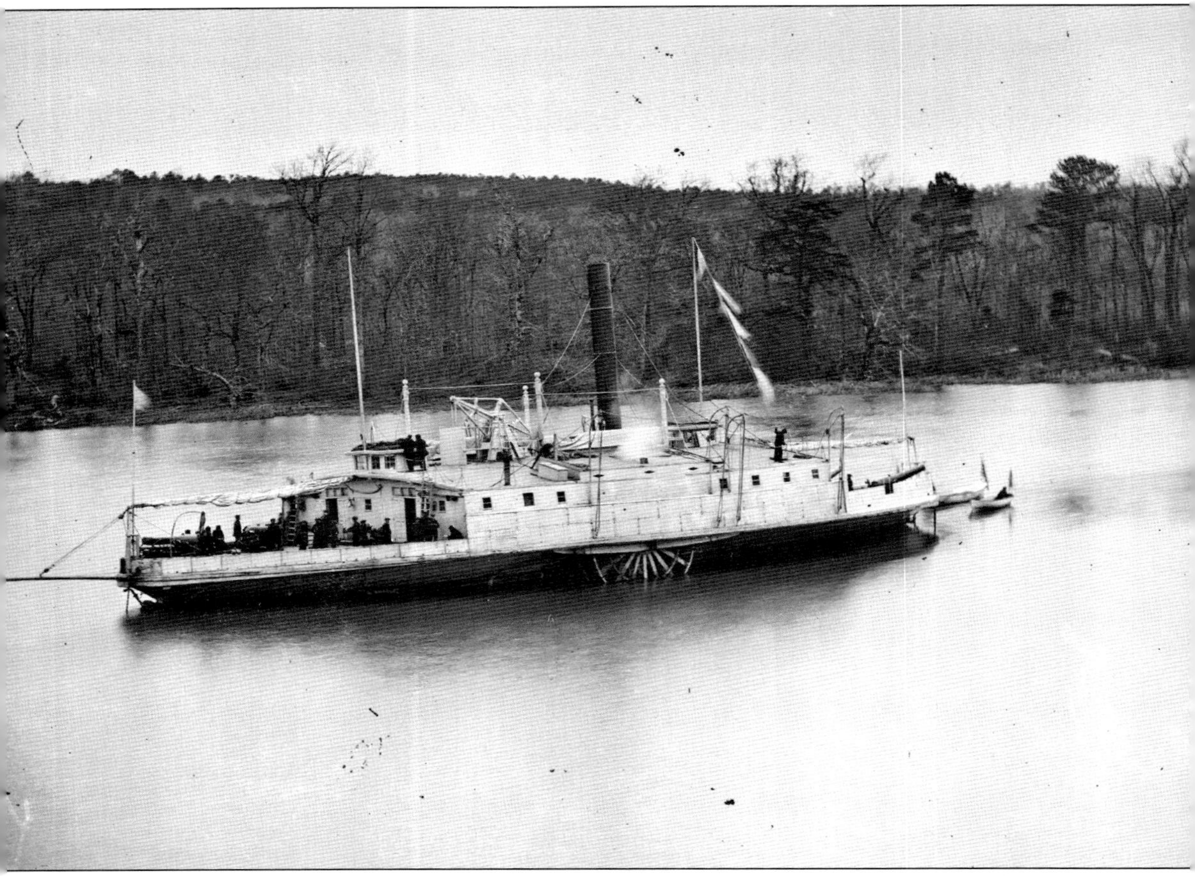

Around the year 1818, a man from Charleston, West Virginia, named Charles Brown bought over 400 acres of land in the area of present-day Winfield. Shortly after acquiring the land, Brown began to operate a ferry that crossed the Kanawha River downstream from Red House, situated on the north bank, and present-day Winfield, on the south bank. Though Brown himself remained a resident of Charleston, later in life his sons inherited the Winfield land and continued to operate the ferry crossing until around the time that an act of the General Assembly of Virginia formed Putnam County out of portions of surrounding counties. After the Brown's family-operated ferry, various other entities operated boat crossings on the river in the area of Winfield, like the ferryboat shown here. The traffic created by travelers moving through the area, coupled with the centrality of Winfield's location, made it an ideal spot to locate the new county seat. (Courtesy of Library of Congress.)

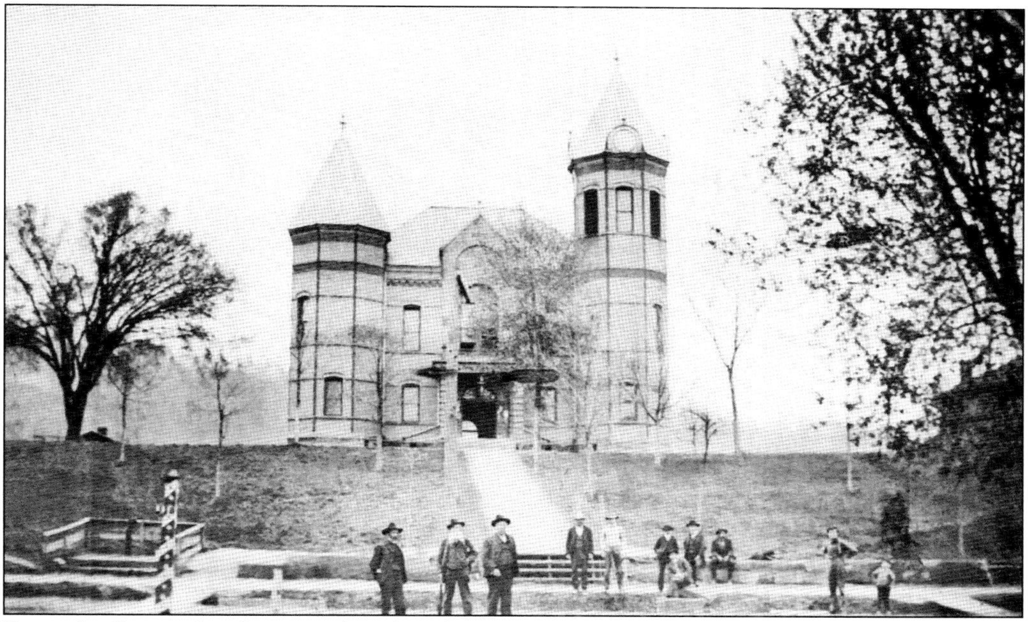

From the Brown family came the plot of ground on which the new county courthouse could be built for Putnam County. Construction of the Romanesque Revival-style courthouse shown here was completed in 1900. In 1848, a courthouse building had been constructed on the site, but in the 1890s, county officials began planning to replace the deteriorating structure. Above is the courthouse shortly after its completion in 1900. The total cost to complete the building was $14,713.31. Frank Pierce Milburn was the architect of the project and is well known in West Virginia for having designed several county courthouses in the state. Shown below is a view of the courthouse soon after completion, with the towers of the building faintly visible in the distance. (Above, courtesy of West Virginia State Archives; below, courtesy of Larry N. Sypolt.)

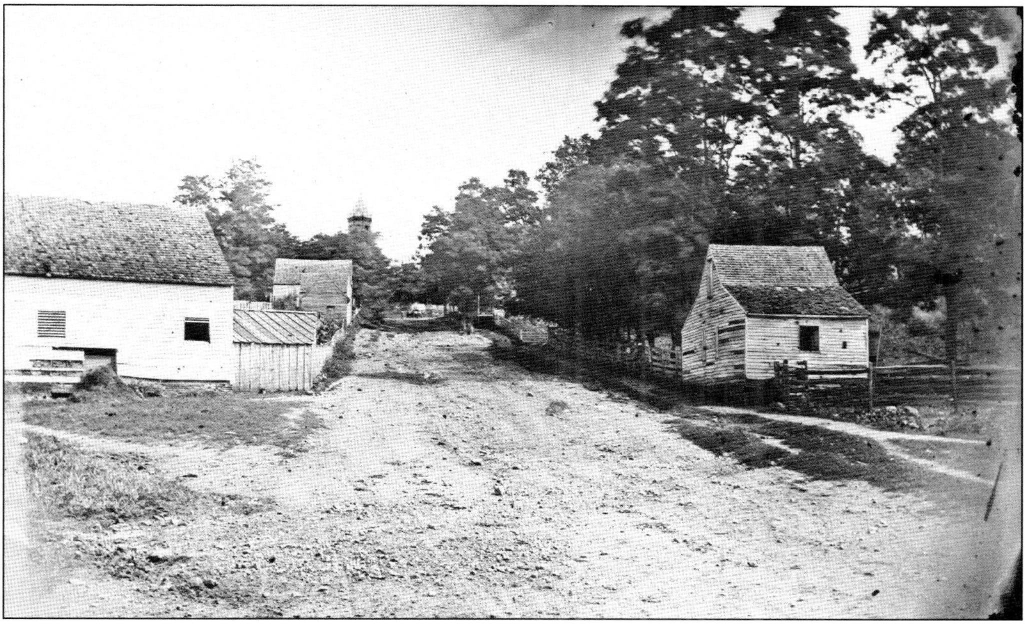

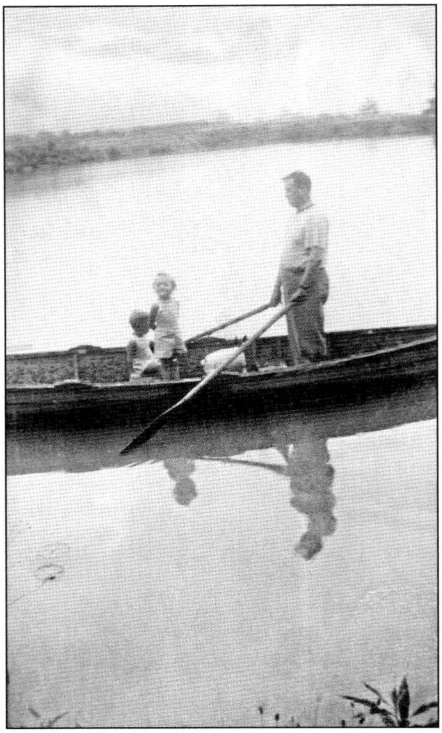

No history of West Virginia's 20th-century labor movements could be considered complete without a mention of William "Bill" Blizzard. Blizzard was not born in Putnam County; rather, he was a native of neighboring Kanawha County. He reportedly began working as a coal miner just after the age of 10 and became active within the United Mine Workers of America labor union during the strife of the Paint Creek-Cabin Creek Strike of 1912 and 1913. During his retirement living near Winfield, West Virginia, Blizzard enjoyed the natural outdoors, as is evidenced in these images of Blizzard and family members in a rowboat on his property. (Both, courtesy of West Virginia State Archives.)

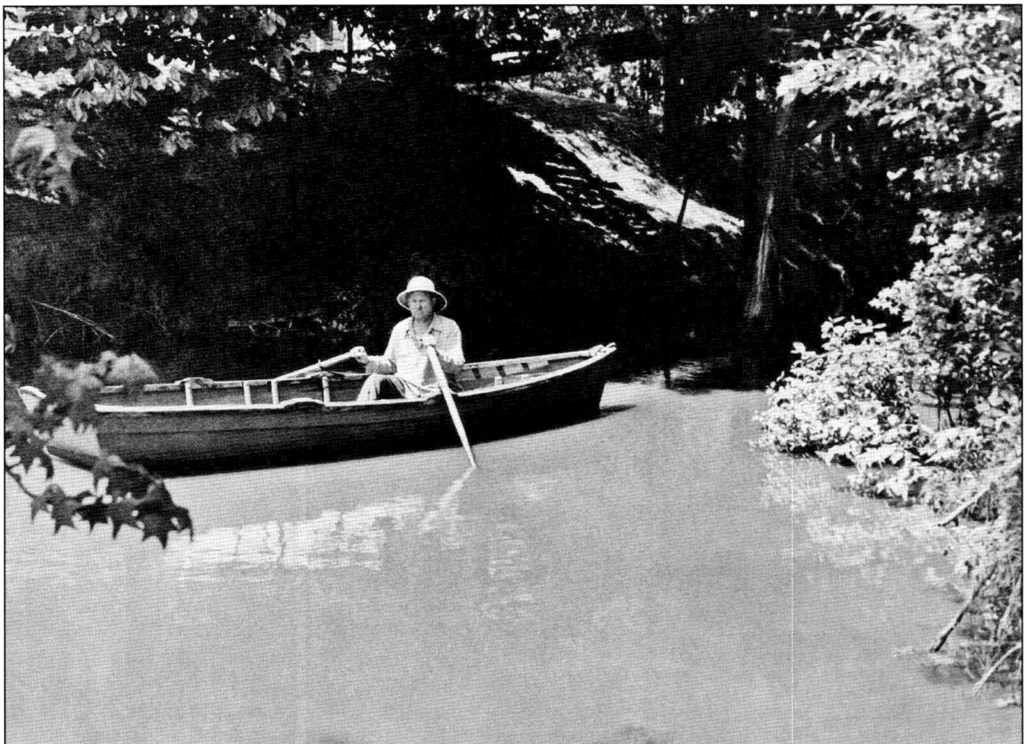

In the latter years of life, Bill Blizzard lived in a lakeside house in the Winfield area of Putnam County with his wife, Lava Rae Cruikshank. In the first decades of the 20th century, Blizzard earned regional fame while leading an army of over 10,000 miners on a march into Logan County, which resulted in a clash with law enforcement entities in what was later dubbed the Battle of Blair Mountain. For his involvement in the clash, Blizzard was tried for treason and murder but was later acquitted of those charges. Shown at right is Bill Blizzard with one of his grandchildren on the family's pony, Pony Bill. Shown below is Blizzard admiring the water lilies by his Winfield home several years before his death from cancer in 1958. (Both, courtesy of West Virginia State Archives.)

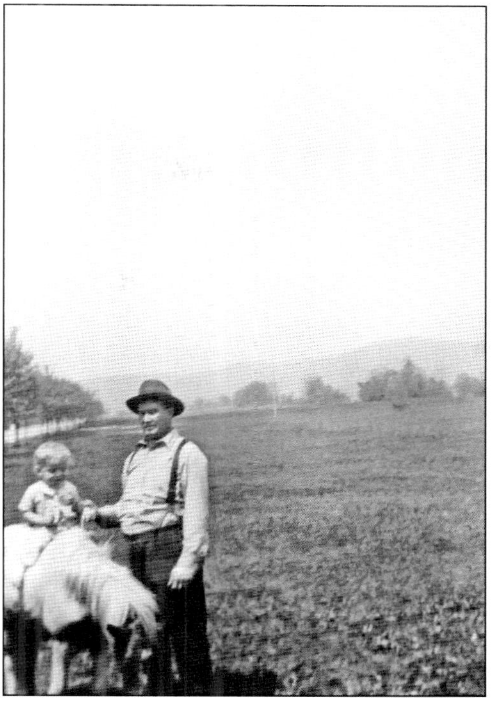

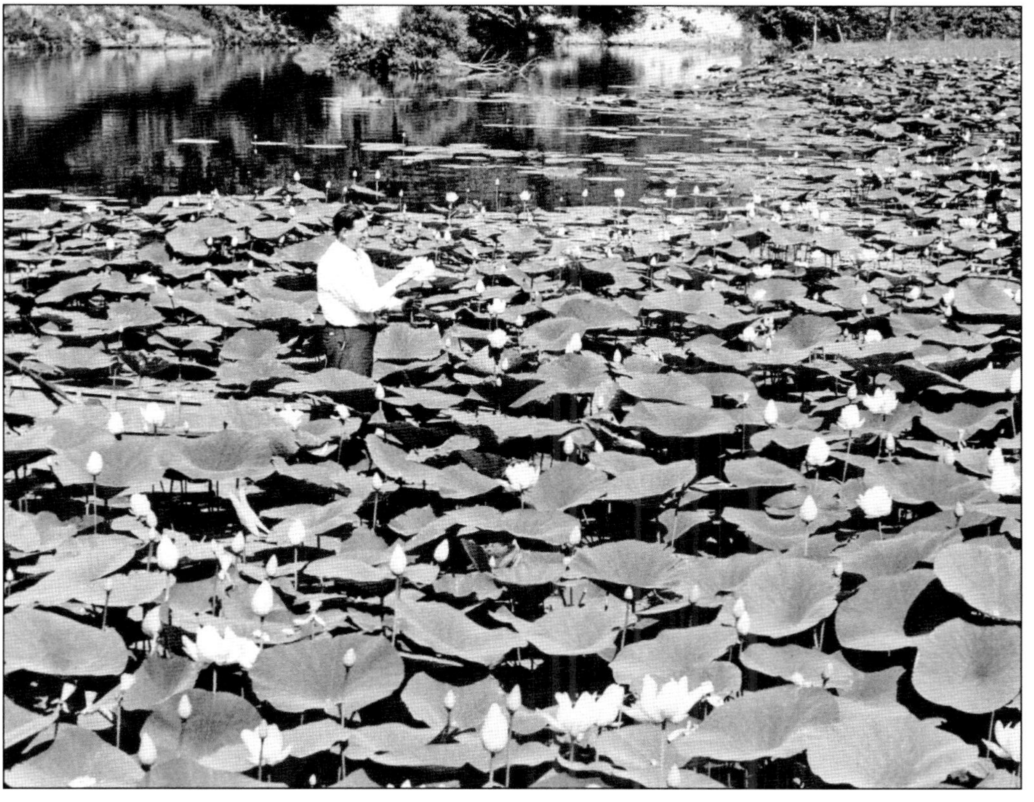

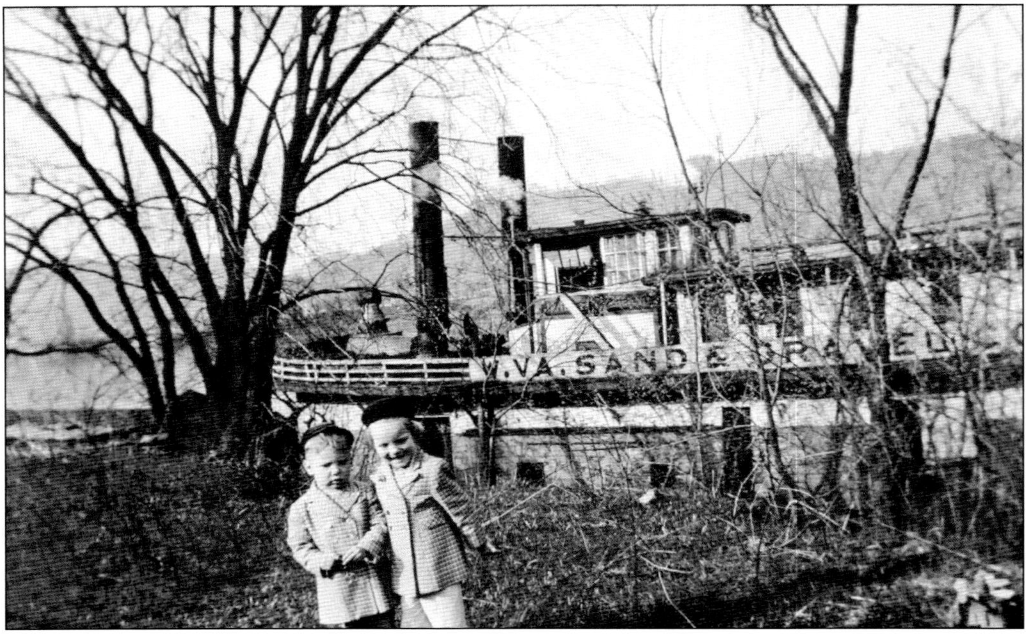

Like the town of Buffalo, Winfield was very much tied to and reliant upon river vessels as a means of transportation and communication in its earliest years. Riverboats were the means by which the town received its mail up through the early 1900s. Additionally, with no bridge over the Kanawha River at Winfield until the Winfield Toll Bridge opened in December 1957—ending nearly 140 years of ferry—residents and travelers through the area often required transportation via steamboats, which could make trips to nearby Red House on the north side of the river seem like quite an endeavor. Photographed here are two grandchildren of William Blizzard posing along the Kanawha in Winfield as a large steamboat passes down the river—a common sight in Winfield at the time. (Both, courtesy of West Virginia State Archives.)

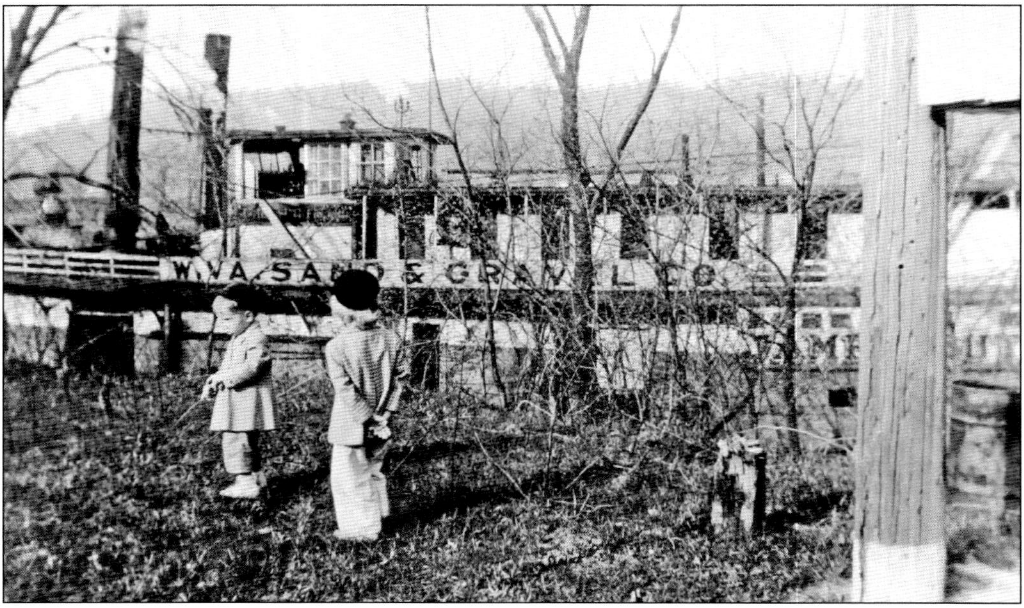

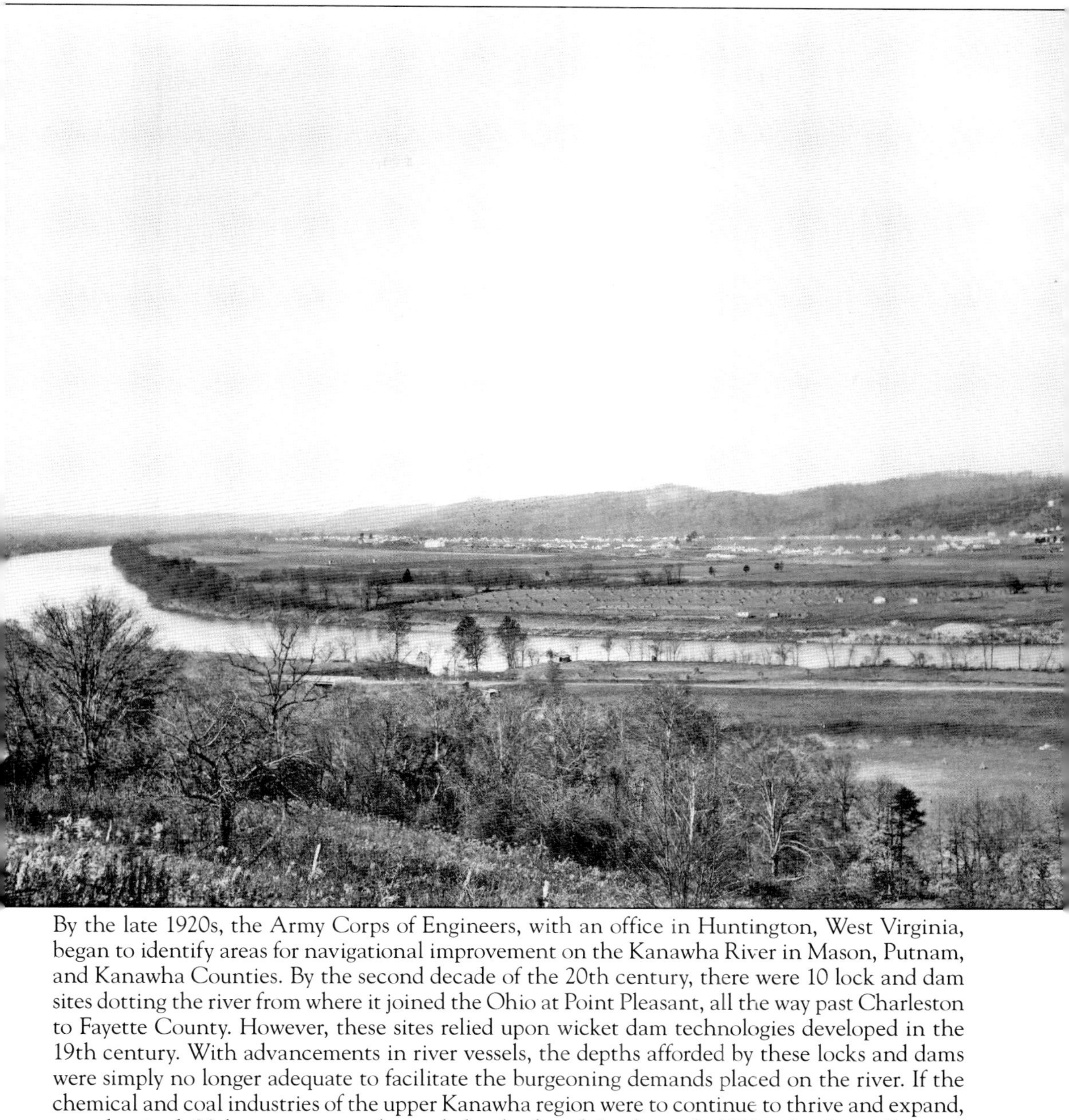

By the late 1920s, the Army Corps of Engineers, with an office in Huntington, West Virginia, began to identify areas for navigational improvement on the Kanawha River in Mason, Putnam, and Kanawha Counties. By the second decade of the 20th century, there were 10 lock and dam sites dotting the river from where it joined the Ohio at Point Pleasant, all the way past Charleston to Fayette County. However, these sites relied upon wicket dam technologies developed in the 19th century. With advancements in river vessels, the depths afforded by these locks and dams were simply no longer adequate to facilitate the burgeoning demands placed on the river. If the chemical and coal industries of the upper Kanawha region were to continue to thrive and expand, a modernized, 20th-century remedy needed to be found. In the early 1930s, the Army Corps of Engineers proposed a series of new locks and dam sites on the Kanawha and Ohio—some of which would update and expand existing locations while others would be placed at previously untouched spots. Winfield Locks and Dam would be the latter instance. The Winfield location, shown above, was placed just a short distance downstream from the town of Winfield. (Courtesy of Army Corps of Engineers.)

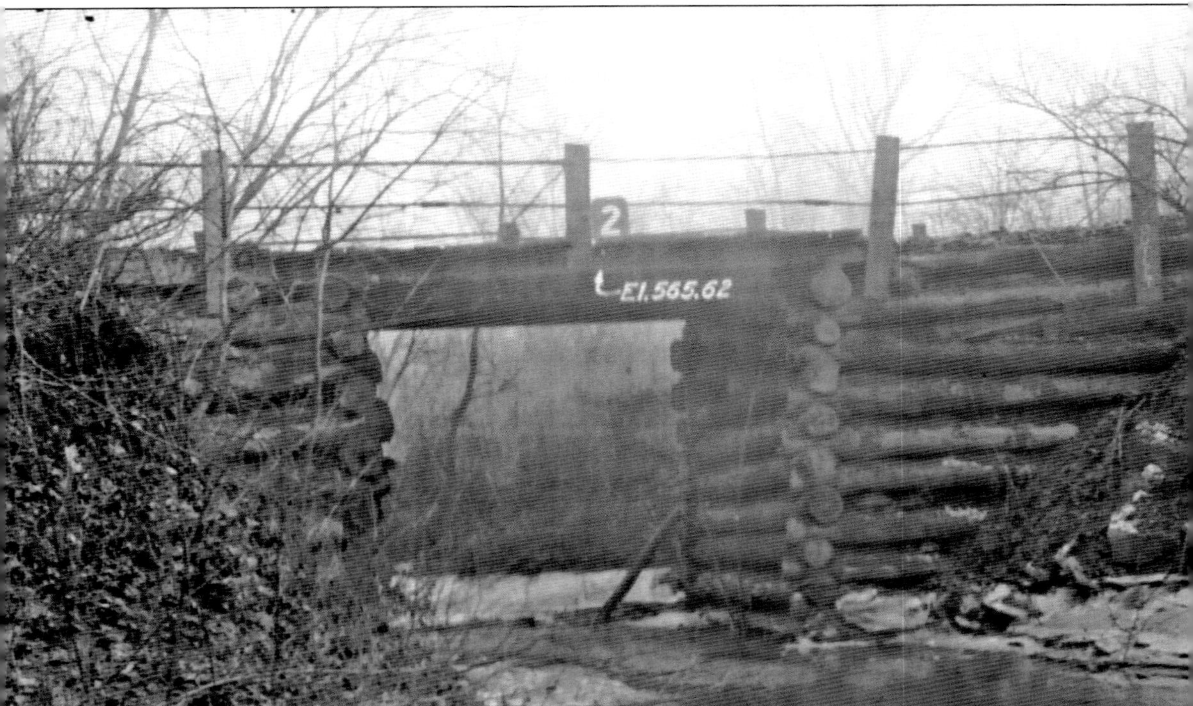

The project of constructing a new dam site at Winfield, by its very nature, meant that water levels upstream from the site, termed the "pool," would be significantly increased. As a result, land bordering the Kanawha River in this area would be directly affected by rising water levels that could claim large areas of previously dry property. Logically, property owners all up and down the river were concerned about the water's encroachments, and they turned their attention to the federal government to have concerns addressed. In 1939, the town of South Charleston wrote their senators, expressing dissatisfaction with the Army Corps of Engineers' responses to property damage claims. In this image, Army Corps photographers documented areas of the Kanawha River that were to be affected by the Winfield project—in this case, a small wooden bridge over the Pocatalico River shortly before its emptying into the Kanawha. The small white arrow at the middle of the bridge shows where the proposed water level would reach once the Winfield Locks and Dam project was completed. (Courtesy of Army Corps of Engineers.)

The view at right offers an impressive glimpse of the entire height of just one of the roller gate piers during a later stage of construction. Beyond the tower is the cofferdam structure, which was a temporary dam barrier made of welded steel that shielded the construction site from the water coming downstream. Though the river was temporarily dammed and diverted around the areas of construction, the river bottom was a damp and soggy base on which to work, as evidenced in the view below depicting two laborers working on the foundation of the lock chamber walls. (Both, courtesy of Army Corps of Engineers.)

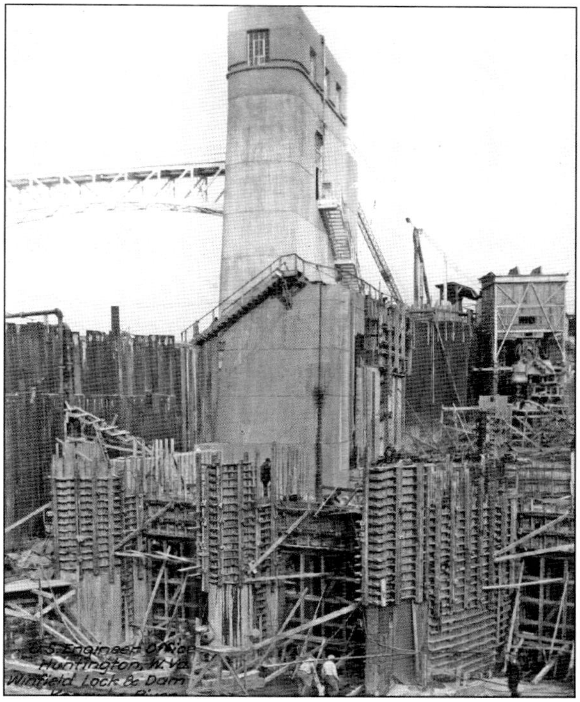

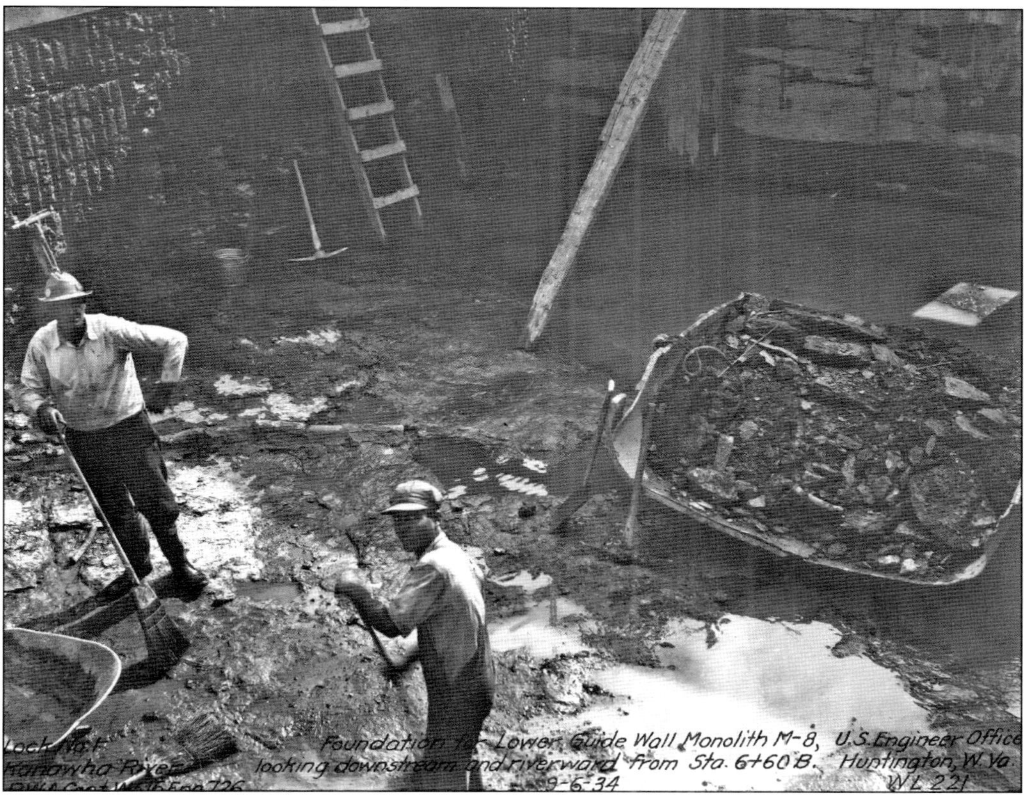

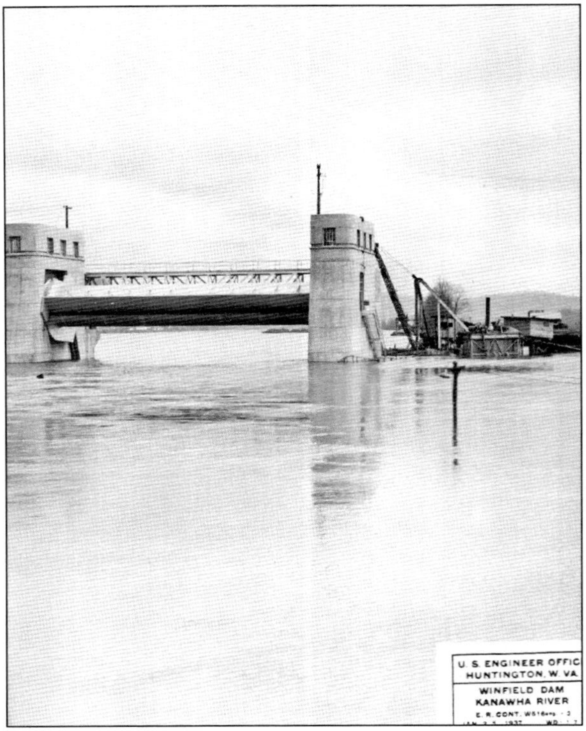

The massive floods that struck the Kanawha River and inundated Buffalo in January 1937 also reached farther upriver to the construction site of the Winfield Locks and Dam project. Shown here, the water levels easily ran only a few feet lower than the dam rollers in a raised position. Many of the project's construction cranes were tipped over or washed away in the torrents of water, while those that remained anchored in place suffered severe damage that delayed some of the latter stages of the project. When the waters finally receded days later, mud and sediment covered much of the project site that was yet to be completed. (Both, courtesy of Army Corps of Engineers.)

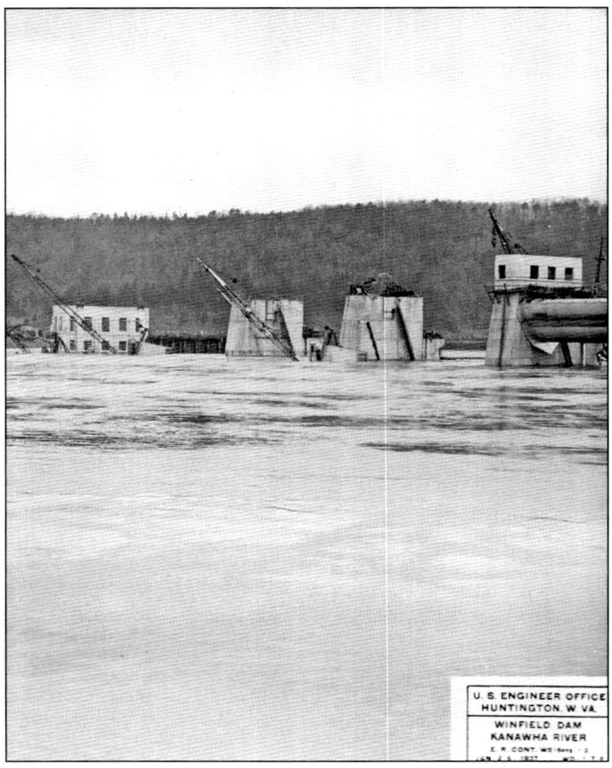

Workers recruited from all over the Kanawha River Valley region and beyond labored in the mud, preparing the lock foundation for one of the two twin lock chambers. The wooden walls depicted in the photograph served as concrete forms for the permanent edifice of the lock chambers. (Courtesy of Army Corps of Engineers.)

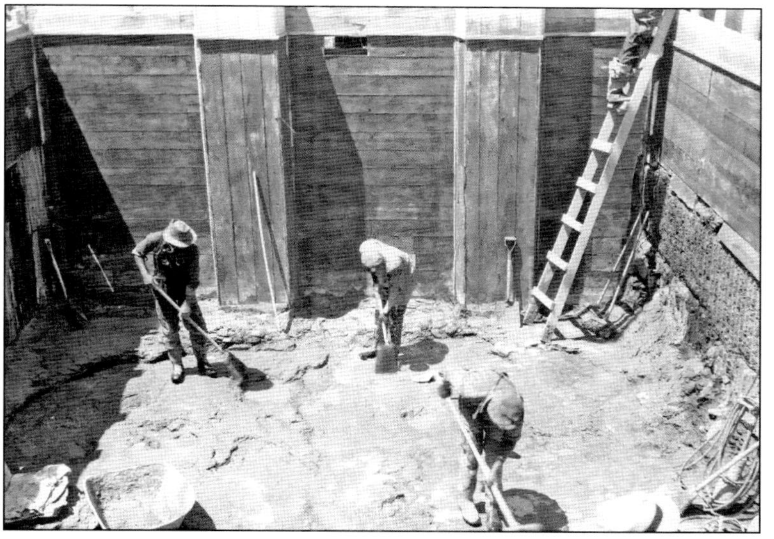

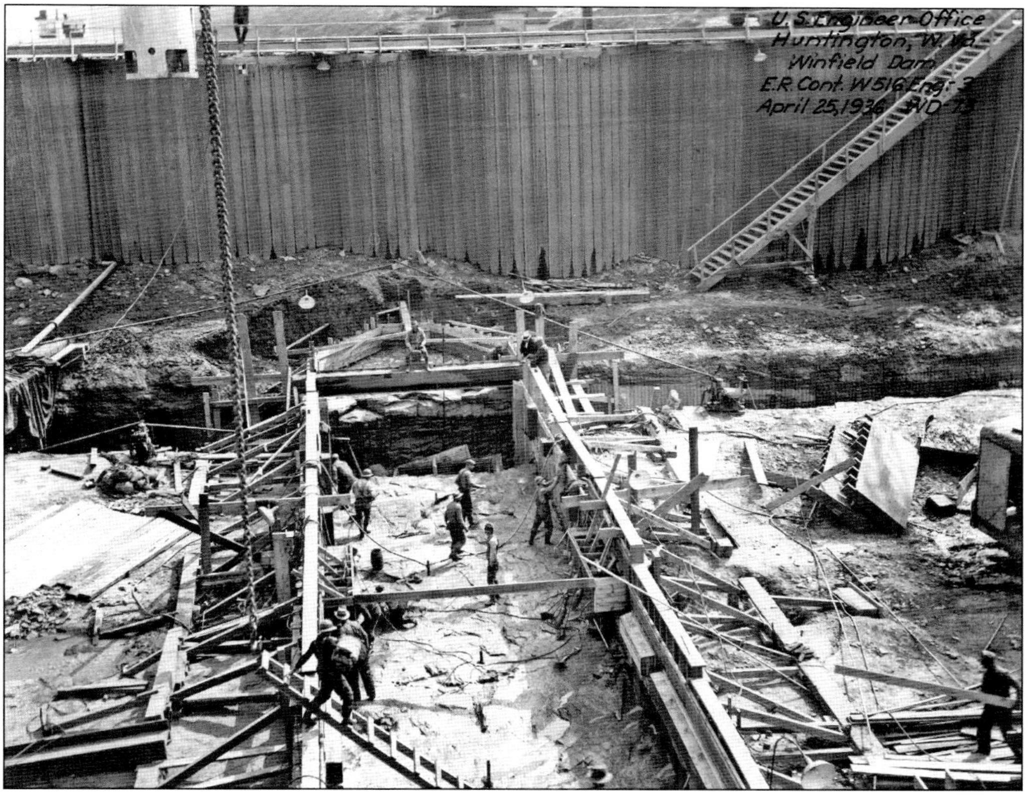

Depicted here is the early stage of construction on just one of the seven pier towers that span the Kanawha at the Winfield Locks and Dam. After excavating downward toward a solid, sturdy base of rock below the sediments of the riverbed, workers erected tons of lumber to form a concrete mold for the shaping of the massive piers. In the upper left-hand corner of the image is a concrete bucket, which was lowered and raised by means of one of a dozen cranes at the site. (Courtesy of Army Corps of Engineers.)

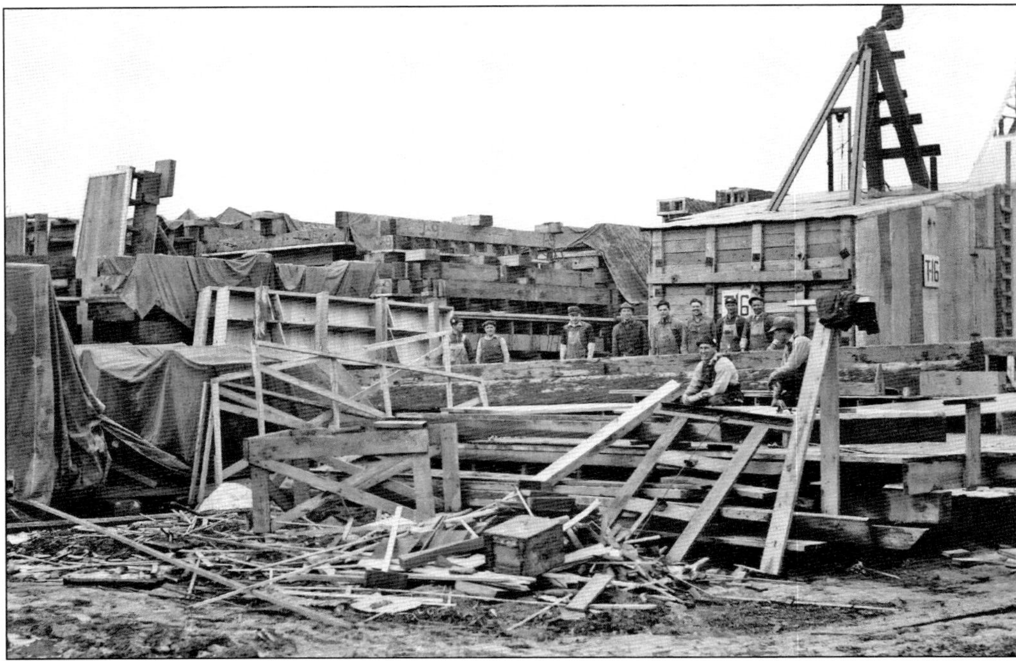

During the construction of the locks and dam, workers assembled temporary sheds, shacks, and garages along the banks of the river to allow for easy and convenient transportation and storage of equipment and building materials. In the above photograph, workers pose amidst the stacks of wooden forms used in the molding of concrete. Below, a team of men work together on the immense task of piecing together a web of lumber, into which concrete will be poured, with the end product being one of the massive piers between which the rollers operate. Even standing on top of the foundation, the men in this photograph are still below the river's water level, which can be slightly seen behind the cofferdam in the background. (Both, courtesy of Army Corps of Engineers.)

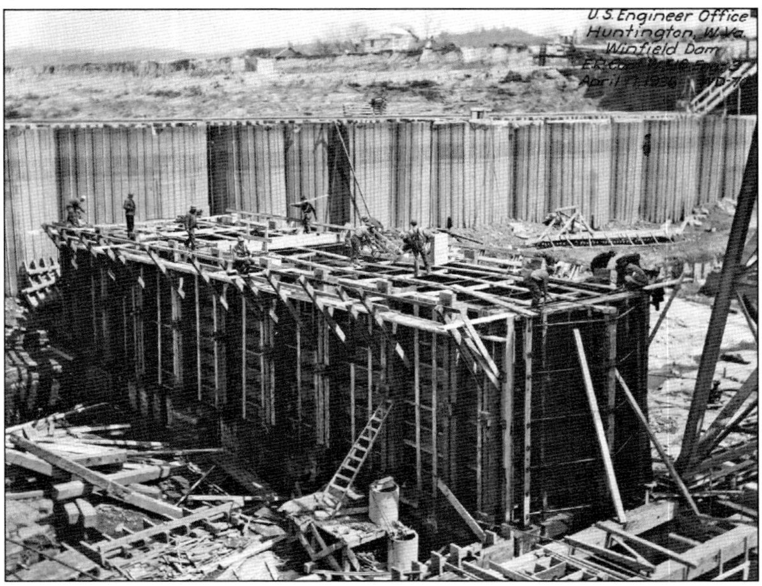

The locks and dam's construction called for large rollers to extend between each of the dam's large piers spanning the river's width. To facilitate the raising and lowering of the completed roller gates, large motors (right) on the top of each pier provided the necessary power for the massive load. The normal operation of moving the rollers was not the most difficult aspect encountered at the site. On August 5, 1936, while trying to move the end of one of the rollers into place, one of two cranes being used buckled under the immense weight, which in turn caused the other crane to fail (below). Luckily, no one was seriously injured. (Both, courtesy of Army Corps of Engineers.)

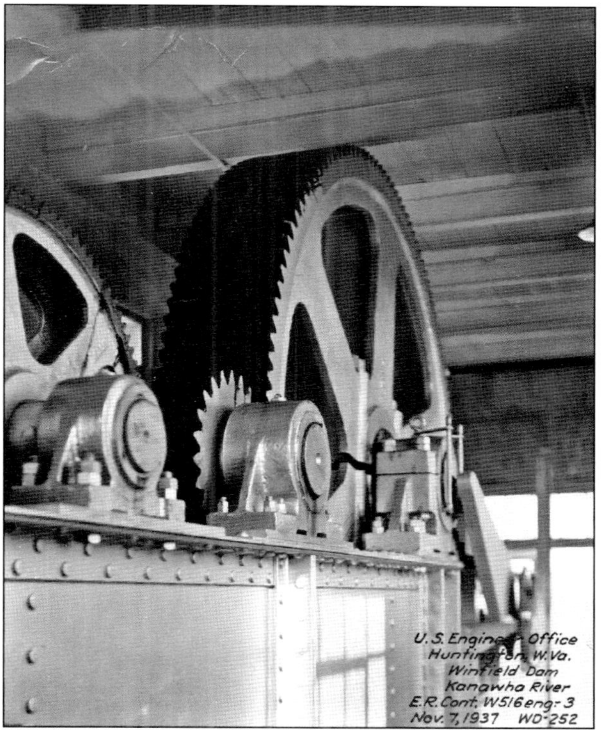

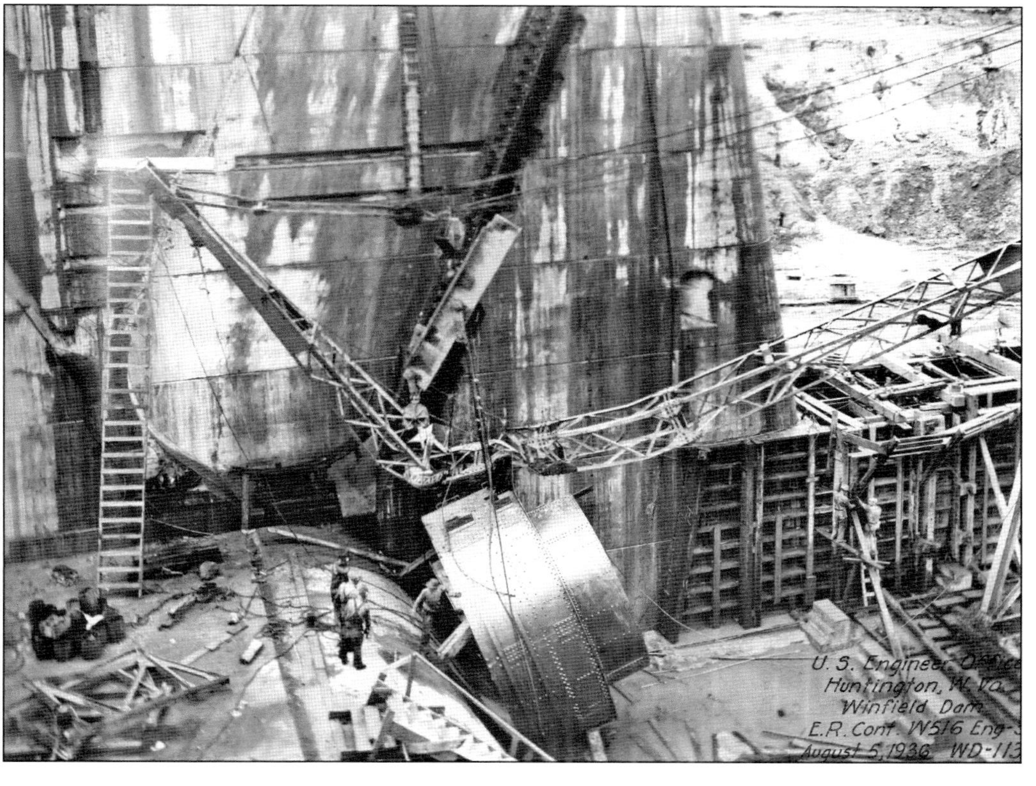

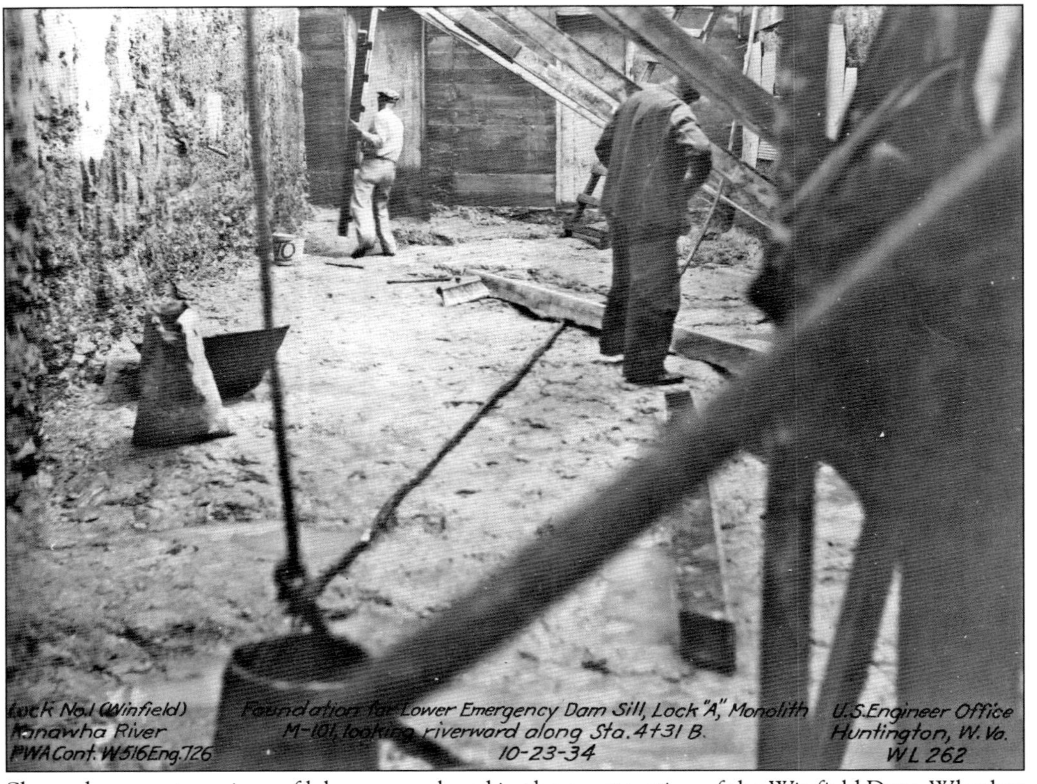

Shown here are two views of laborers employed in the construction of the Winfield Dam. Whether they were assigned to work on the building of the dam's sill foundation (above) or to the crews reinforcing the temporary cofferdams at the hydroelectricity facility (below), all were subject to a series of New Deal regulations that were new and somewhat revolutionary—and sometimes unpopular. The main regulation was the strict enforcement of the eight-hour workday. Roosevelt's administration in Washington, DC, required early on in the Kanawha improvement projects that the Public Works Administration's guidelines be followed, including this limitation on the length of work shifts. Unfortunately, Dravo Contracting Company had many issues with finding qualified, skilled workers to perform certain tasks, which was further complicated when the limited number of highly qualified men were allowed only eight hours of work per day. (Both, courtesy of Army Corps of Engineers.)

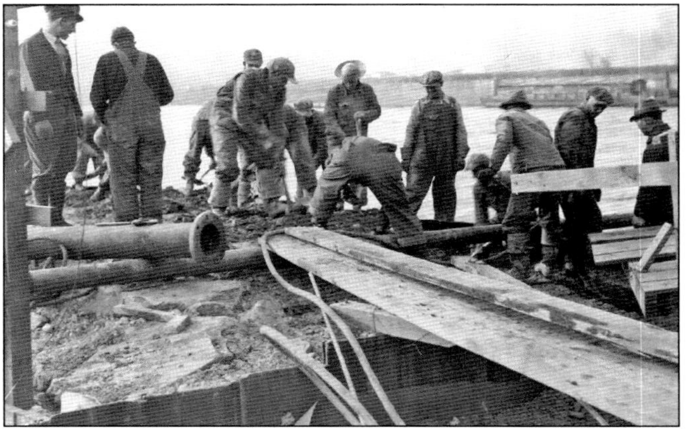

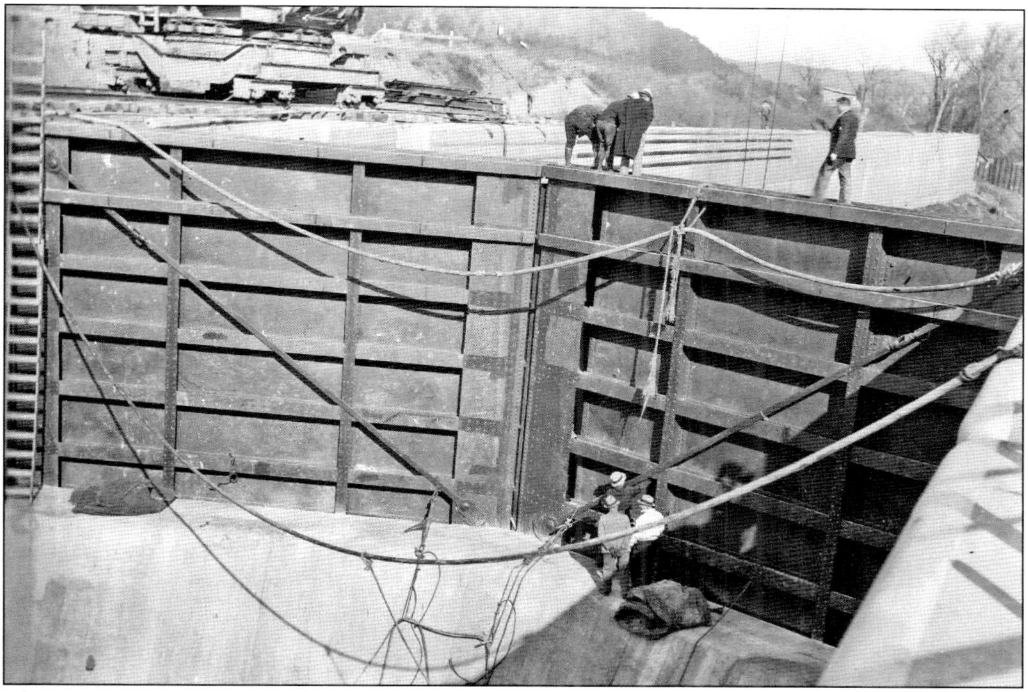

The Army Corps of Engineers' project at Winfield called for the construction of two lock chambers—each measuring 56 feet wide by 360 feet long. With miter gates on both ends of the lock chambers to hold out water in conjunction with controllable valves, water was flowed into and out of the space, which allowed gravity and buoyancy to essentially raise and lower a river vessel that entered either of the locks. Shown here in November 1934, workers test the newly assembled miter gates, each of which closed at an approximately 18 degree angle, providing extra strength because of the arch shape that was formed. (Both, courtesy of Army Corps of Engineers.)

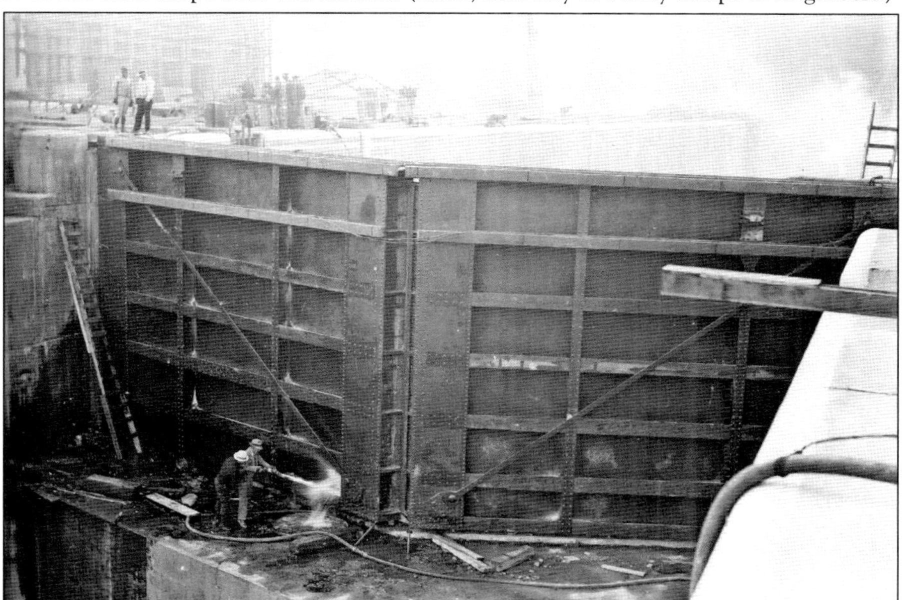

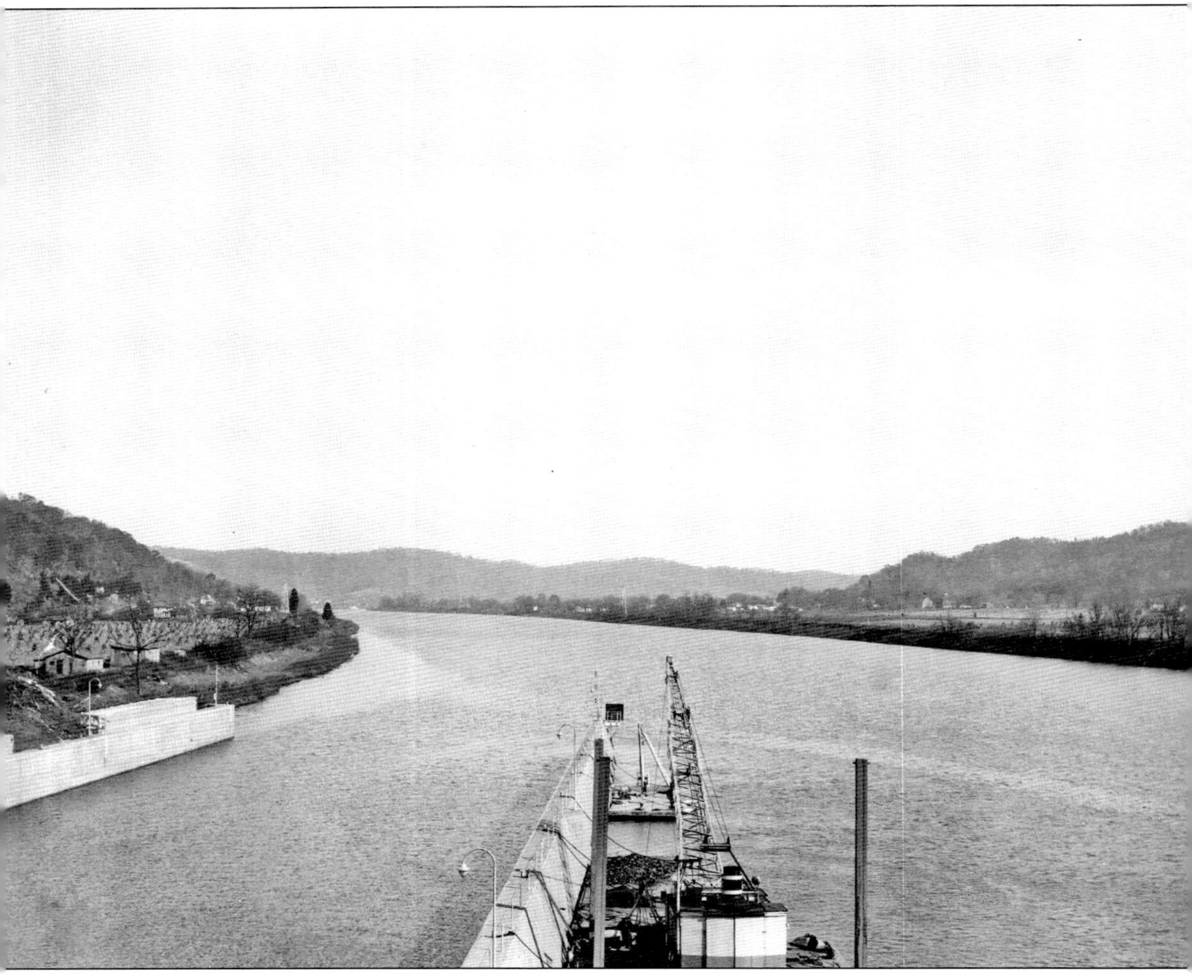

Taken from atop one of the tall piers spanning the river, this view looks upstream at the pool created by the dam. In the distance can be seen the faint outlines of houses and a water tower, all part of the town of Winfield. Today, the Winfield Toll Bridge would be prominently seen spanning the width of the river from this angle; however, construction of the bridge did not begin until 1955. The left-hand portion of the photograph shows the approach to the lock chambers. Once the roller gates were operational and able to control the levels of the river, the depth of the upstream pool was increased to around nine feet, which greatly enhanced the navigability of the river by barges and other river craft. (Courtesy of Army Corps of Engineers.)

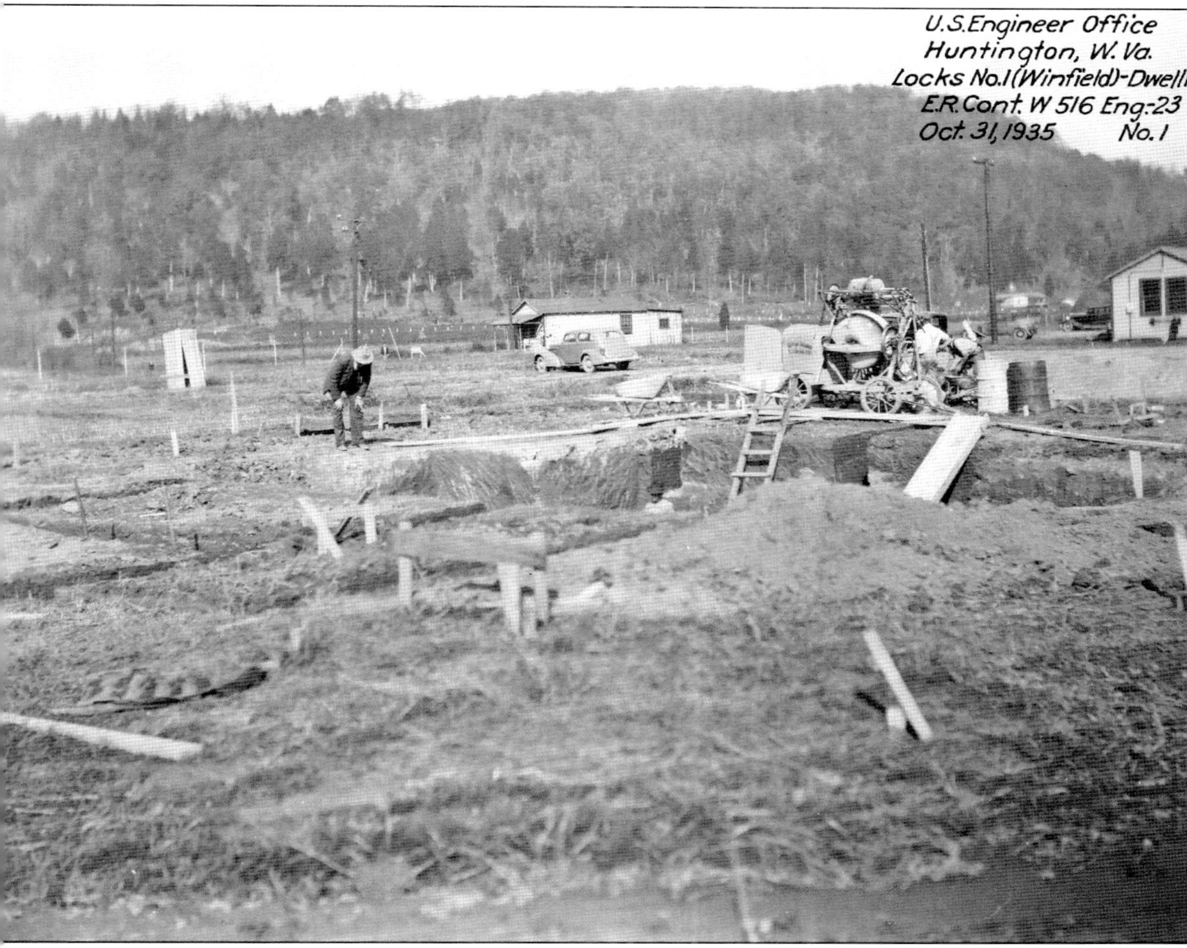

As part of the Winfield Locks and Dam project, two housing quarters were constructed on the grounds of the project to be occupied by the future lockmaster and assistant lockmaster. The area of ground on the north bank of the Kanawha River where the houses were constructed is the same tract of land on which stood the domicile of George Washington's nephew, Lawrence Augustine Washington. The property included over 3,000 acres of agricultural land and, after 1811, was the location of Lawrence's family residence. In the second decade of the 1800s, the Virginia legislature granted Washington the right to construct a wing-dam system on the Kanawha River, which was meant to deepen the center depth of the Kanawha River along Red House shoals. Photographed here, the project foreman inspects the basement excavations for the lockmaster house. (Courtesy of Army Corps of Engineers.)

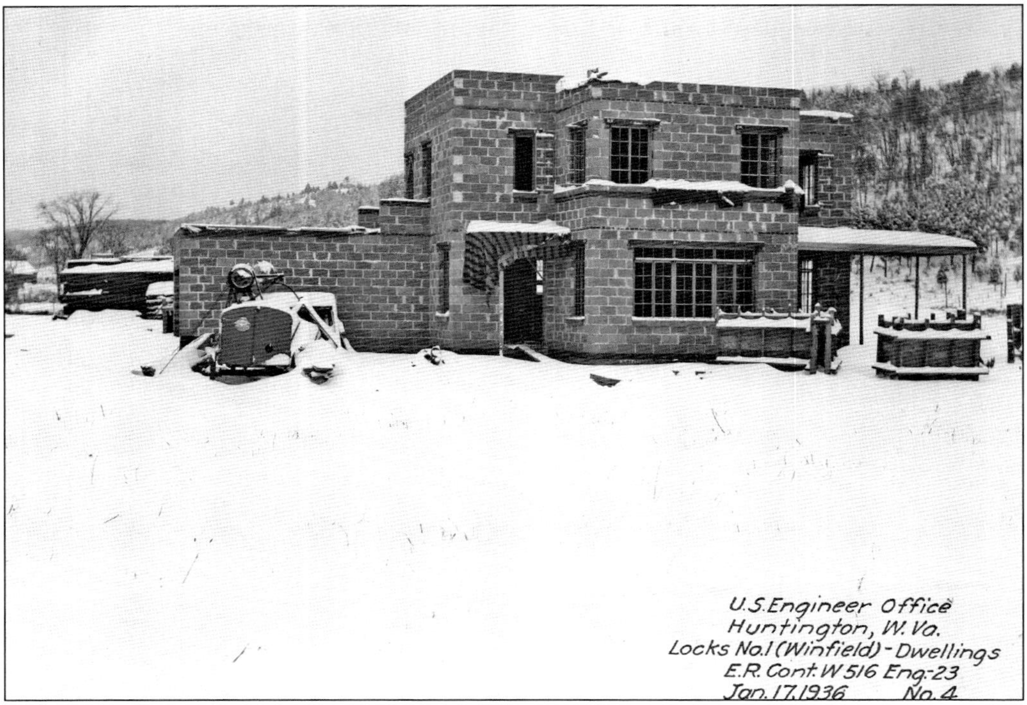

Like the houses constructed in the nearby town of Eleanor around the same time, the two lockmaster residences were built of a simplistic cinder block design. Though a solid and durable method, the use of blocks resulted in persistent moisture problems within the houses. Shown here is the lockmaster house after the initial framing of the structure, photographed in the aftermath of a strong nor'easter snowstorm that temporarily halted the teams of construction crews on the site in the middle of January 1936. Records indicate that when temperatures rose sharply a week later, the resulting melting of snow caused minor flooding in the muddy construction site, which further delayed work. (Both, courtesy of Army Corps of Engineers.)

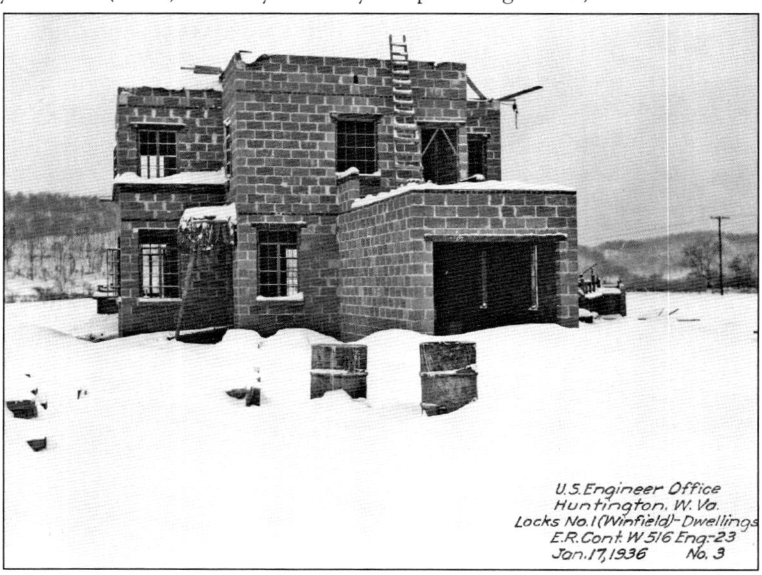

The lockmaster's and assistant lockmaster's houses were both completed by mid- to late 1936—well in advance of the 1937 completion of the entire locks and dam project. Having housing at the site of the locks and dam was rather standard at the time for the Army Corps of Engineers, just as in coastal locations where government-built and -operated lighthouses often had a caretaker's residence. These two lockhouse dwellings were in existence until the 1980s. The ground on which they stood was heavily excavated and altered during the 1990s addition of a third lock chamber on the northern end of Winfield Locks and Dam. (Both, courtesy of Army Corps of Engineers.)

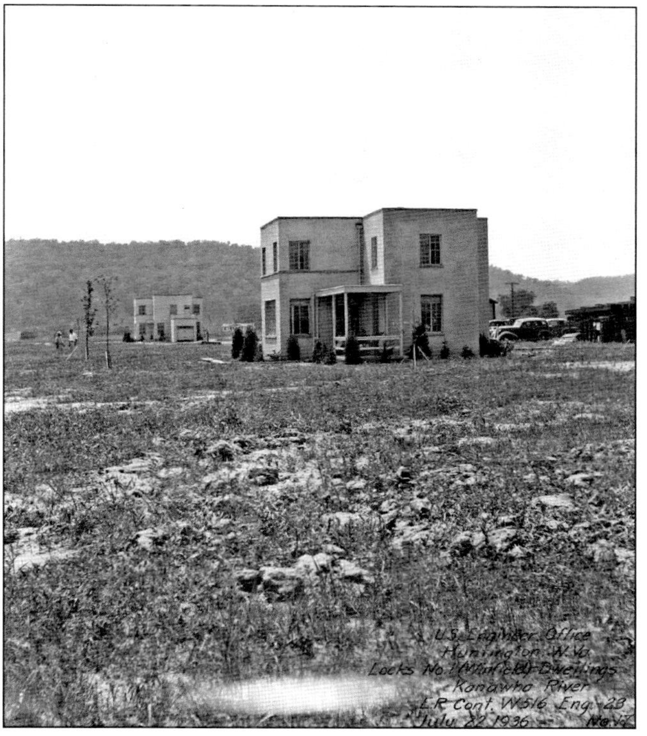

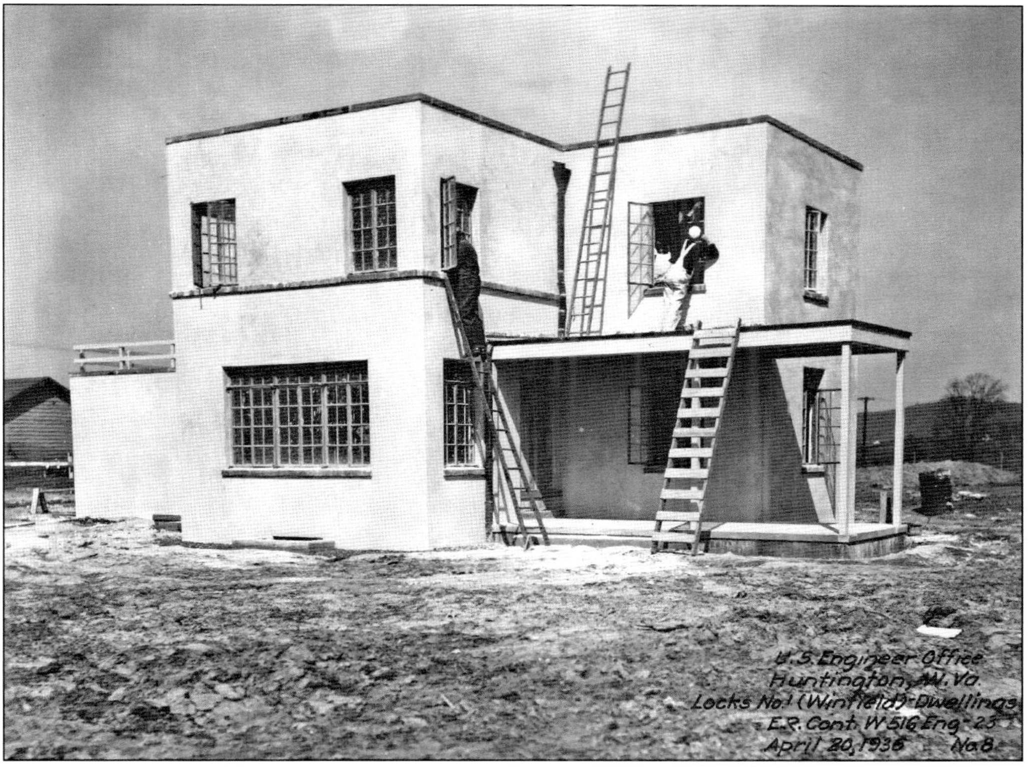

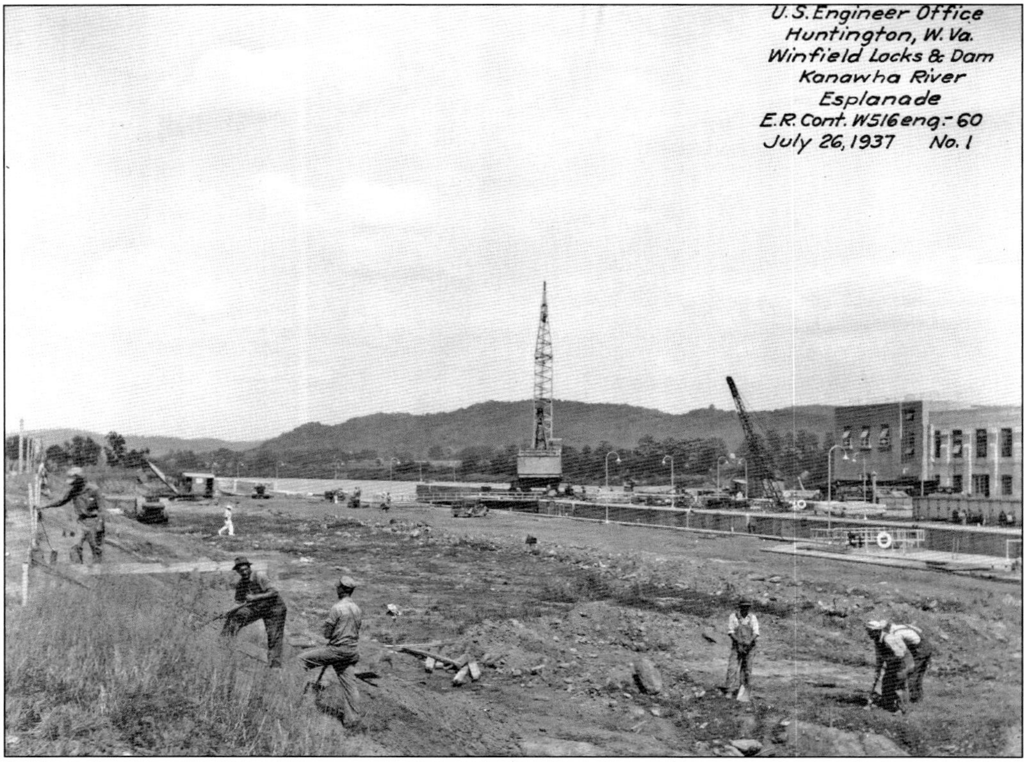

In the latter stages of the construction of the Winfield Locks and Dam, crews turned their attention toward the finishing touches of landscaping at the site. Running along the entire northern bank bordering the lock chambers, workers constructed an esplanade and flood bank to run between the lockmaster houses on higher ground and the locks and dam at river level. Above, workers amassed a steep 45-degree bank that sloped down to the locks. Below, large mechanical rollers were used to flatten and surface the esplanade area, which basically served as a parking lot for the locks and dam site. (Both, courtesy of Army Corps of Engineers.)

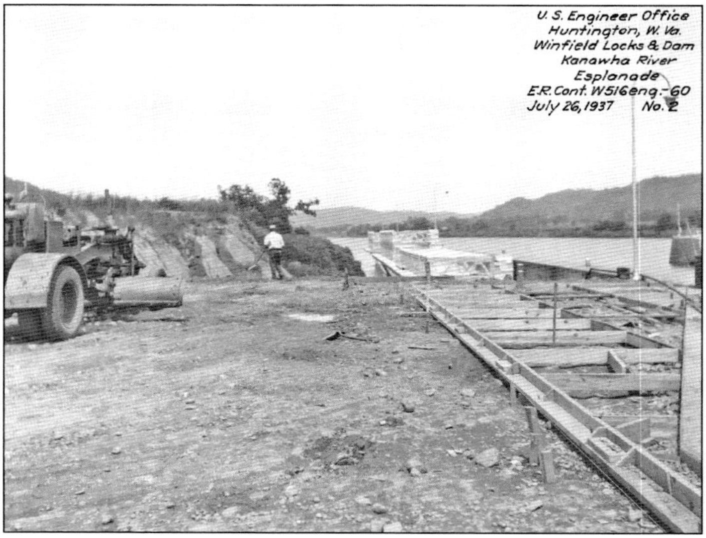

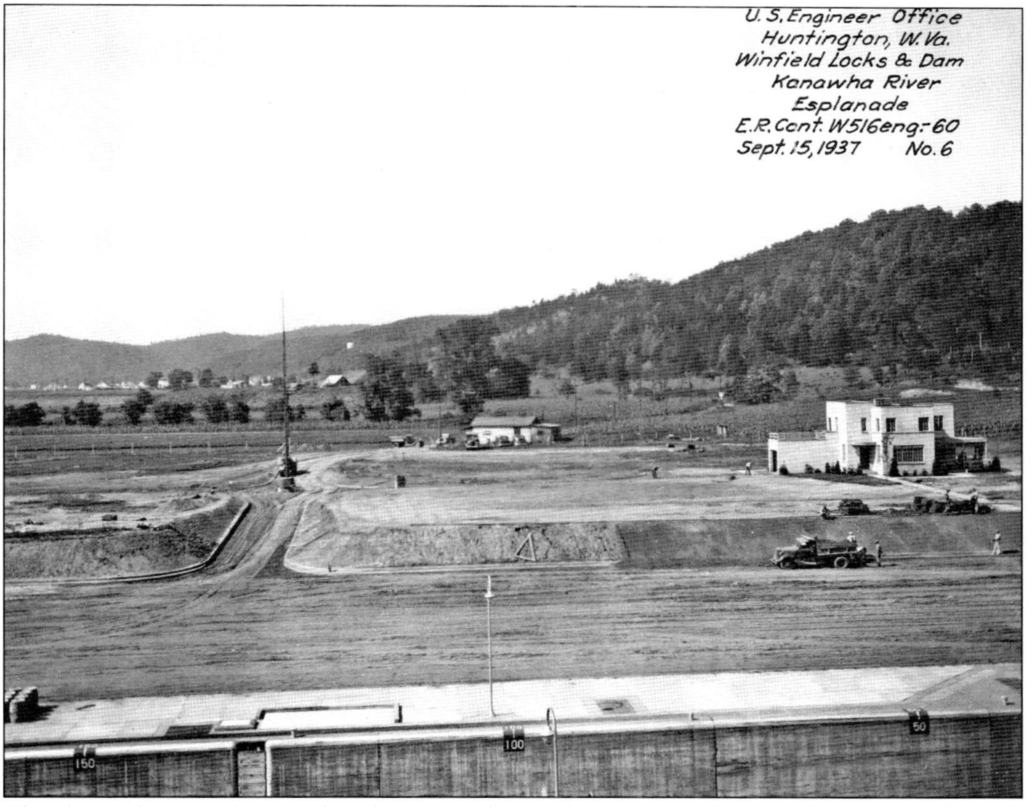

The above photograph was taken from atop the northern pier, with the walls of one of the lock chambers visible in the immediate foreground. The wooden structure near the center surrounded by cars and trucks served as a temporary foreman's office and storage building during the entire construction of the locks and dam. Interestingly, the newly constructed white houses of distant Eleanor are visible in the far left background. The image below portrays the half-dozen men who were needed in September 1937 to erect the flagpole in the center of the previous photograph—a fixture at every Army Corps of Engineers site. (Both, courtesy of Army Corps of Engineers.)

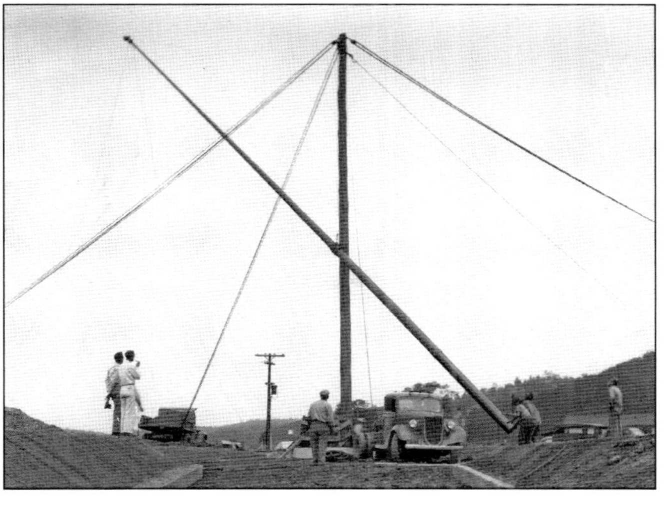

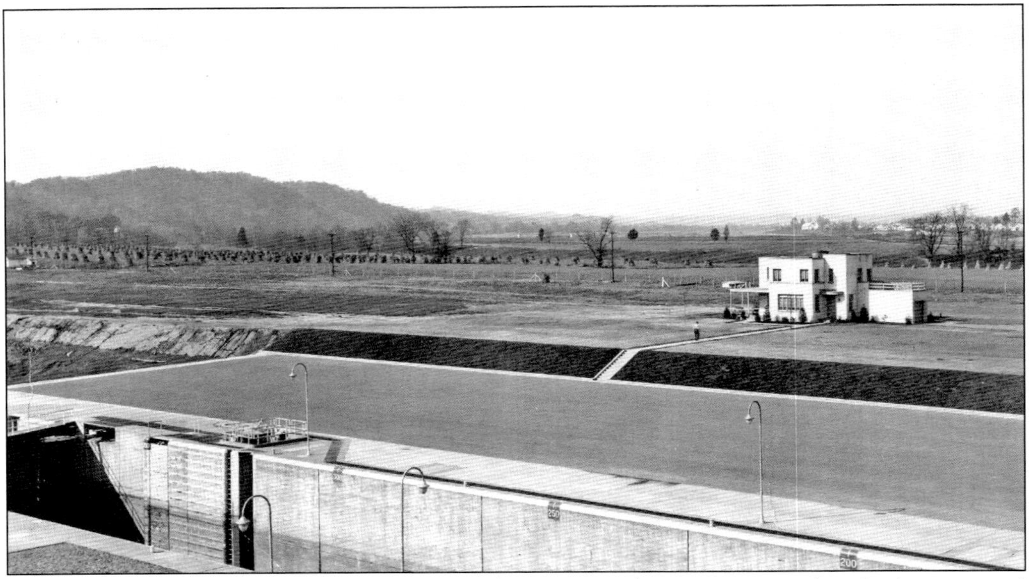

The above photograph, captured from atop the site's northern pier, was taken looking toward the northwest at the angle at which the Kanawha River turns as it meanders downstream from Winfield Locks and Dam. When this photograph was captured, the lock and dam was complete except for the ongoing hydroelectric project on the opposite shore of the site. The lockhouse in the photograph was that of the assistant lockmaster. Seen below is a photograph taken from the south bank of the Kanawha, showing the roller gates in operation after the removal of the temporary cofferdam. Both lockhouses and esplanade are visible in the background. (Both, courtesy of Army Corps of Engineers.)

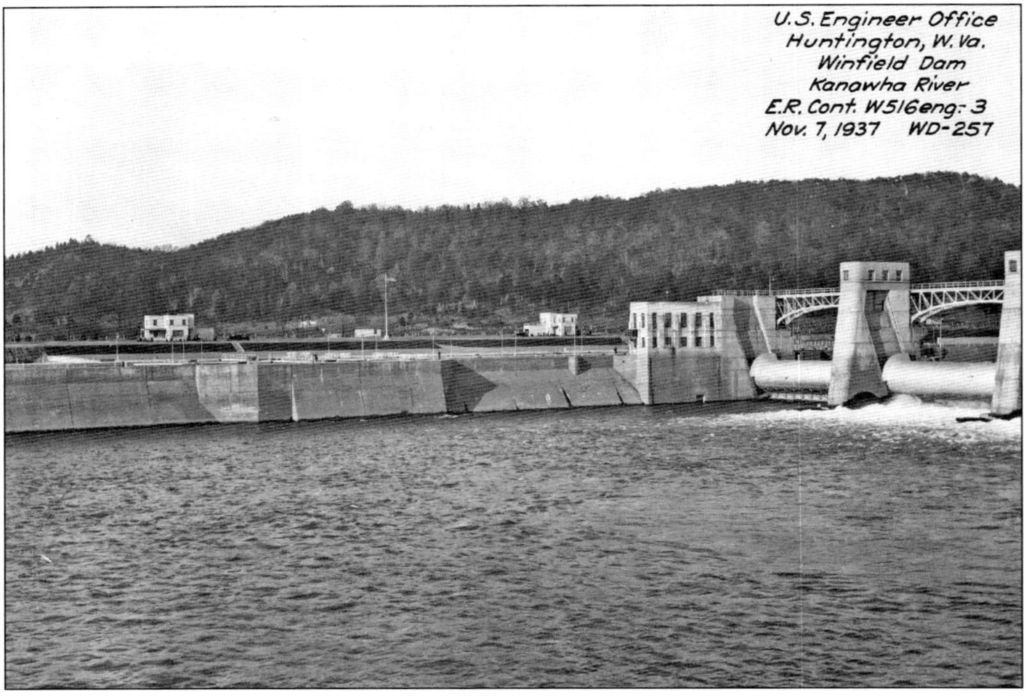

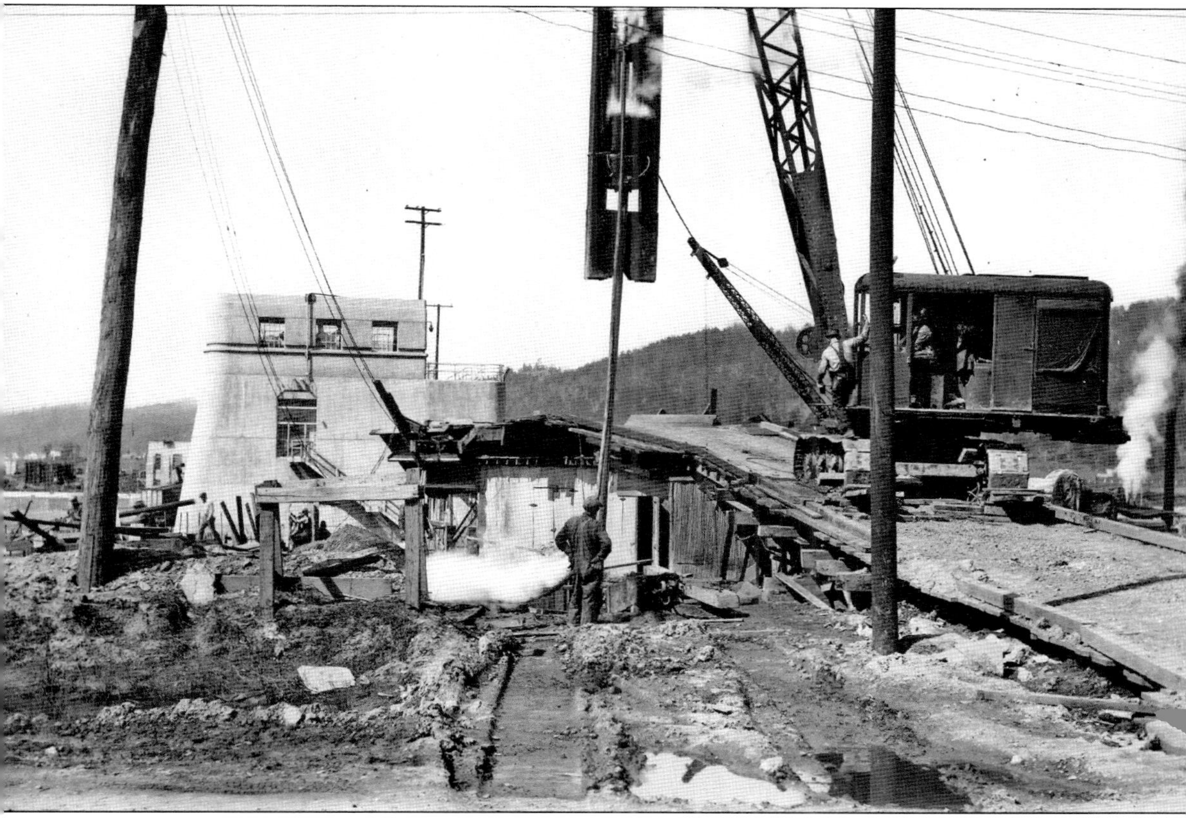

The government legislation that authorized the series of river navigation improvement projects along the Kanawha was not concerned solely with creating a deeper navigable channel by which river vessels could ply the water safely and easily. Rather, the project also called for a federally operated power project that would harness the power of the Kanawha River through the use of hydroelectric plants at various sites along the waterway. At Winfield, the hydroelectric plant was to be built on the southern portion of the locks and dam site. The use of powerful water currents for production of electricity in West Virginia was no new idea at the time. Since at least the early 1920s, federal and state government entities had been looking into the feasibility of constructing hydroelectric plants at various sites throughout the state. Even private companies had found great success in West Virginia hydroelectric endeavors, including the Electro-Metallurgical Company's successful completion of a plant near Hawks Nest along the New River. (Courtesy of Army Corps of Engineers.)

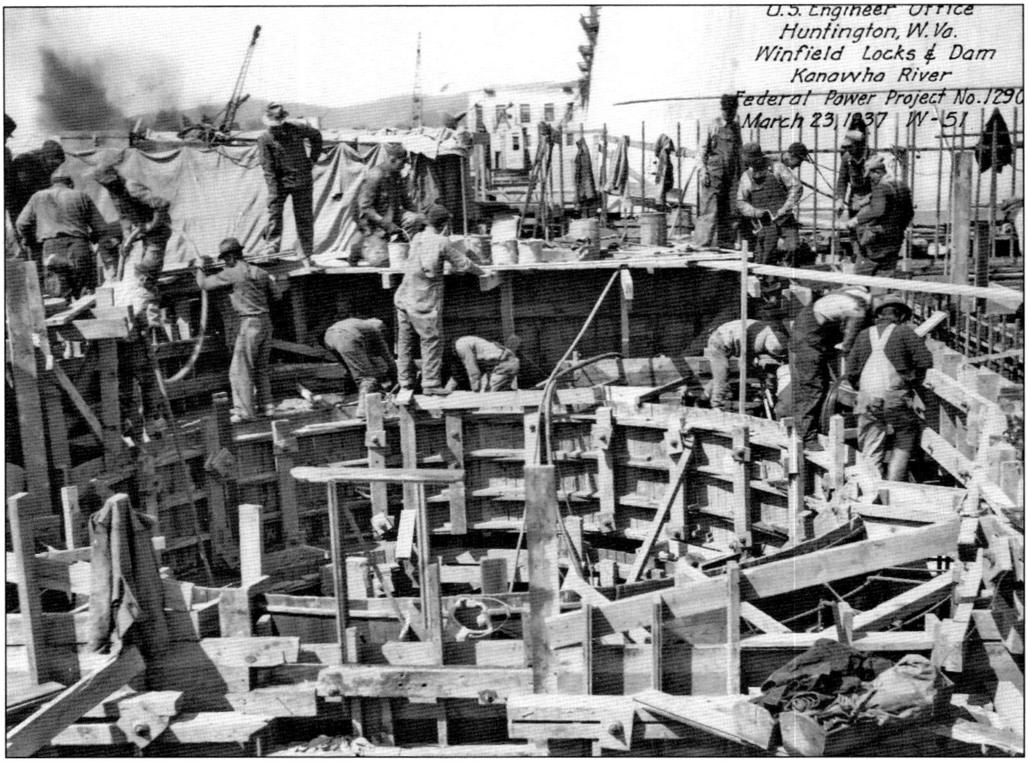

In the above photograph are the scores of workers hired to work on construction of the turbine pits that were to be the focal point of the hydroelectric plant at Winfield. At this stage of the construction process, workers framed out the circular pit with timber, which was then filled with concrete. In total, there were three of these turbine pits constructed at the site. At hydroelectric plants built at large dams that were used for flood control, water levels upstream greatly fluctuated, which in turn could adversely affect power output and reliability. However, with locks and dam sites like Winfield, where roller gates provided for a constant level of water (nine feet) upstream, the success of hydroelectricity seemed likely. The photograph below depicts the same site several months later, after the hydroelectric plant powerhouse had been constructed. (Both, courtesy of Army Corps of Engineers.)

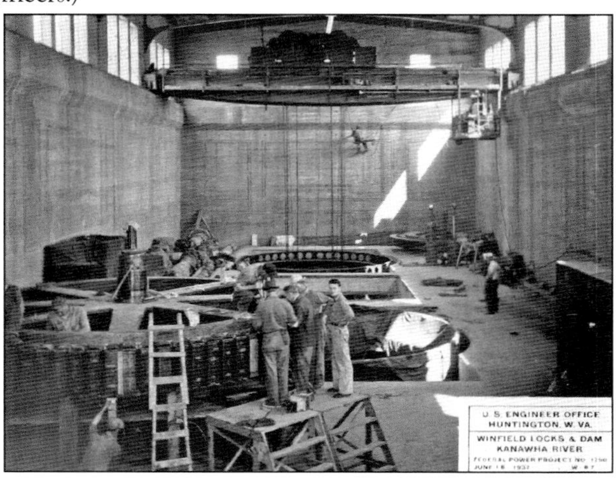

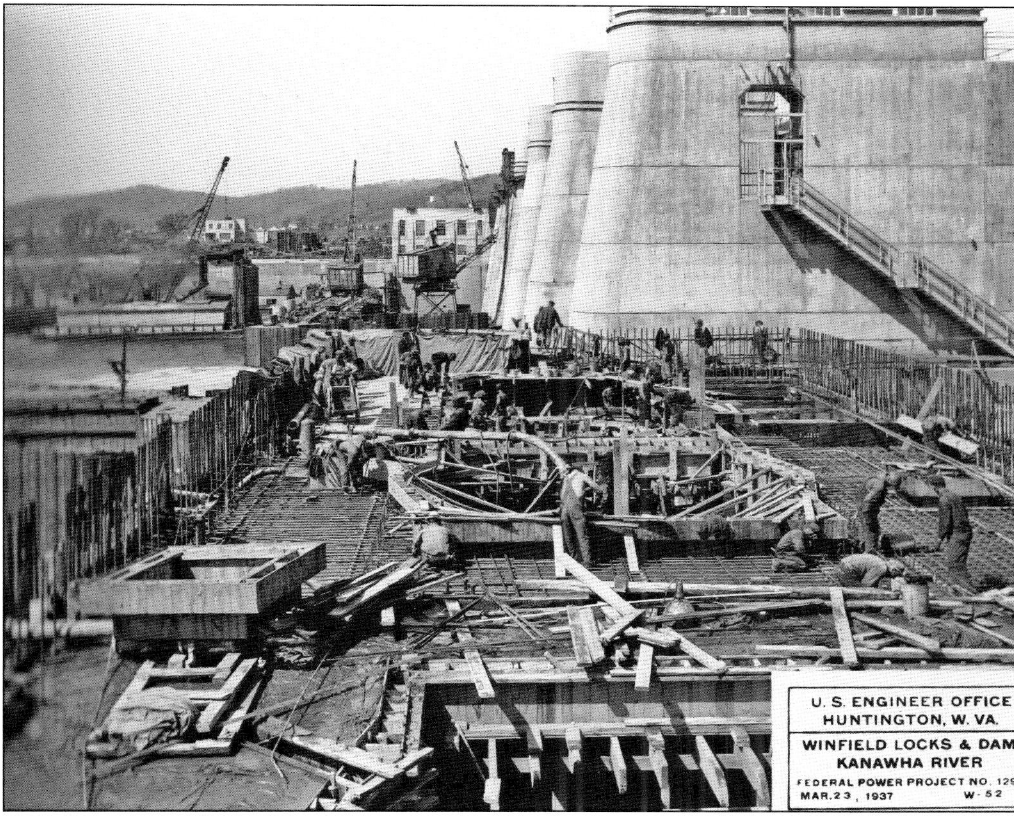

All three of the turbine pits are visible in the above view of the hydroelectric power plant construction site. Taken in March 1937, this photograph just barely captures the presence of water passing through the roller gates, signifying that the site was operational even while the power plant was being completed. The cranes in the background were located at the lock chambers on the north shore of the river. At right, work crews in late 1937 completed construction of the transformer station that sits adjacent to the hydroelectric plant, from which river-generated electricity is distributed from the site to power the surrounding region. (Both, courtesy of Army Corps of Engineers.)

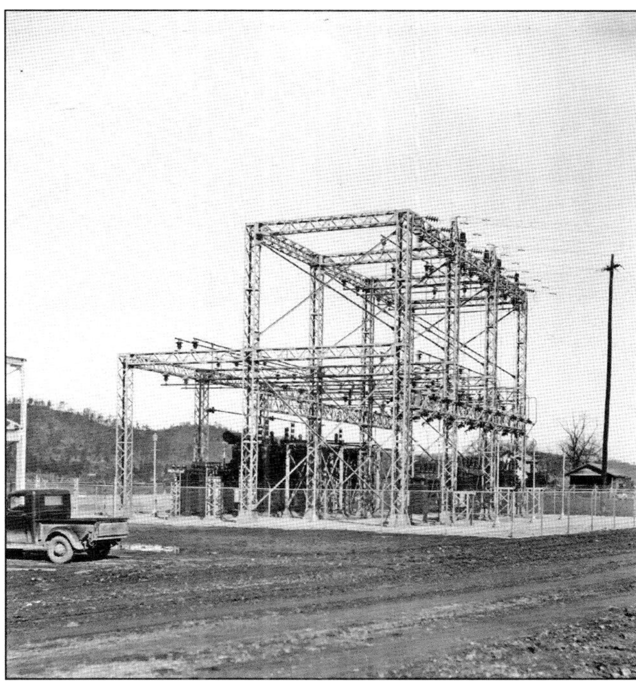

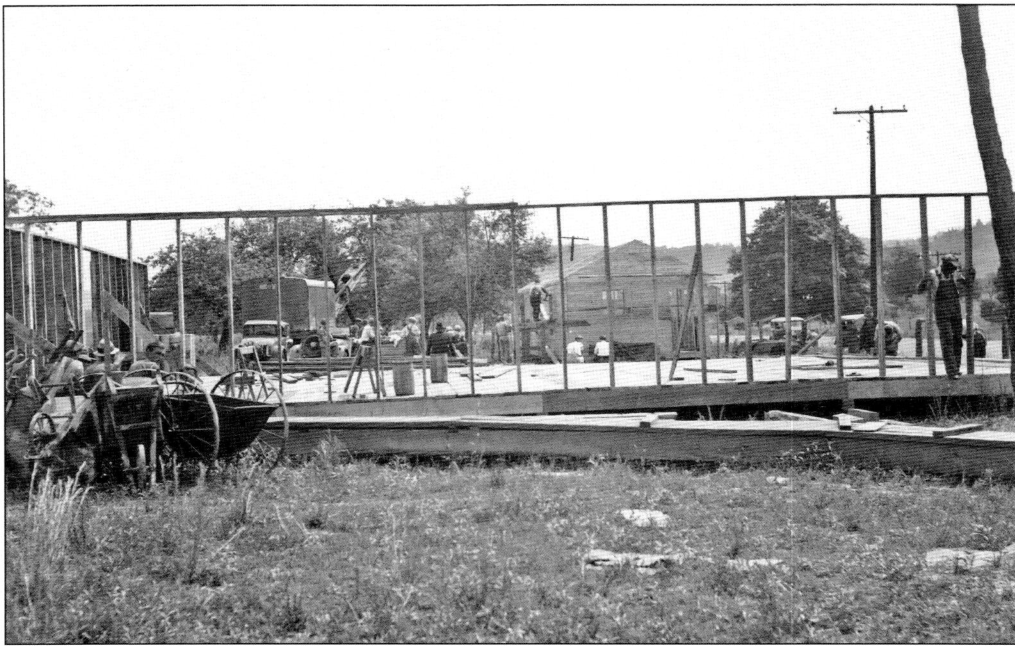

Above are workers erecting a series of temporary frame buildings to serve as garages and storage sheds during construction of the hydroelectric plant at Winfield. These structures stood for several years along modern Route 817, which runs along the south side of the Kanawha River. The structures provided safe storage for equipment, such as the wheelbarrows in the left corner, and for concrete framing equipment. The image below is taken from downstream of the Winfield project, showing an overall view of the completed site in 1937, with the hydroelectric power house on the right, seven piers spanning the river, and the two lock chambers on the left. (Both, courtesy of Army Corps of Engineers.)

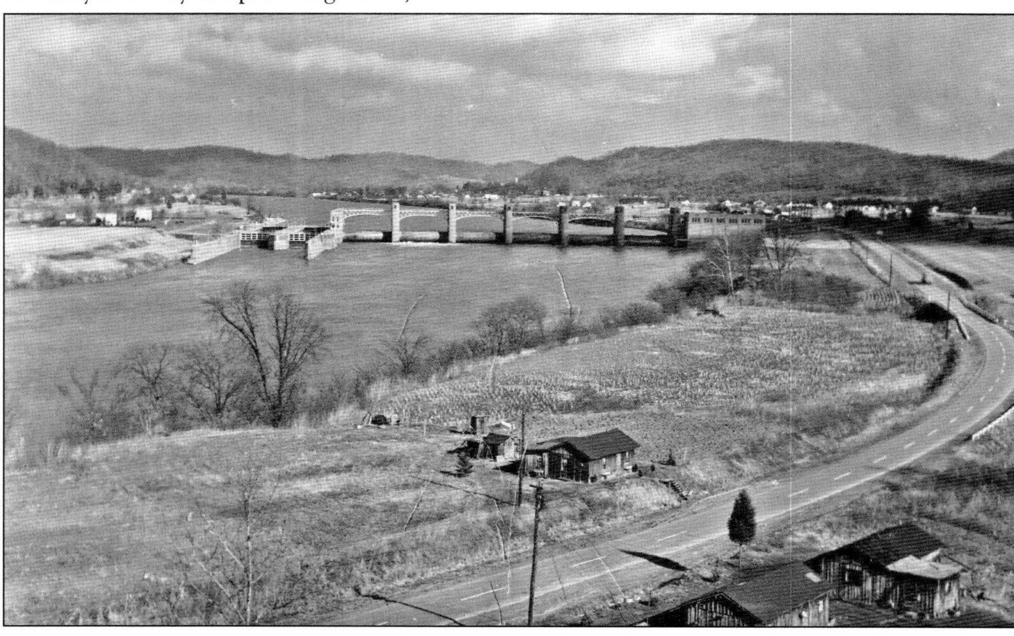

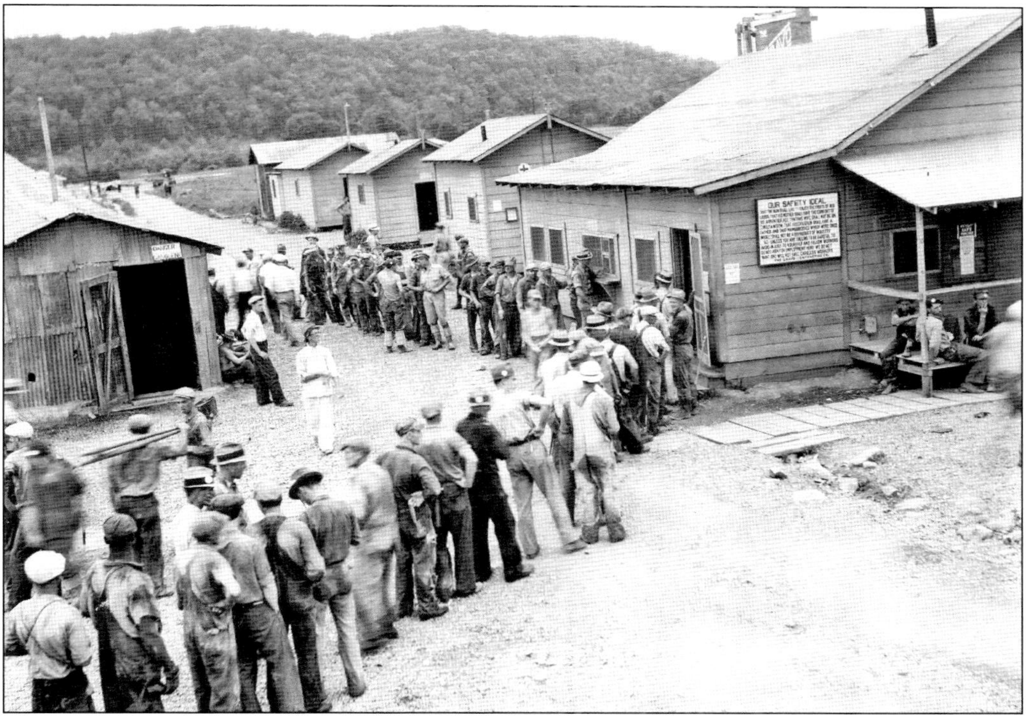

The series of locks and dam projects constructed along the Kanawha River at Marmet, London, and Winfield, in addition to the site at Gallipolis on the Ohio River, provided much welcomed employment for laborers who had been facing bleak job prospects for months and even years. President Roosevelt's National Industrial Recovery Administration Act contained the framework under which people were recruited and hired for work on the Winfield Locks and Dam. Interestingly, residents of the nearby homestead community of Eleanor were not allowed to be recruited into the workforce at Winfield because they had all been employed by a separate New Deal relief office. Shown above are workers at Winfield waiting in line on payday. Below, a worker sits in a delivery vehicle adjacent to the construction site. (Both, courtesy of Army Corps of Engineers.)

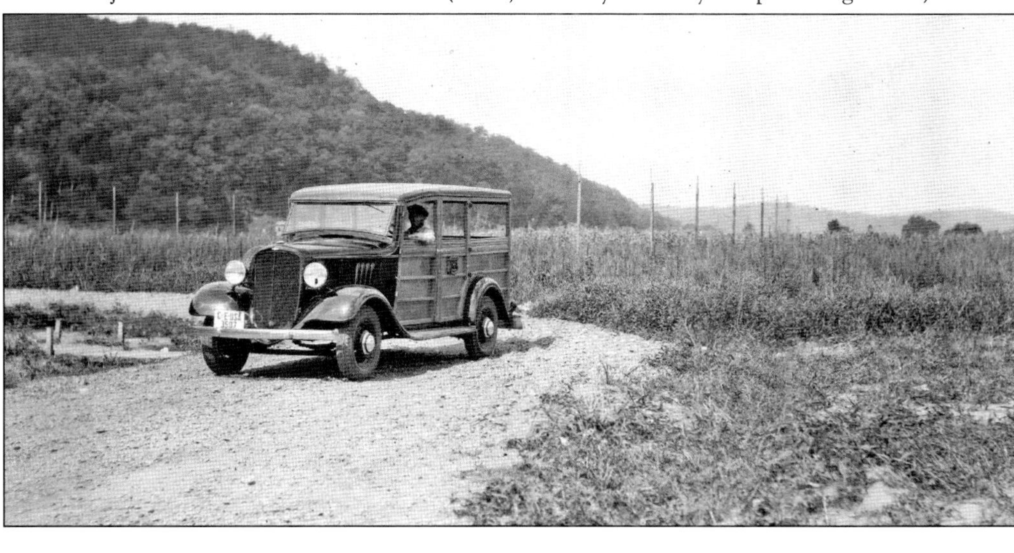

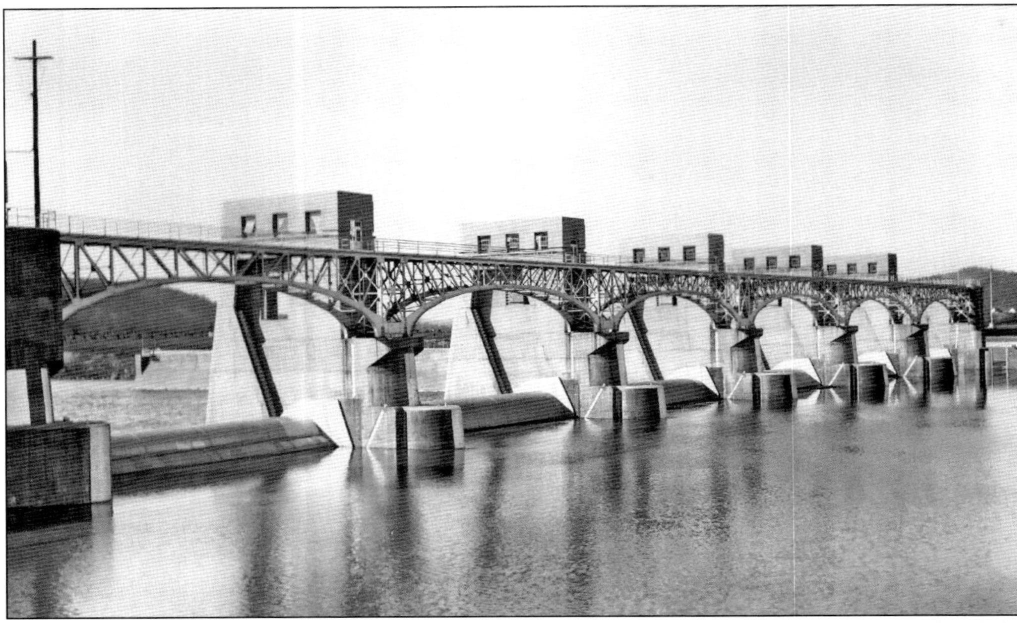

The two photographs seen here, both taken from different locations on the south side of the river, show the completed locks and dam. In the above photograph, the completed roller gates' functionality can be readily seen. The gates are in a lowered position, and the tracks on which the gates were raised can be seen running diagonally up all of the piers' sides. In the scene below, the two smokestacks and rear paddle wheel can be discerned of a riverboat entering one of the lock chambers on the far, upstream portion of the site. Once again, buildings on the outskirts of the Eleanor homestead community appear in the far left background. (Both, courtesy of Army Corps of Engineers.)

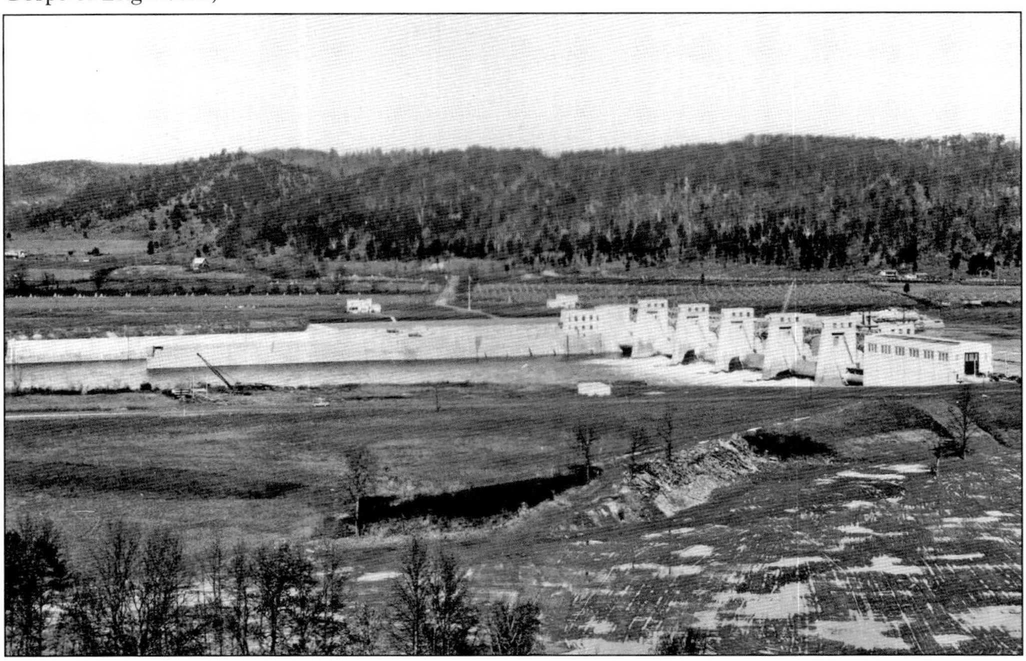

Three

Eleanor
Hope in the Great Depression

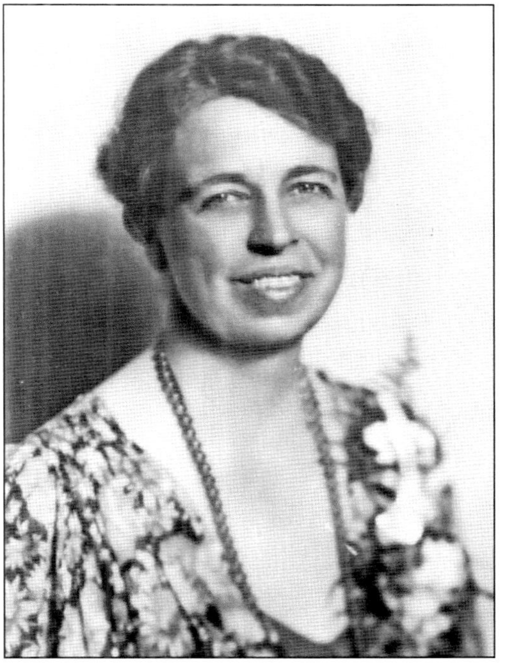

While the 19th-century town of Winfield owes its name to an icon of one era of American history, just to the north of the Kanawha River and several miles downstream, a 20th-century town also owes its name to an icon but of different times and circumstances. As far as the history of the Kanawha River Valley goes, the town of Eleanor is a rather recent arrival. For years before its establishment, local entities had attempted to establish a town in the area—going so far as to survey housing lots and future streets. However, a tepid response from interested buyers put any plans for a settlement on hold. With the onset of the Great Depression, however, and the introduction of a new federal homesteading program, plans were initiated for a town at modern-day Eleanor. For this particular town, and many similar homestead towns all over the country, the popular First Lady Eleanor Roosevelt, shown here, would become an unabashed ally. (Courtesy of Library of Congress.)

Shown here is a view of the homestead community of Eleanor taken from the south looking northward. To local residents of the region—especially those who already lived in the immediate vicinity of the new town—the rapid appearance of the homestead was an awe-inspiring and almost miraculous accomplishment to behold, especially amidst all of the economic hardships and decreases in productivity brought about by the terrible first years of the Great Depression. The faint outlines of utility poles can be seen in the center of the photograph, signifying where Route 35 (modern-day Route 62) ran through the center of town from southeast to northwest. The portion of the road within the town was renamed Roosevelt Boulevard. The farm fields in the immediate foreground were first owned and cultivated by George Washington's nephew, Lawrence A. Washington. (Courtesy of Library of Congress.)

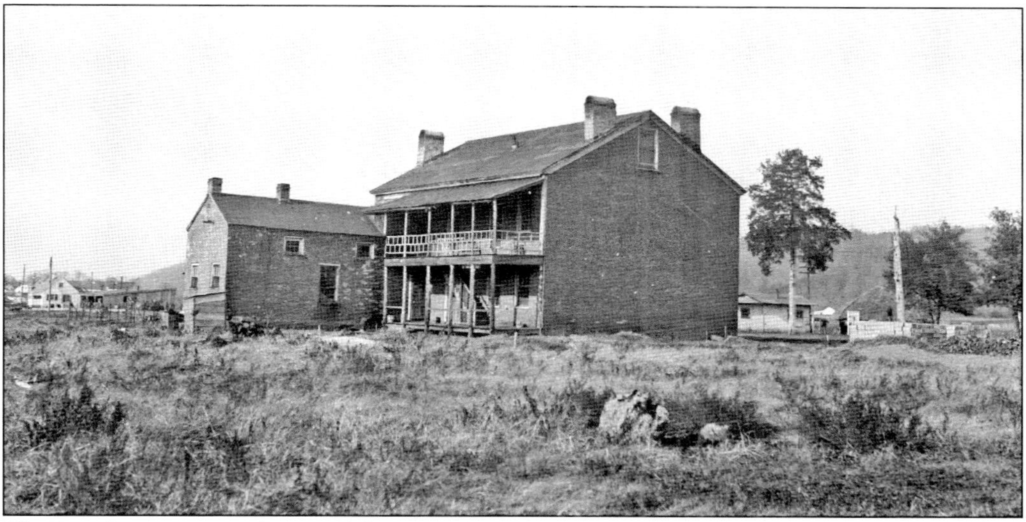

The Revolutionary War hero and first president of the United States, George Washington owned huge tracts of land all over the developing frontier land on the western fringes of the original 13 colonies. He had visited the Kanawha River Valley earlier in life and through the years acquired lands all up and down the mighty river. One tract of property encompassed the ground on which the town of Eleanor was erected over 130 years after his death in December 1799. Sometime during the first few decades of the 19th century, a man named Benjamin Ruffner acquired much of the land in present-day Eleanor, on which he erected a large redbrick house. This building, shown above, is today the Eleanor Town Hall. Aside from Ruffner's large red house, the immediate area had been sparsely populated before Eleanor's creation. The Red House Taxi Line, shown below, was located on Route 35, south of where Eleanor is now located. Owned by D.F. Little, it offered many services in addition to a taxi line, including gasoline and automobile parts. (Both, courtesy of Library of Congress.)

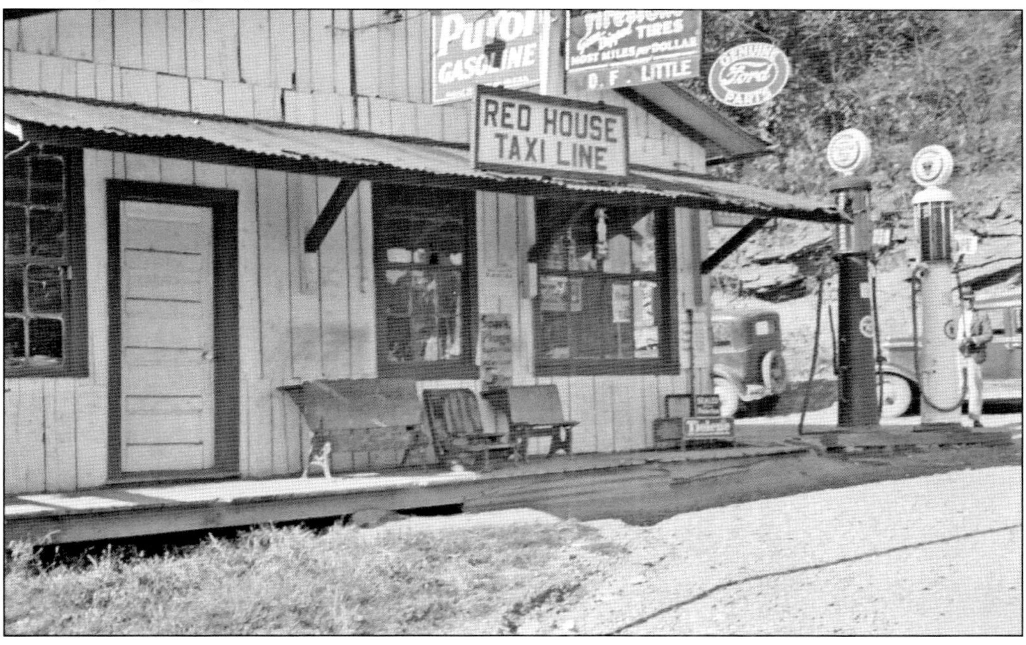

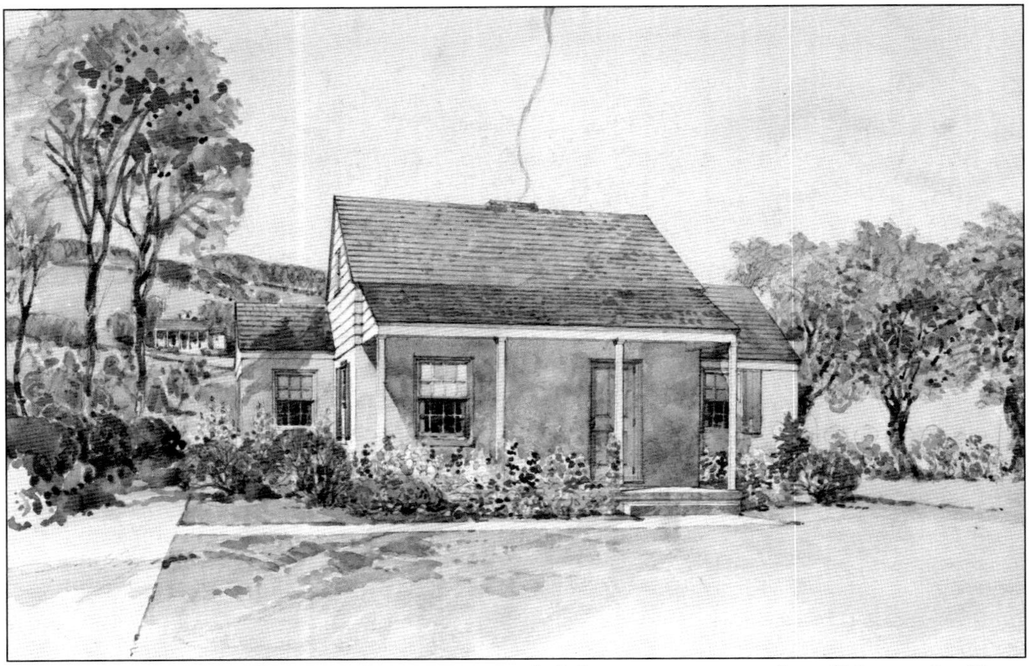

The Great Depression homestead program entailed the construction of small house dwellings to be occupied by families that were selected for participation in the program. The houses were constructed on small, three-quarter acre lots. Each home had a garden, with many also having a chicken coop and garage. In total, there were over 10 different designs for the homes, ranging in a few different sizes and shapes, and eventually 150 of these homes were completed in the Eleanor project. The appearance of the homes was mainly utilitarian in design, but these watercolor design portraits show that the intent was for structures that blended well with natural surroundings. (Both, courtesy of West Virginia State Archives.)

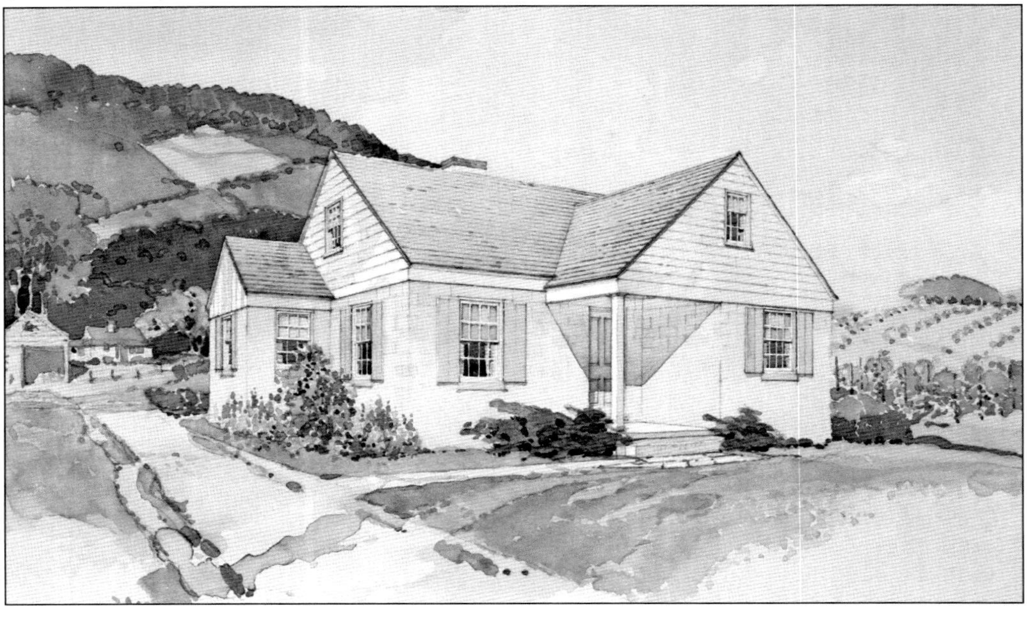

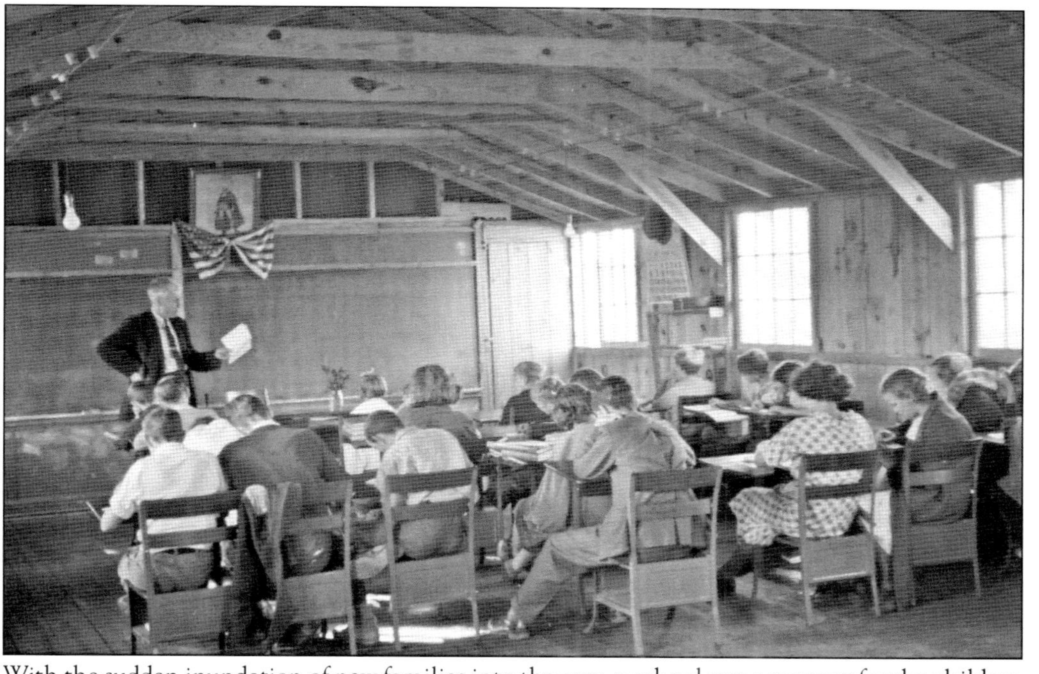

With the sudden inundation of new families into the area, a school was necessary for the children of the homestead project. Years earlier, during the 1920s, at the time of the failed attempt to establish a community in the area, a school called Oak Dale had been present in the vicinity of Eleanor; however, the school closed its doors around 1928. With the establishment of Eleanor, a new school was needed. At first, a temporary school was held in the communal barracks of the town before finally receiving a permanent home. Seen here, young residents of Eleanor learn their school lessons from their instructor. (Both, courtesy of Library of Congress.)

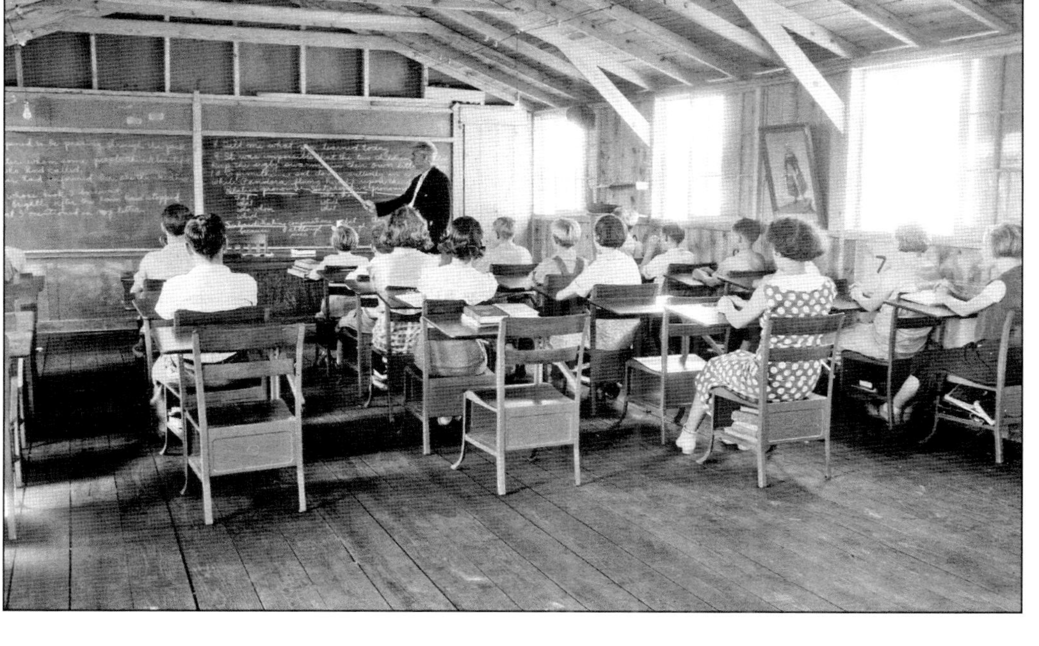

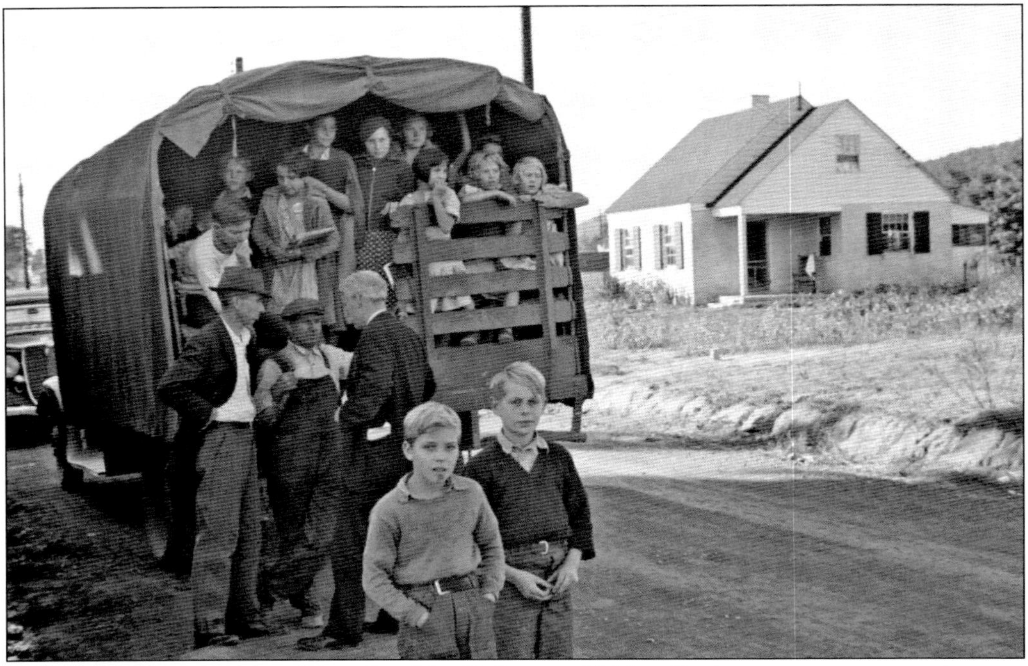

One of the core principles of Pres. Franklin D. Roosevelt's New Deal programs was not only to try to alleviate the suffering and misery caused by the Great Depression, but also to provide education and betterment that would leave Americans better off and personally better equipped after the economic downturn had passed. These two photographs of Eleanor's residents provide a visual example of the idea behind homestead settlements, like the one tried at Red House; the communal-style living allowed strangers to become helping neighbors who all pulled together to survive the nationwide economic disaster. The Ford truck shown here served in Eleanor's early days as a form of mass transportation for Eleanor's residents. (Both, courtesy of Library of Congress.)

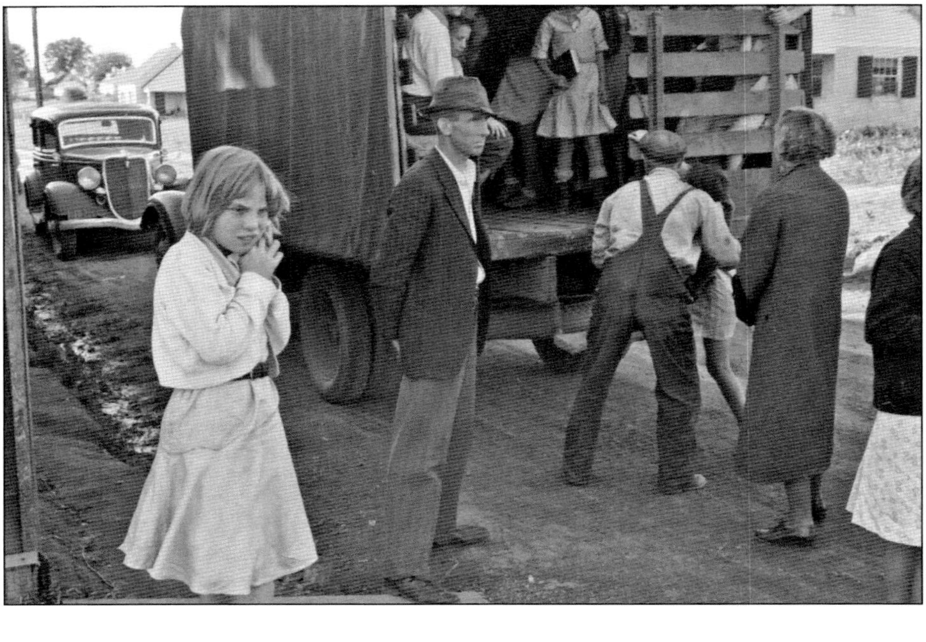

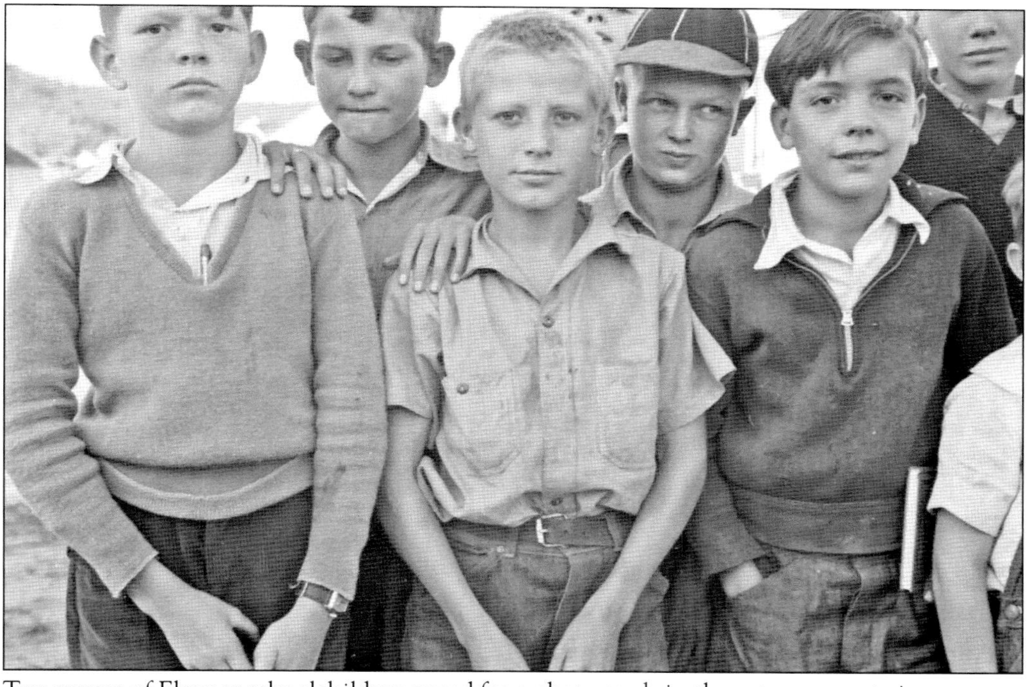

Two groups of Eleanor schoolchildren posed for a photograph in these twc separate images: one of the boys, one of the girls. Though the names of the individuals shown are not recorded, the image is representative of the scores of children who called Eleanor home at some point during the 1930s and 1940s. In Wintz's *History of Putnam County*, Eleanor resident Eurgene Hudson described the sometimes cramped conditions of families with several children: "My mom and dad used one bedroom, my three brothers the other bedroom, the four girls slept upstairs in the attic and *we had a big house*." Over 240 children attended the Eleanor school and were instructed by eight teachers. (Both, courtesy of Library of Congress.)

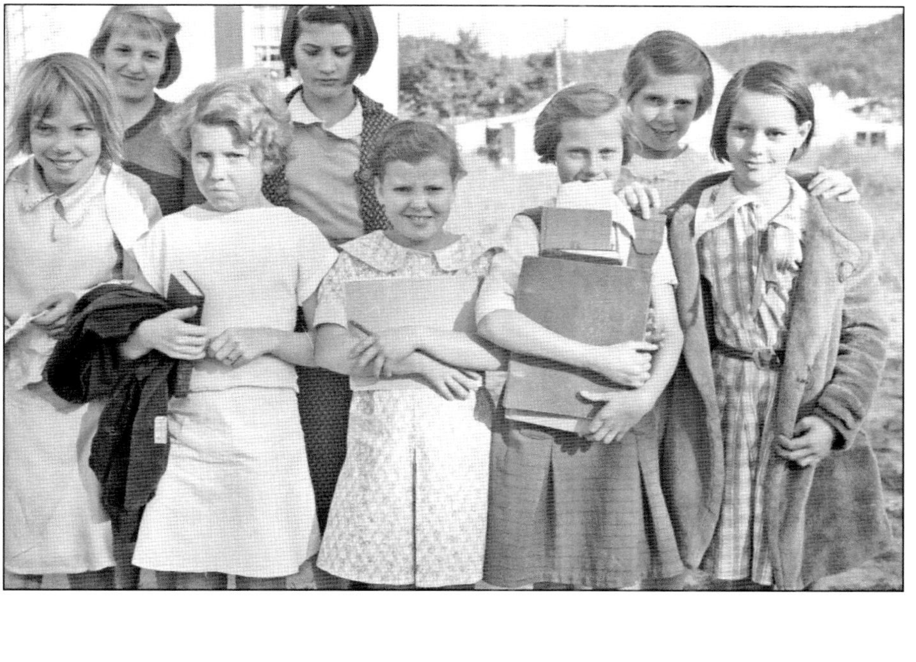

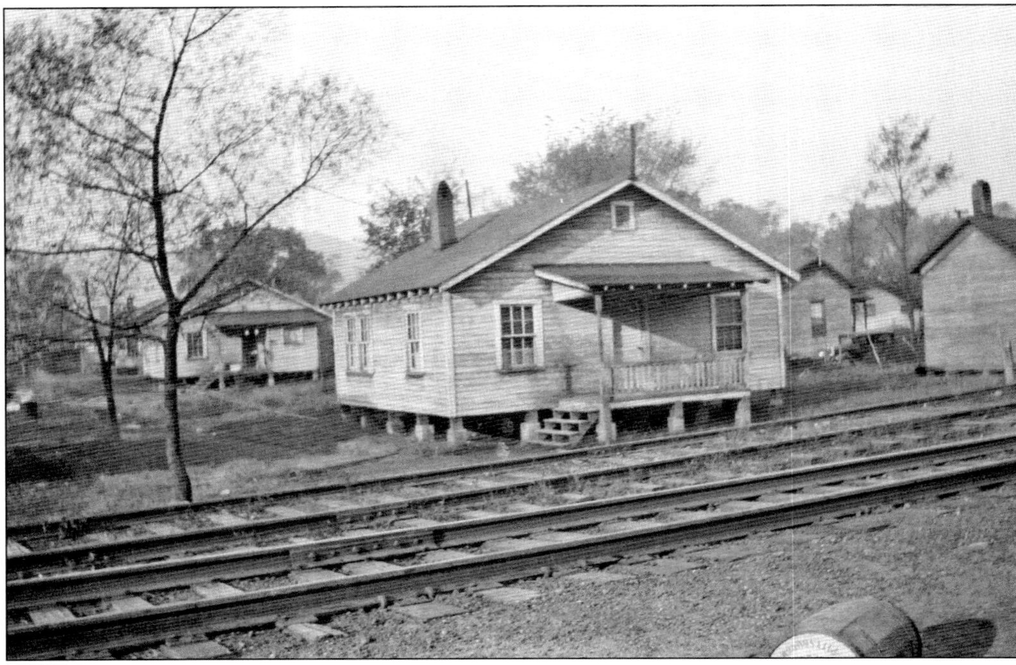

Five miles away from the new town of Eleanor was a sizable pocket of homes inhabited mainly by individuals who worked for the Plymouth coal mines. These small wooden structures were located five miles east of Eleanor along the Kanawha River. The above photograph shows a typical home of the area, which was four rooms in size. Unlike in Eleanor, however, more than one family often resided in one of these single units. The tracks in the foreground belonged to the New York Central Railroad. The photograph below was taken because of the infamous subject recorded; this typical mining household was the scene of a horrific event that captured the attention of the area's residents. A Plymouth mining foreman who lived in the house, while drunk, began beating his wife, for which he was subsequently killed by his son. (Both, courtesy of Library of Congress.)

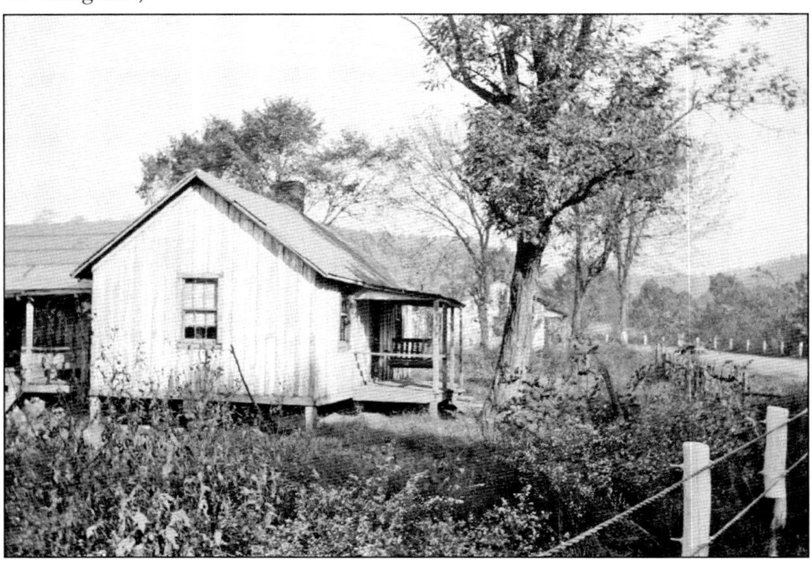

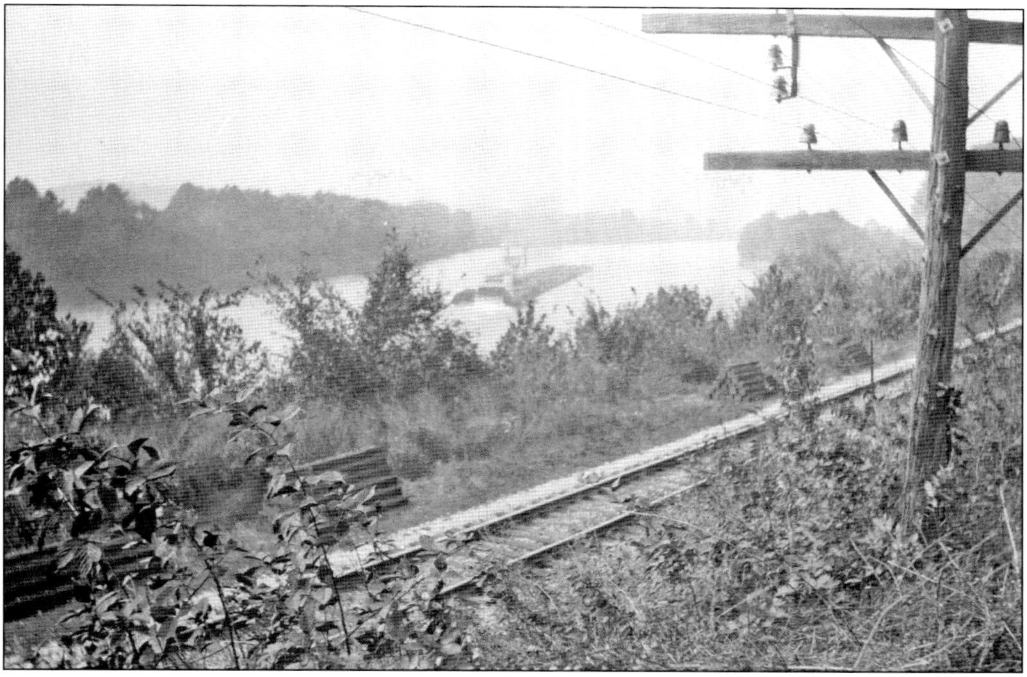

By the first few decades of the 20th century, Putnam County employed over 1,000 coal miners, and in their peak years, the mines within the county produced nearly 500,000 tons of coal. The Kanawha River offered the easiest means of transporting these large amounts of coal to its markets via the Ohio River. Around this time period, the view of a vessel moving coal downriver would have been a common one, as seen in the above photograph taken around 1930 from a high ridge southeast of Eleanor. The railroad is the New York Central. At right, George Roach—who lived east of Eleanor and was a native of Putnam County—had a background in mining and in the 1930s was a vocal area supporter of the homestead project. (Both, courtesy of Library of Congress.)

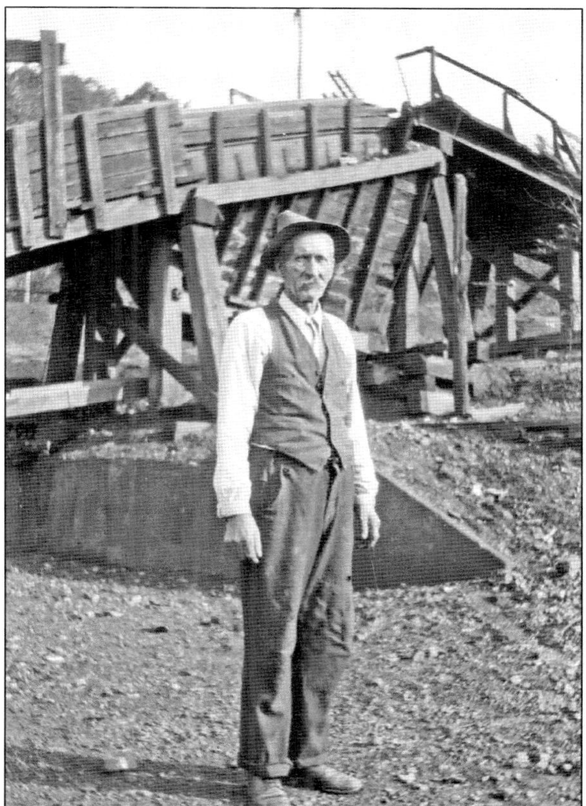

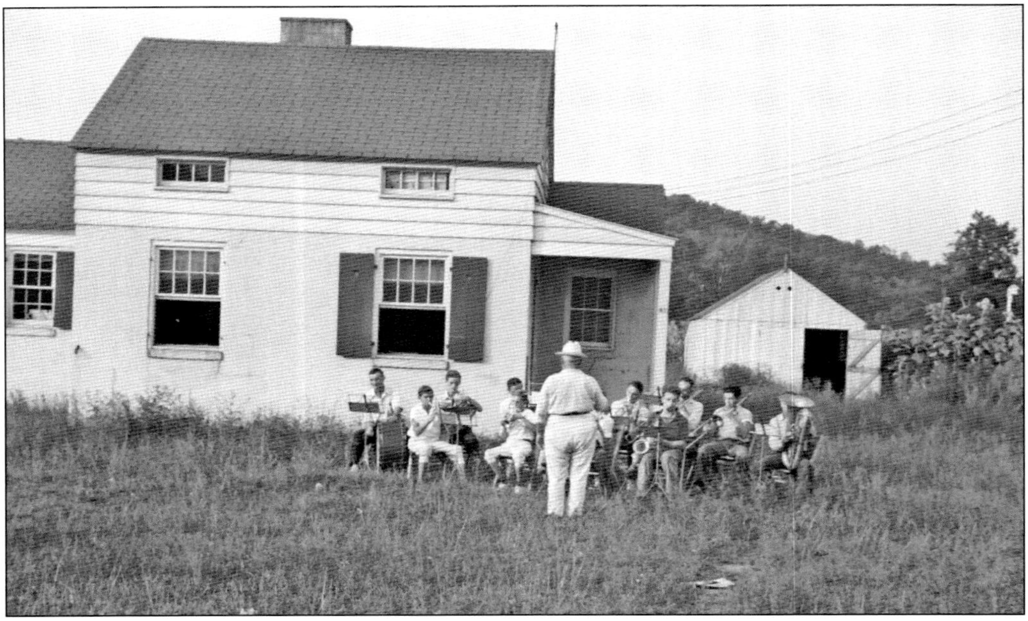

The main aim of the homestead projects at Eleanor and elsewhere was to provide economic opportunity for displaced families in need of work. However, not everything was work with no play. Though made up of strangers initially, the residents of Eleanor came to create a rather harmonious community that had its share of leisurely pastimes and hobbies for enjoyment. Shown here, the Eleanor band holds its practice on one of the town's lots. The band was made up of a wide range of musicians, ranging from young schoolchildren to some of the older adults in town. The band played at special events throughout the year, including small holiday concerts. (Both, courtesy of Library of Congress.)

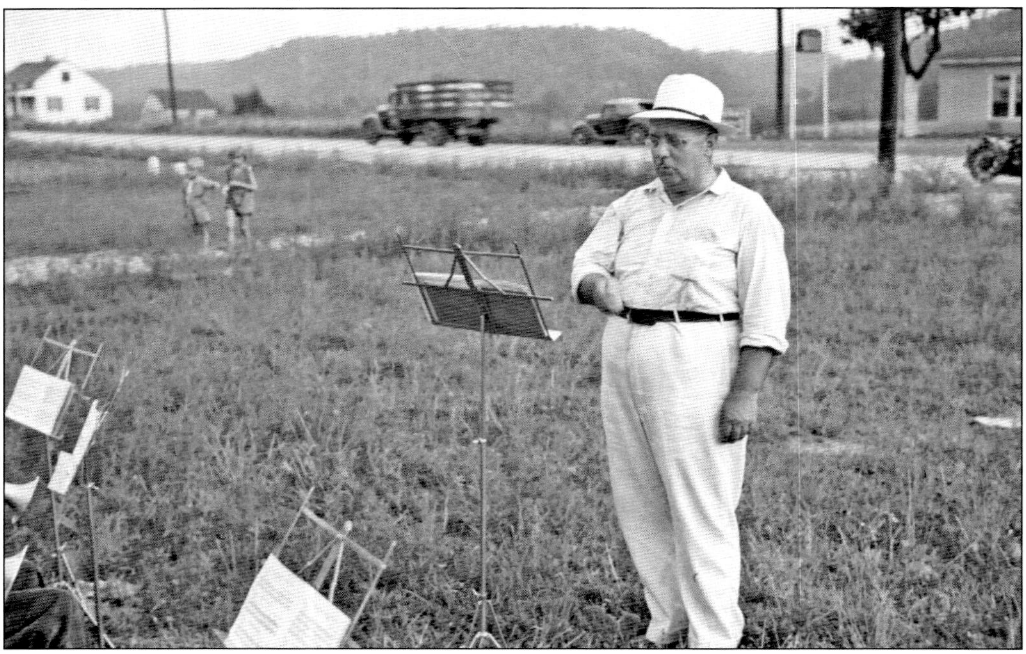

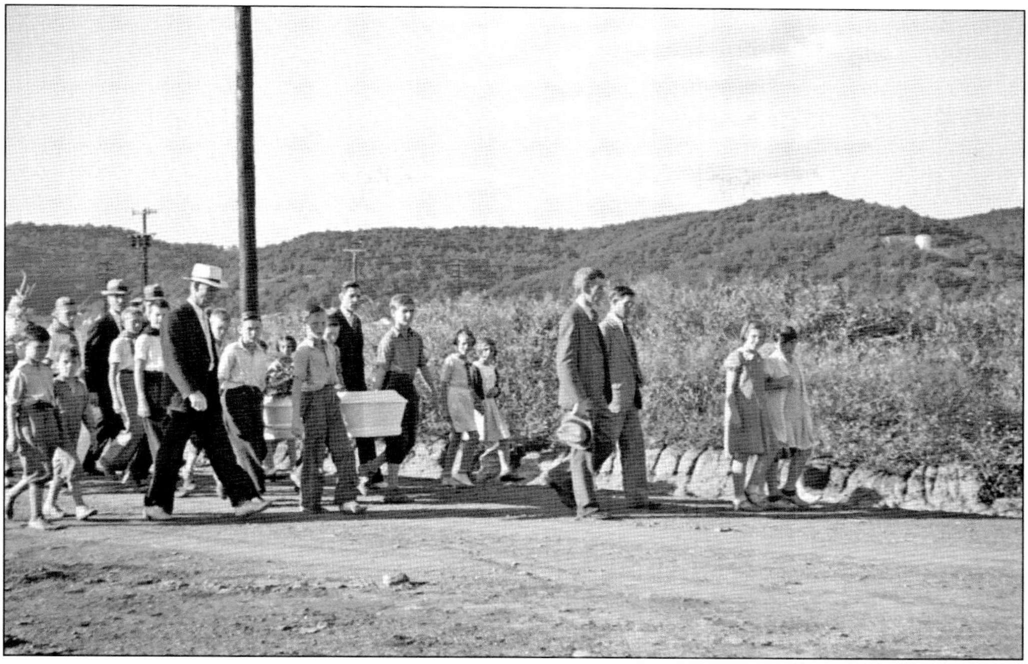

Not even a year into the life of the new community of Eleanor, tragedy struck one of the homestead families with the death of a five-year-old boy in September 1935. The funeral service for the young lad was held in the town barracks before this large funeral procession, composed of friends and family, made its way up the hill outside of town to the boy's final resting place. The image below affords a clear view of the back side of Ruffner's Red House, which was used as the administration building for the homestead project. The building has been extensively remodeled and added to in the past 80 years. (Both, courtesy of Library of Congress.)

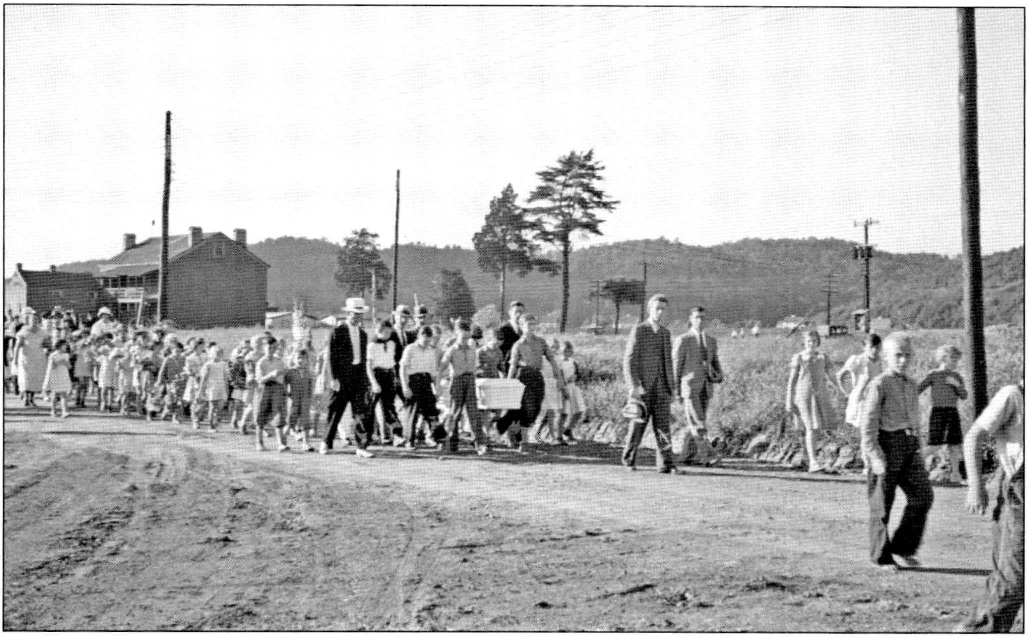

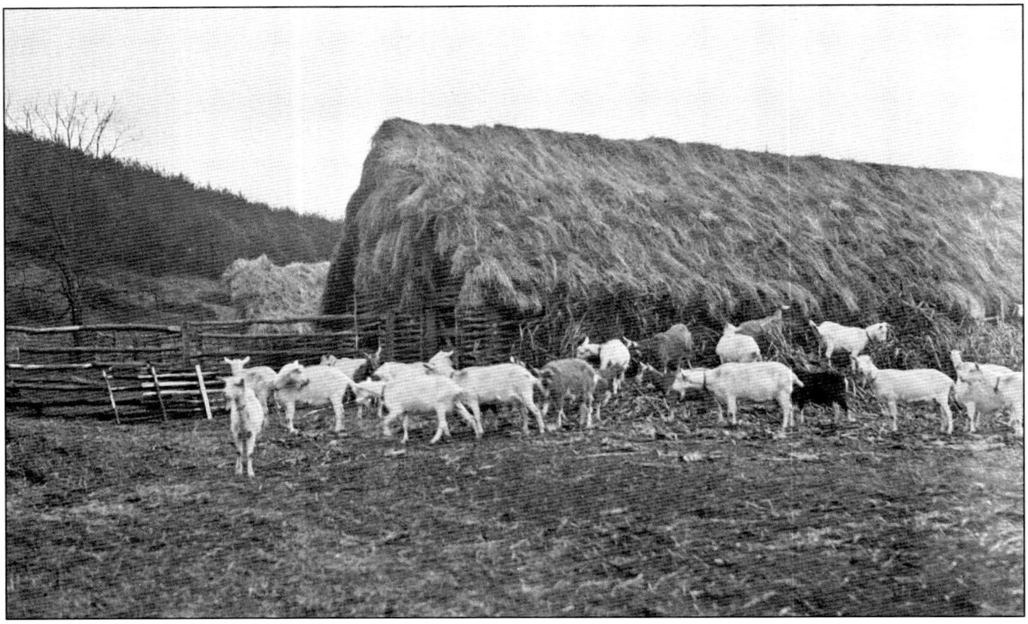

When the homestead community was first established at Eleanor, planners allowed for the raising of a large number of goats as part of the town's economy, to be cared for by the residents. However, according to recollections of the time, people in town quickly developed a dislike for the taste of goat milk. A year or two into the establishment of the community, funds were raised to procure dairy cows. The introduction of cows to the fields around Eleanor did not result in expulsion of the goats, as both were allowed to add to a diverse livestock that even grew to include sheep and other traditional farm animals. (Both, courtesy of Library of Congress.)

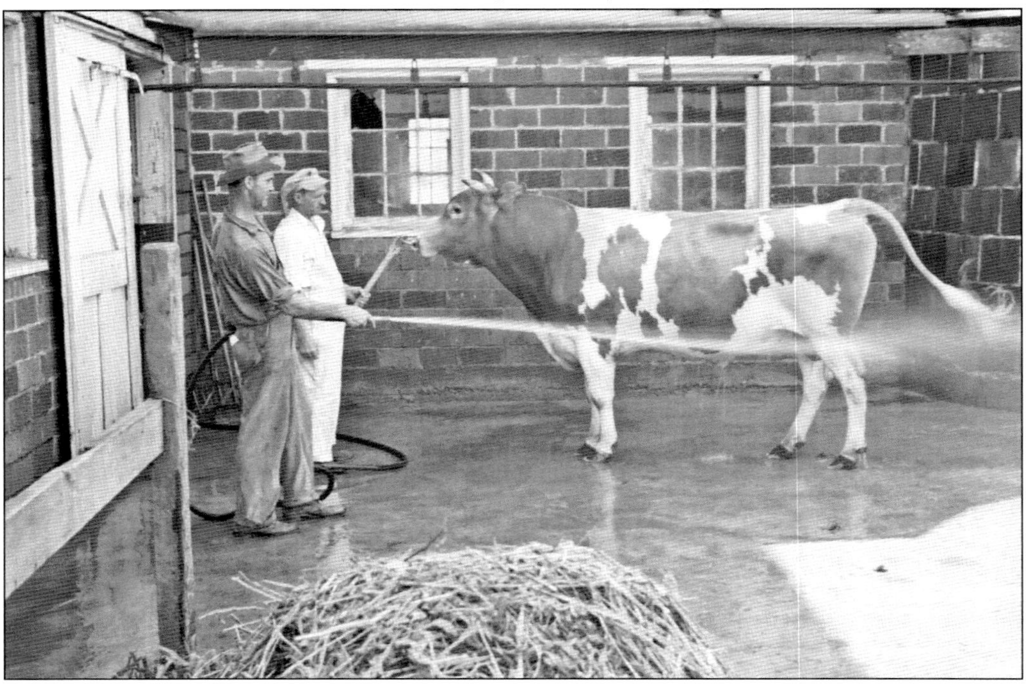

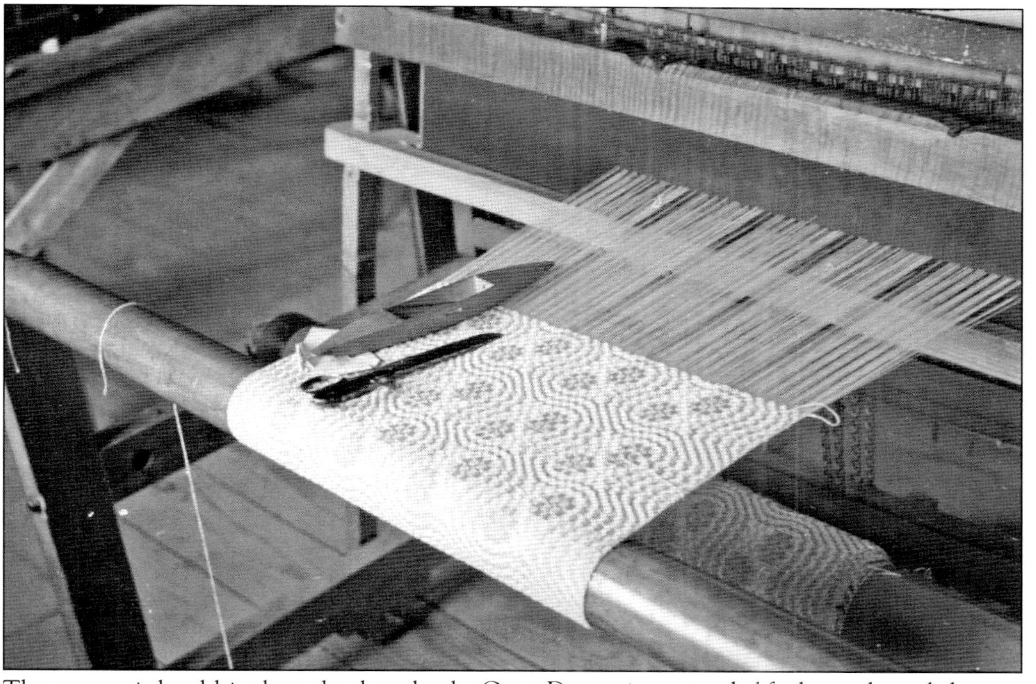

The economic hardships brought about by the Great Depression extended far beyond simply having a roof over one's head and food on the table for one's family. The 150 families who called Eleanor home during the Depression era pooled and expanded their talents into alleviating many areas of hardship, including adequate clothing. Photographed here are weaving looms that were used primarily by the women of Eleanor to provide clothes for family members. When materials and supply were plentiful enough, excess finished products could be sold outside of the town in nearby areas, or as far away as Charleston or Point Pleasant. (Both, courtesy of Library of Congress.)

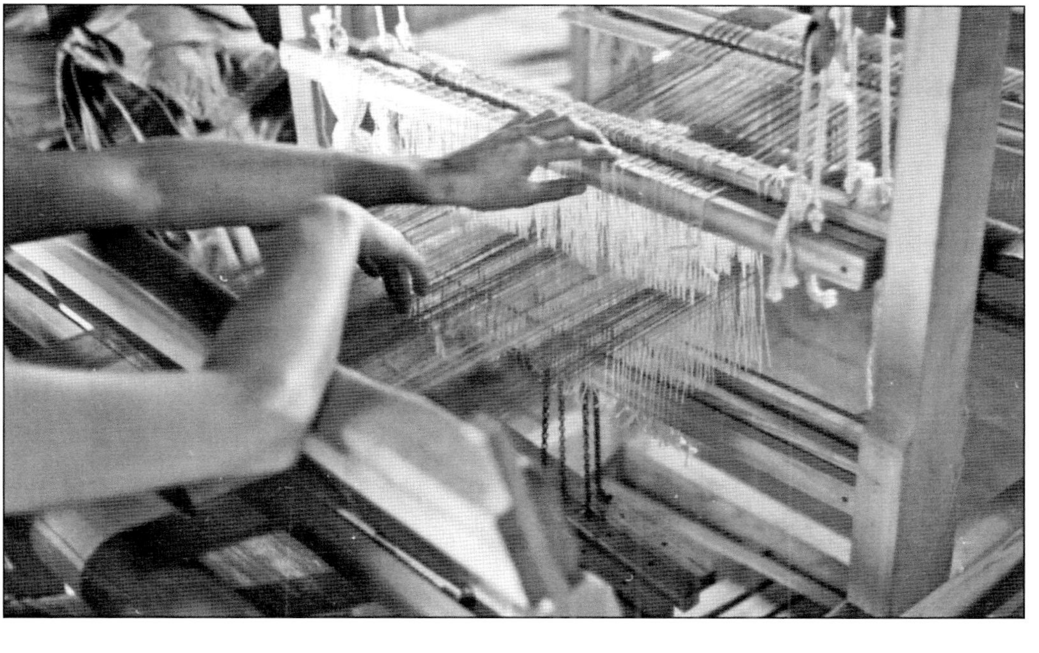

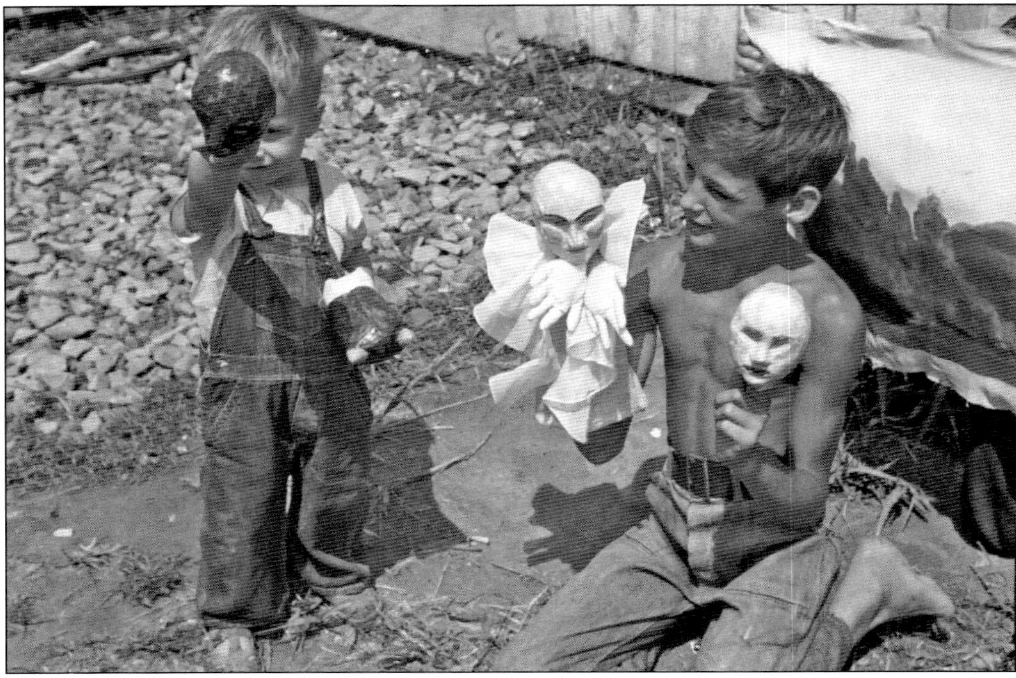

The social opportunities available in the town of Eleanor were numerous and diverse. Early on in the project, newly arrived families established social clubs, church groups, fraternal societies, and various sports teams. During holidays, the town's school-age children performed plays and recitals, while the adults hosted community banquets and festivals. Seen here are children of Eleanor during rehearsal for a small puppet show. In the above photograph, a painted canvas can be seen on the right, which was used in coordination with the homemade puppets that are being held by the two young children. (Both, courtesy of Library of Congress.)

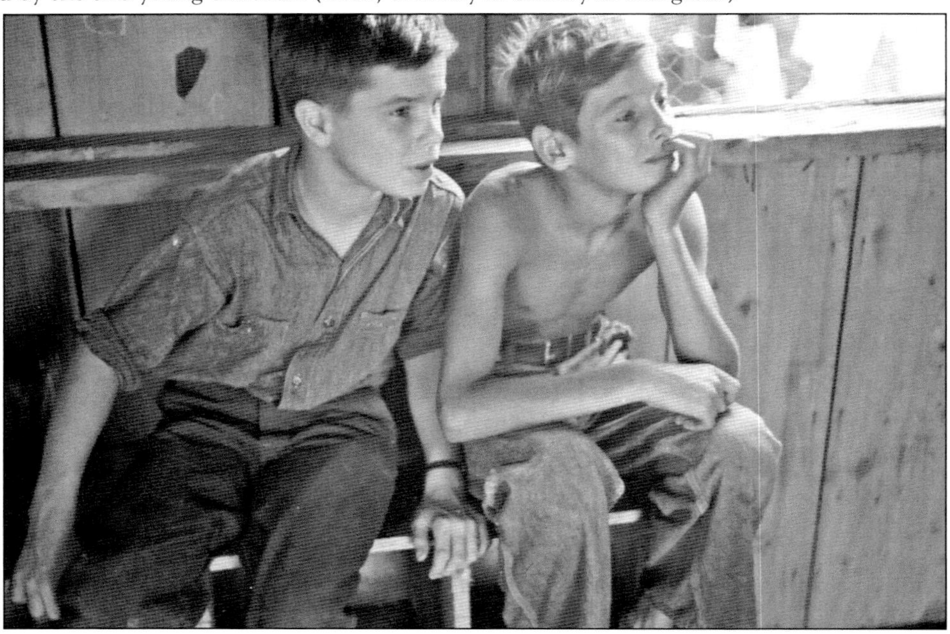

Four

NITRO
WORLD WAR I BOOM TOWN

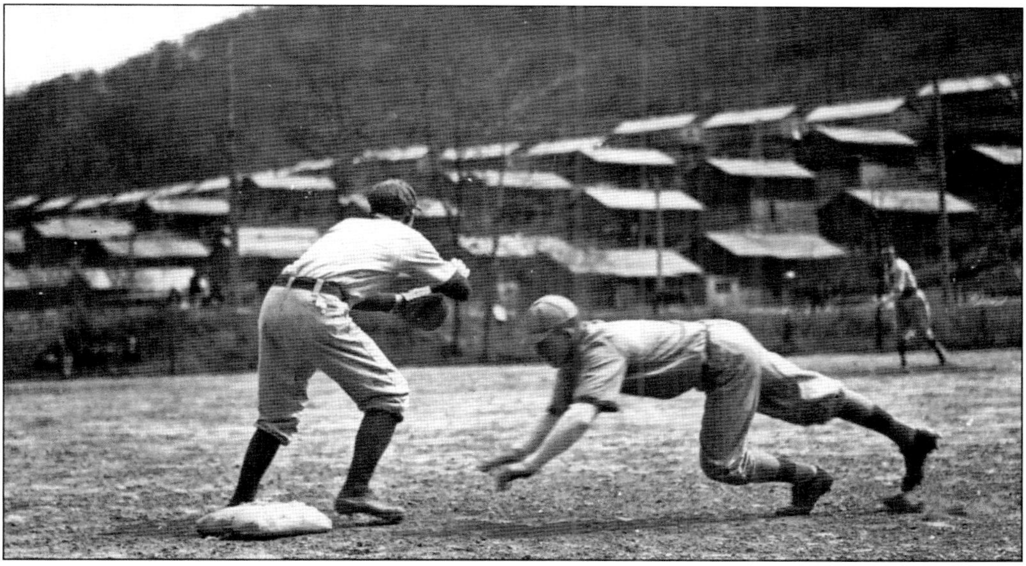

Nitro was built as a military-operated city created explicitly to aid the United States war effort as the nation entered World War I in 1917. However, wherever there is a gathering of young men and women together in one place, social recreation is bound to find expression through various means. Photographed here in what would have been a common sight around town during the height of the war effort, workers of Nitro's munitions plants engage in a spirited game of baseball on the athletic fields that were constructed within the city. Teams of men from Nitro played against one another as well as against teams formed from nearby locales, such as Charleston. The connection to baseball in Nitro extended beyond the World War I recreation. Lew Burdette, a Major League Baseball player in the 1950s and 1960s, was born in Nitro. He is most remembered for his outstanding record as a pitcher, which included helping the Braves to win three games in the 1957 World Series against the Yankees. (Courtesy of City of Nitro.)

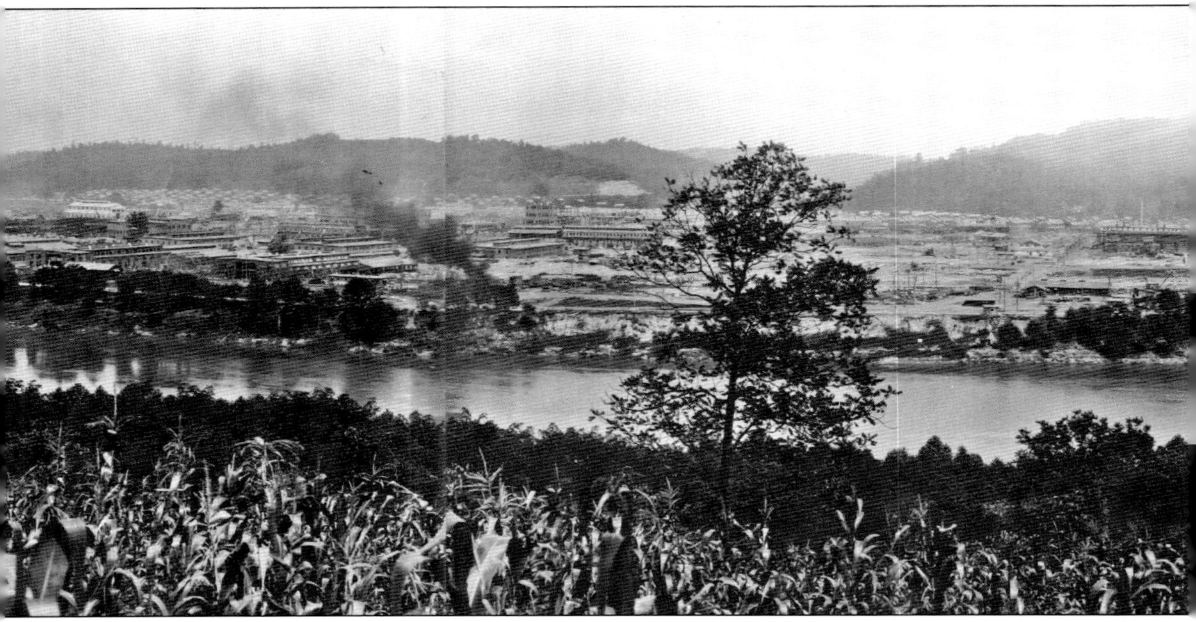

A 1918 view of Nitro from the heights opposite the town, with the Kanawha River in the foreground, speaks to the immense magnitude of the entire project. In late 1917, the flat grounds in the photograph had been only farm fields and sparsely separated houses and barns. With the entrance of the United States into World War I, the nation's military identified locations in which to locate

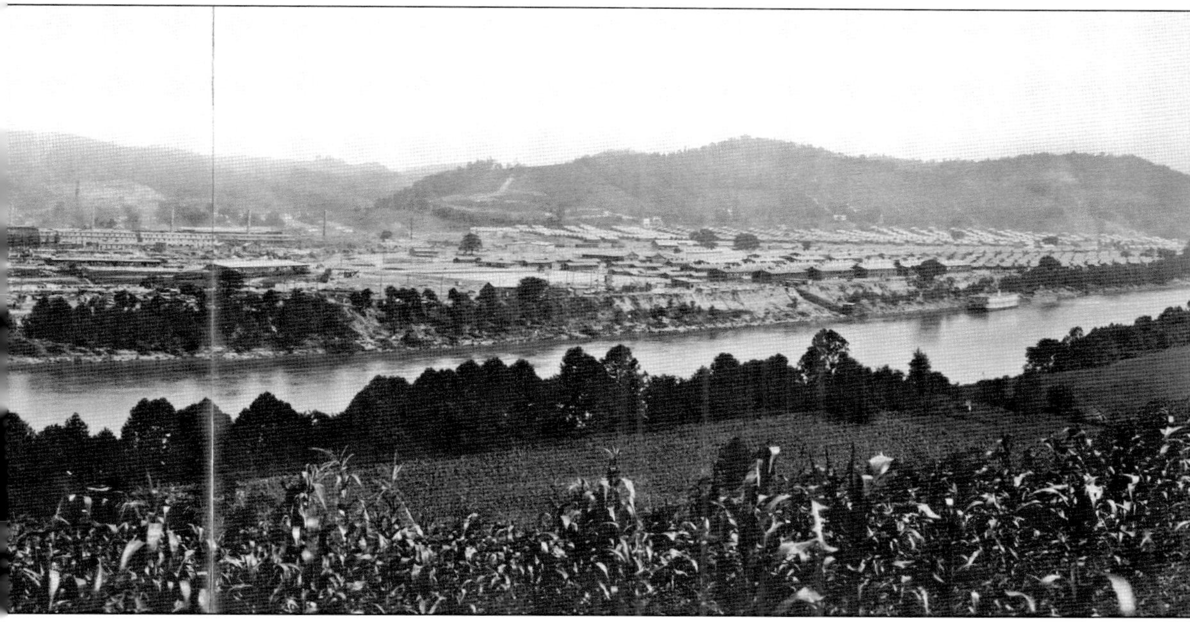

powder plants to serve the war effort. Nitro was identified because of its proximity to river and railroad transportation as well as its moderate climate. Official word of the plant's construction was announced in November 1917 in the Charleston newspapers. (Courtesy of Rich Hively.)

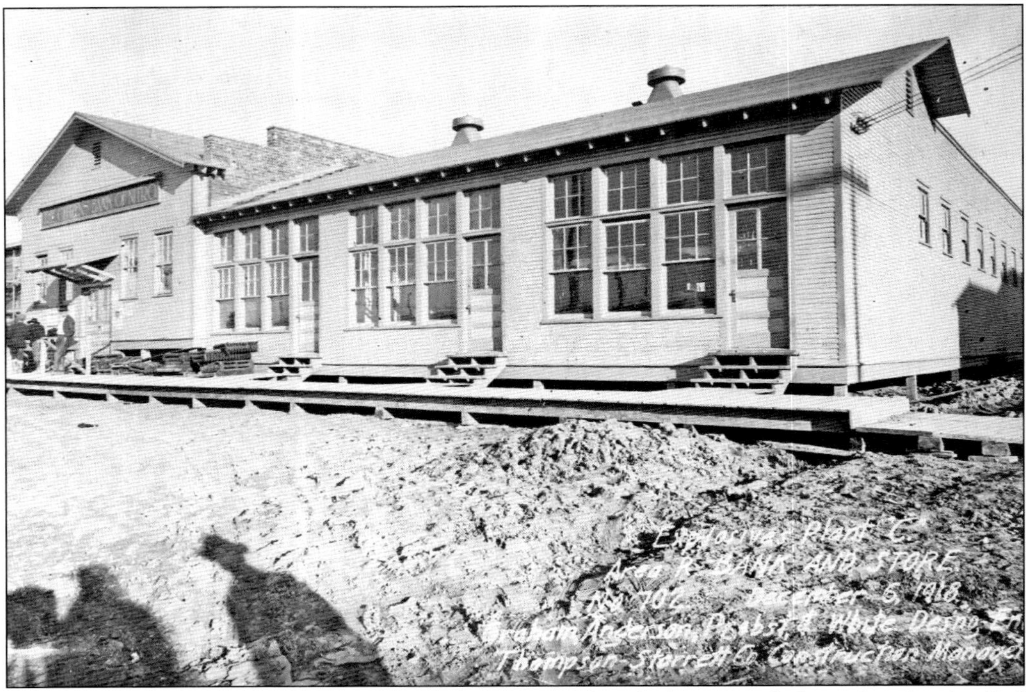

Erecting a new, mostly self-contained community in what had previously been farmland called for the construction of a wide multitude of multifunctional buildings. Because the settlement had no immediately close neighboring towns, public services such as banks and stores had to be built from scratch. Shown above, the Citizens Bank of Nitro was located on what is now named Bank Street. The structure was shared by one of several stores within the town that sold products to the residents of Nitro, all of which were operated by the US Commissary. Today, an H&R Block building stands on this site. Below, another building provided a multifunctional use, with a store on the bottom level and offices above. (Both, courtesy of Rich Hively.)

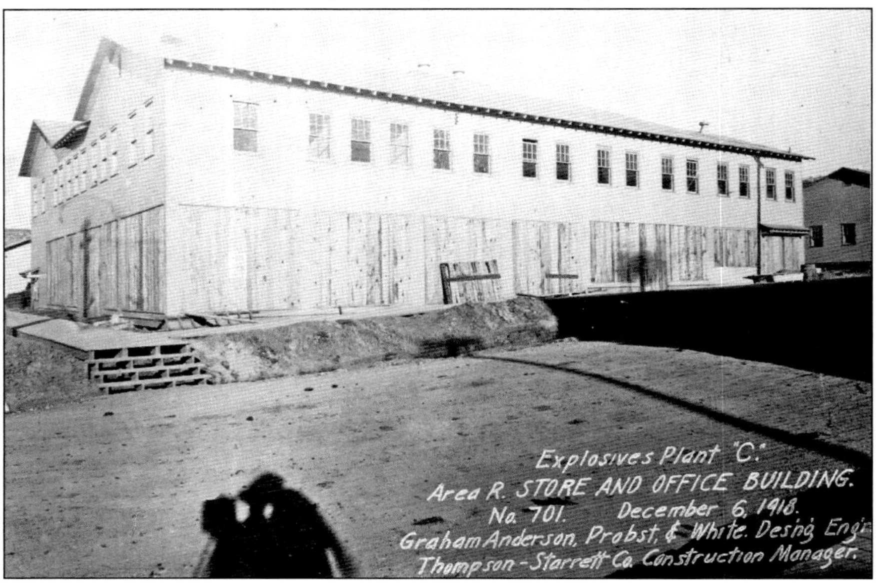

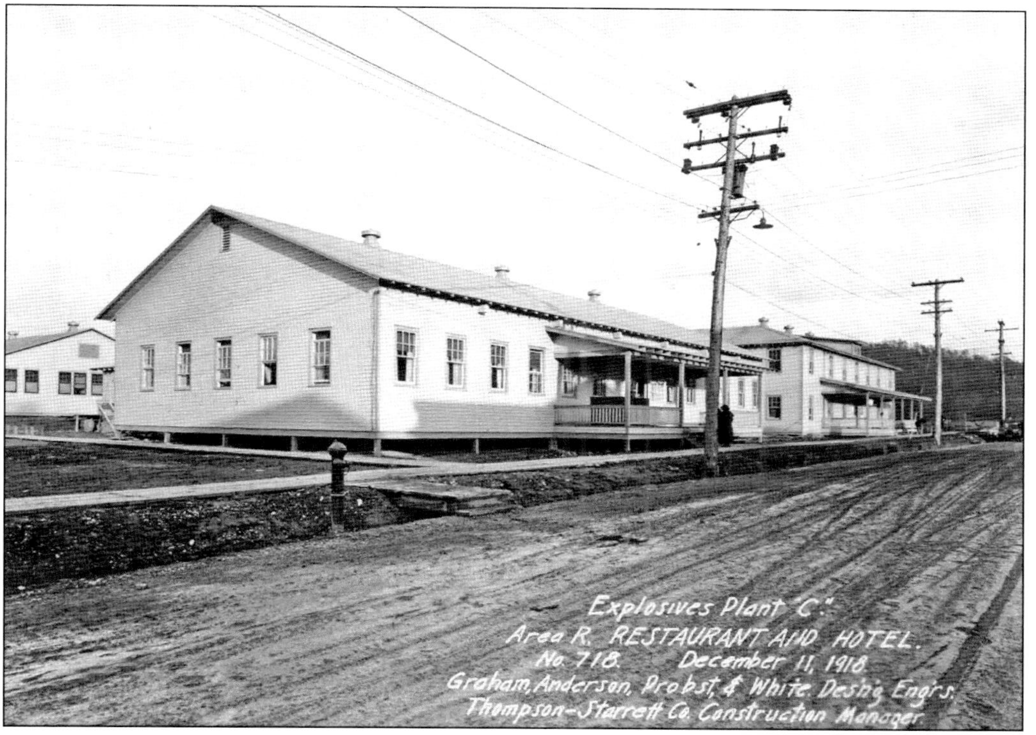

Shown here is one of several restaurants in the town, in the foreground, and a hotel farther down the street. The dirt road on which these buildings sat is today Twenty-first Street. The hotel caught fire several years after construction, and, today, the First Presbyterian Church of Nitro is located on this property. (Courtesy of Rich Hively.)

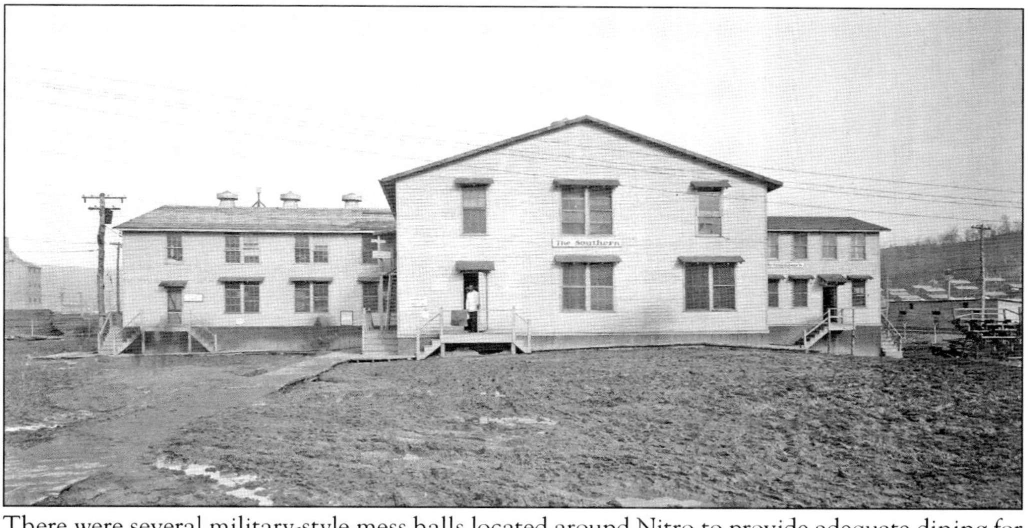

There were several military-style mess halls located around Nitro to provide adequate dining for the burgeoning populations of construction laborers and factory workers. This building, referred to as the "Administration Messes," was probably located in the same area of town as the hospital. The sign on the wall indicates that the establishment was also referred to as the "Southern." (Courtesy of Rich Hively.)

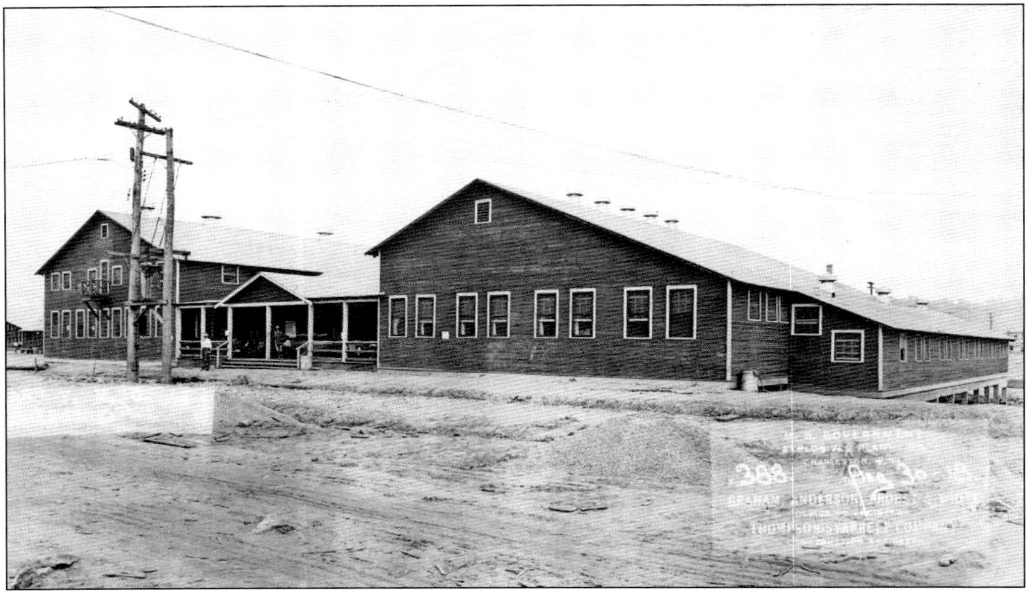

Following military protocol, the Young Men's Christian Association was set to operate two separate buildings in Nitro, one for whites and one for blacks. Historian Bill Wintz records the story that during construction of the two structures, the whites-only YMCA building was completed and ready for operation first, so leaders of the organization made the decision to open the facility to all residents of the town; whether they were white or black made no difference. In size and appearance, the whites-only YMCA (above) and blacks-only YMCA (below) were of similar characteristics. The blacks-only facility was located on present-day Eleventh Street. (Both, courtesy of Rich Hively.)

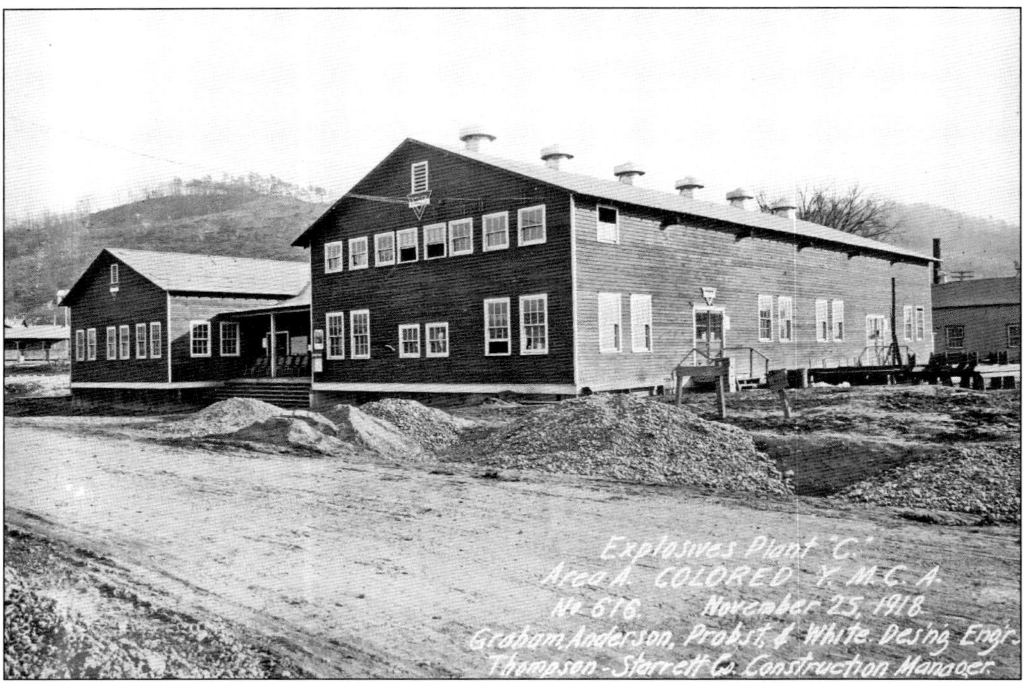

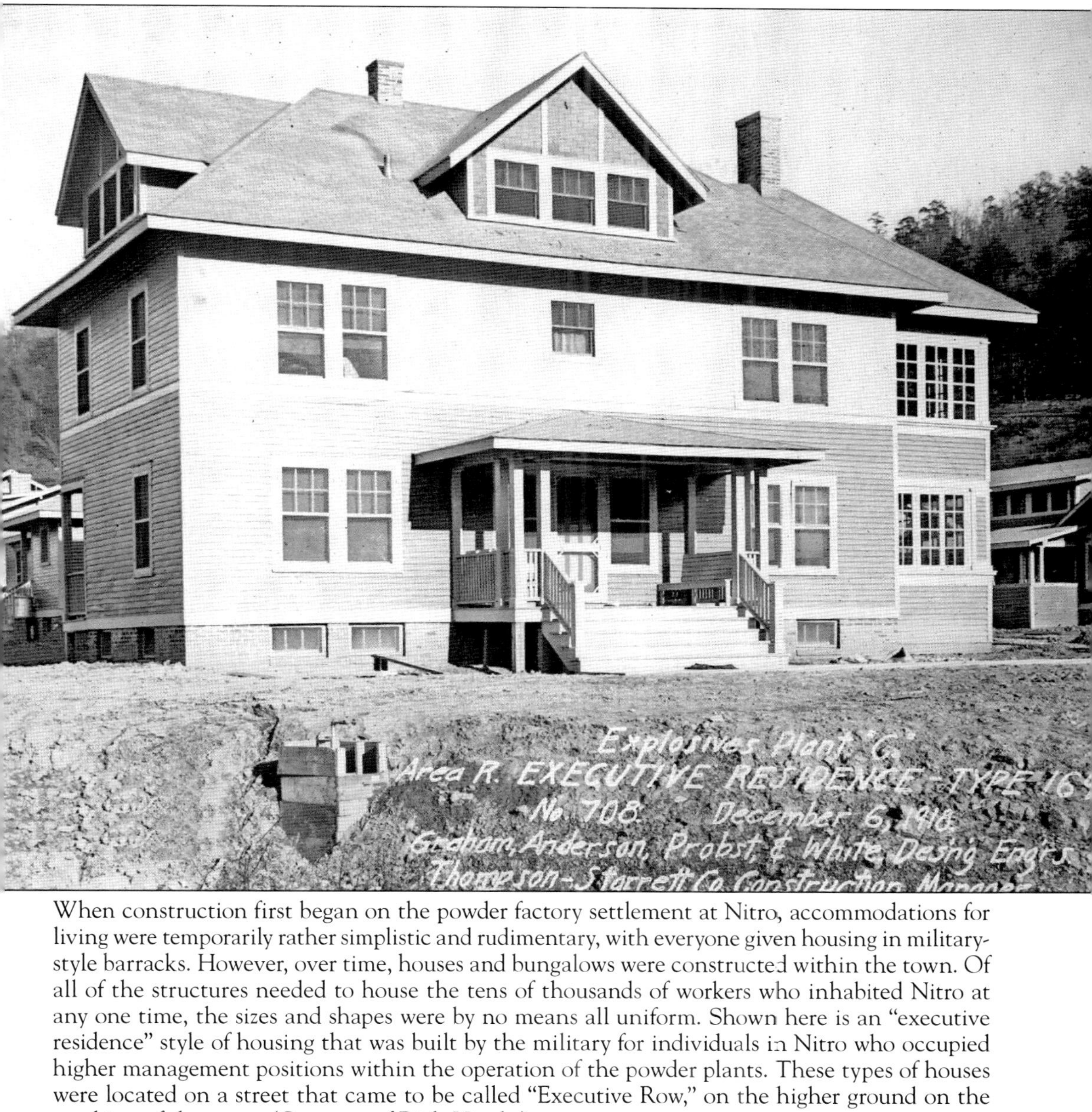

When construction first began on the powder factory settlement at Nitro, accommodations for living were temporarily rather simplistic and rudimentary, with everyone given housing in military-style barracks. However, over time, houses and bungalows were constructed within the town. Of all of the structures needed to house the tens of thousands of workers who inhabited Nitro at any one time, the sizes and shapes were by no means all uniform. Shown here is an "executive residence" style of housing that was built by the military for individuals in Nitro who occupied higher management positions within the operation of the powder plants. These types of houses were located on a street that came to be called "Executive Row," on the higher ground on the outskirts of the town. (Courtesy of Rich Hively.)

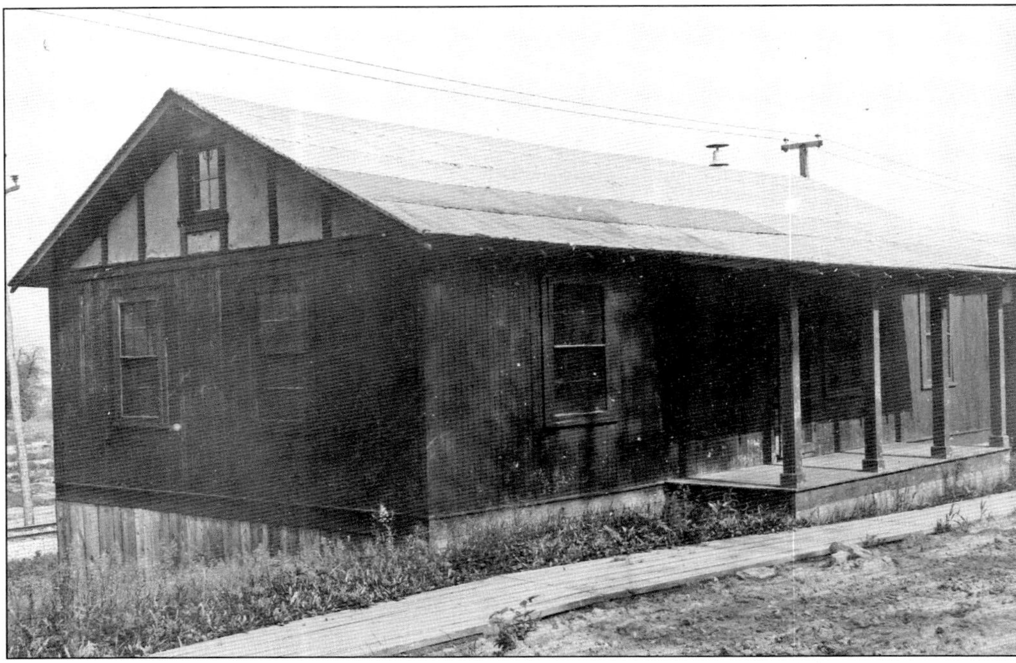

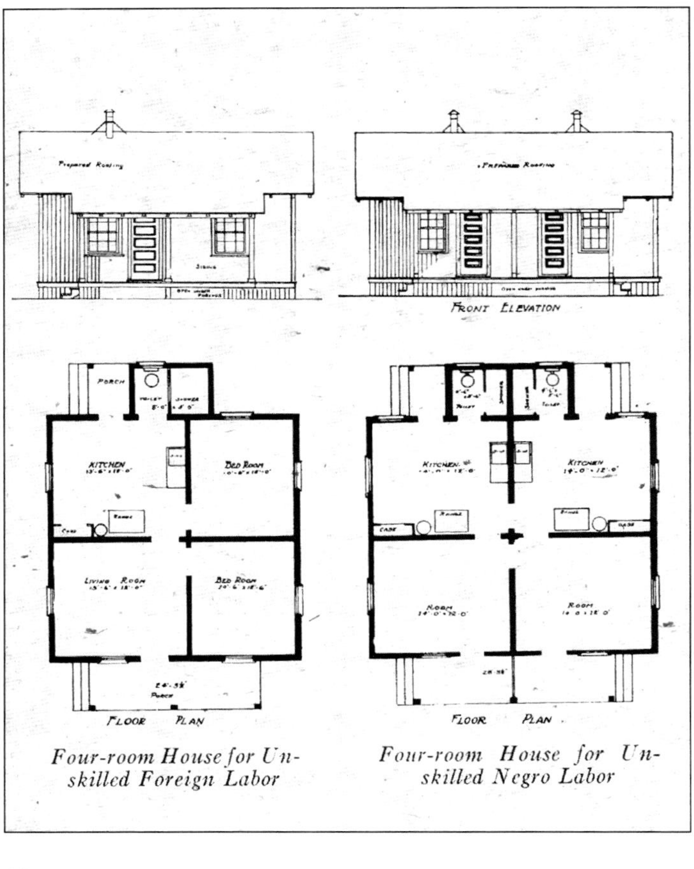

One of the many delineations made between the workers and residents of Nitro was based upon race. Since racial integration within the United States military did not occur until Pres. Harry S. Truman's time in office at the end of World War II, the World War I town of Nitro adhered to the US armed forces' established aspects of racial segregation. Shown above is a typical bungalow that was allotted for use by African American workers of Nitro. The illustration at left shows an architectural drawing of two types of segregated housing in Nitro, a bungalow for unskilled foreign labor on the left and a bungalow for black unskilled workers on the right. (Above, courtesy of Rich Hively; left, courtesy of National Archives.)

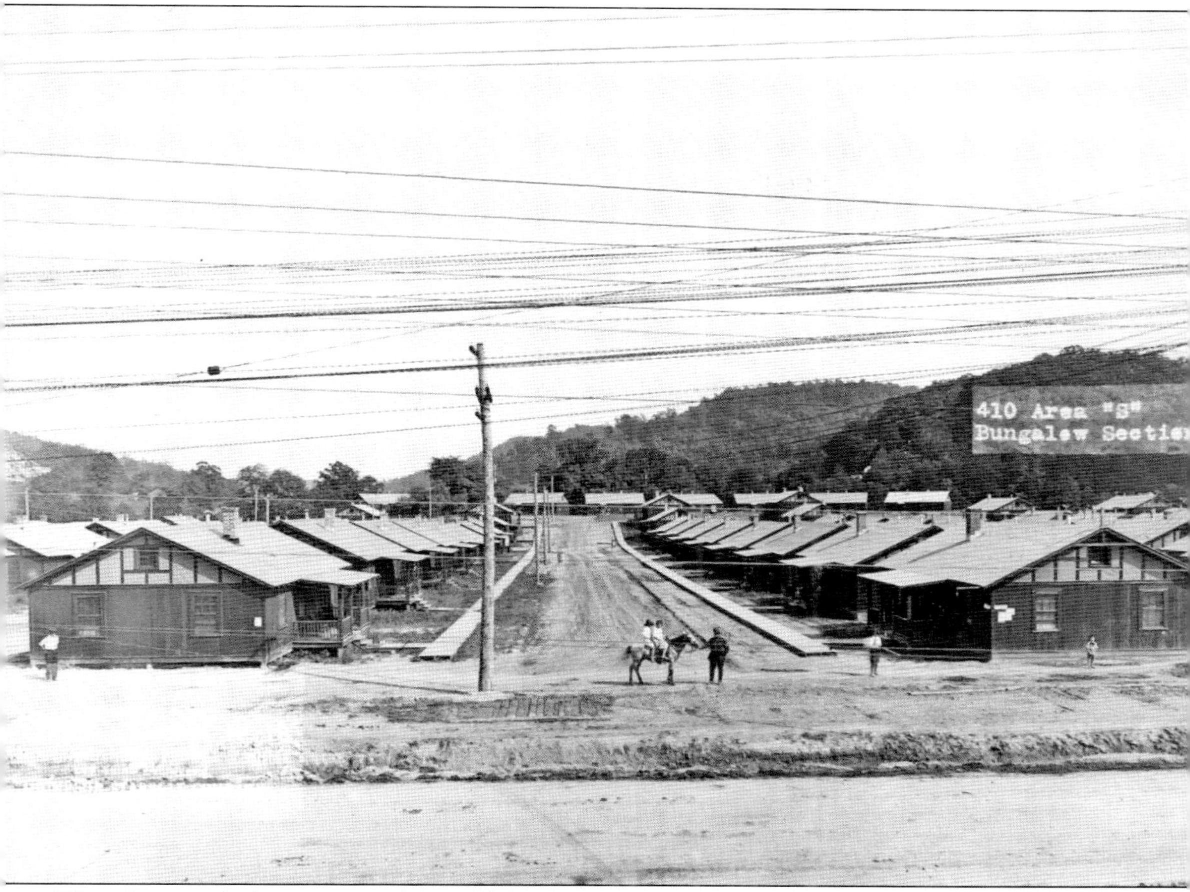

This photograph shows a typical view of the street and neighborhood layouts found in Nitro at the height of its use as a military industrial plant. The frantic pace at which the communities were constructed and the overarching goal of supporting the war effort meant that the design and layout were essentially utilitarian in nature. Raised, wooden sidewalks provided necessary safeguards against the muddy, wet environment that was ever present in the town that had been farm fields and pastures only a year or two earlier. Anecdotal stories from the time tell of workers who sometimes had trouble finding their home at the end of the day due to the uniform look of the entire settlement. (Courtesy of Rich Hively.)

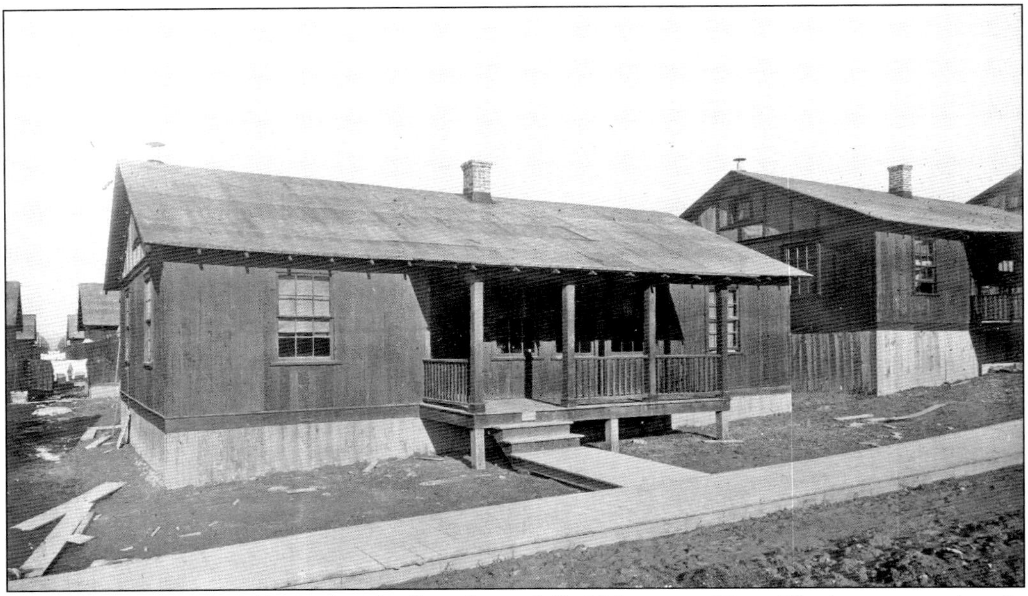

Shown above is a typical bungalow dwelling for unskilled laborers in Nitro. The houses were largely predesigned and fabricated away from the actual site, though on-site calculations and variations were often necessary in order to remedy differences in the landscape's elevations. Shown below is an inside view of the living room in a typical five-room bungalow. The standard features included a brick and mortar fireplace, along with wicker and simple wooden furniture. Smaller bungalows, such as the four-room unskilled foreign laborer homes, had a similar appearance—especially the brick fireplace as the focal point of the space. (Both, courtesy of Rich Hively.)

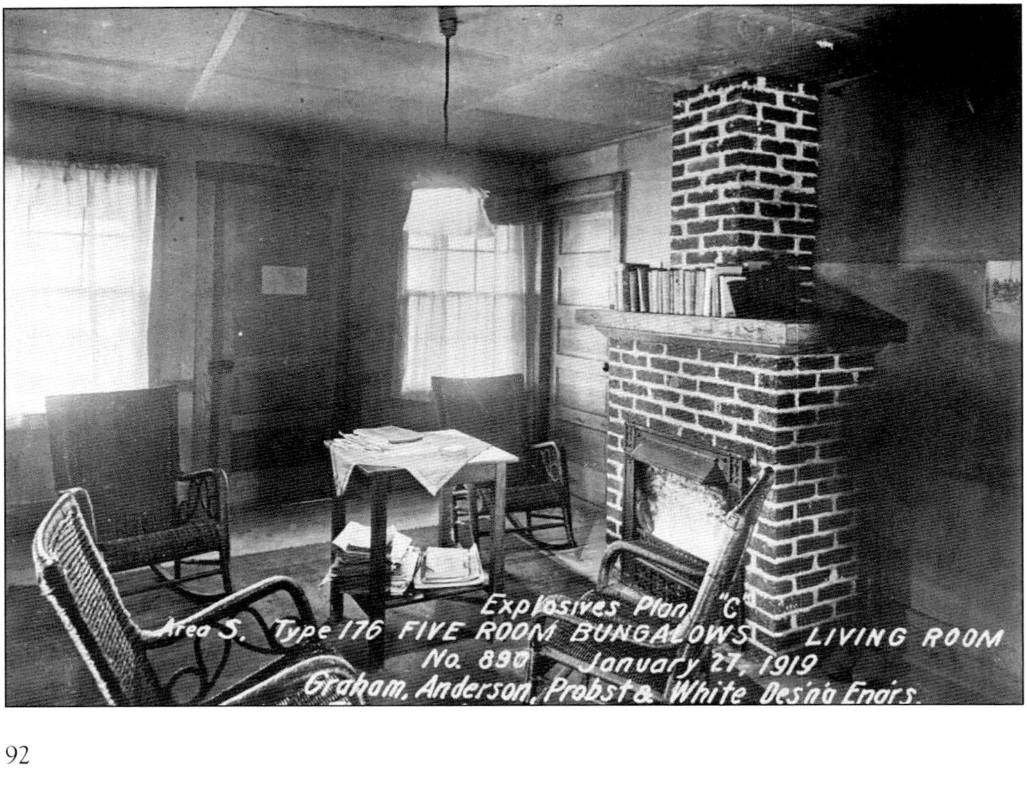

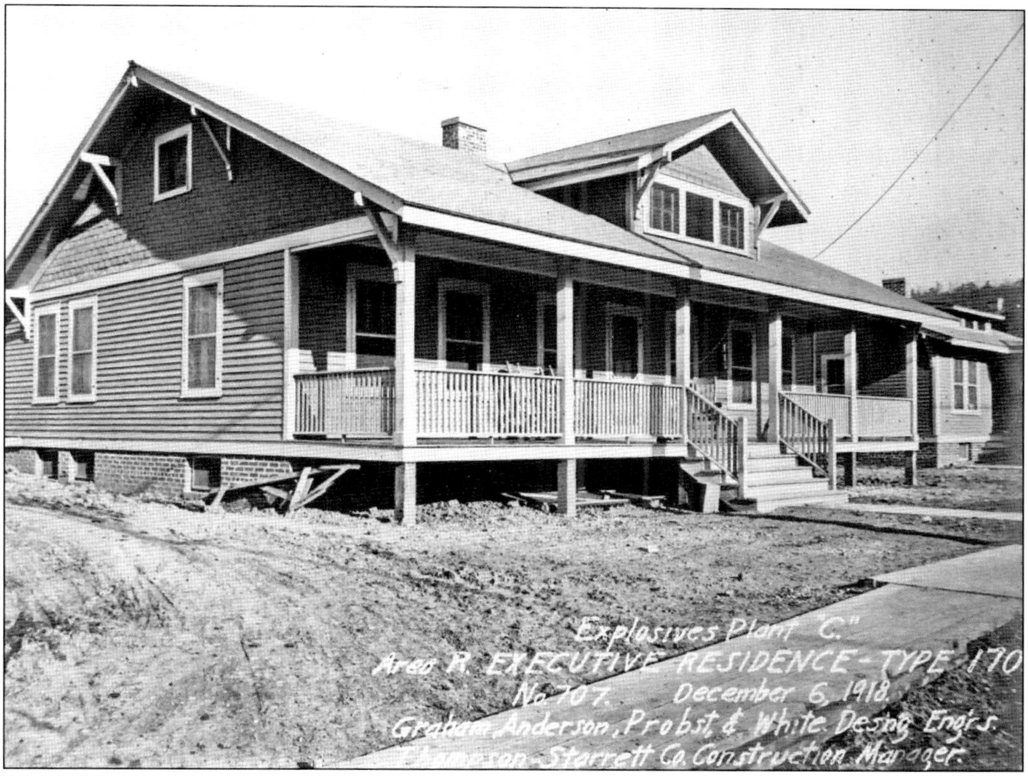

Shown in the above photograph is an example of one of the smaller executive residences that were built in Nitro. Though not as elaborate as the two-story executive residences, these houses were located in the same area of Nitro along Executives Row. The photograph below illustrates the nicer accommodations provided in the more expensive executive homes, including additional space, light fixtures, and even crown molding. Though the bungalows were provided almost entirely with furniture, and even kitchenware, executive residences often were stocked with personal belongings brought along when the houses' new residents moved to Nitro. (Both, courtesy of Rich Hively.)

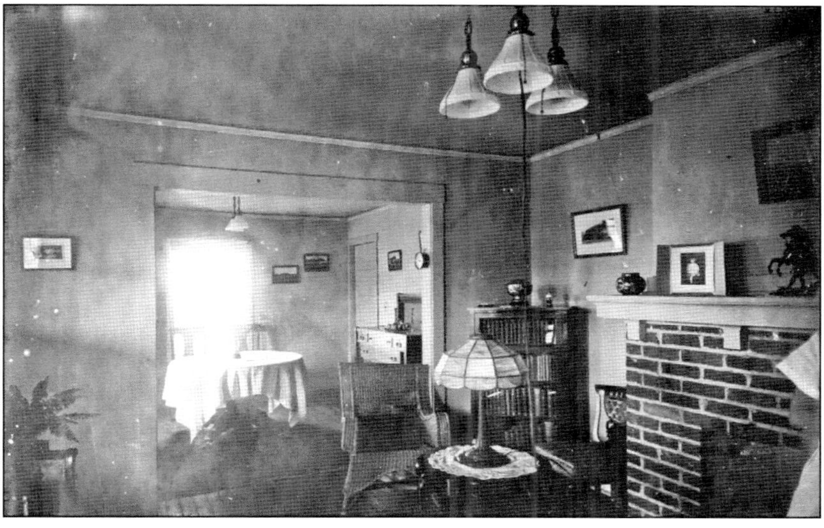

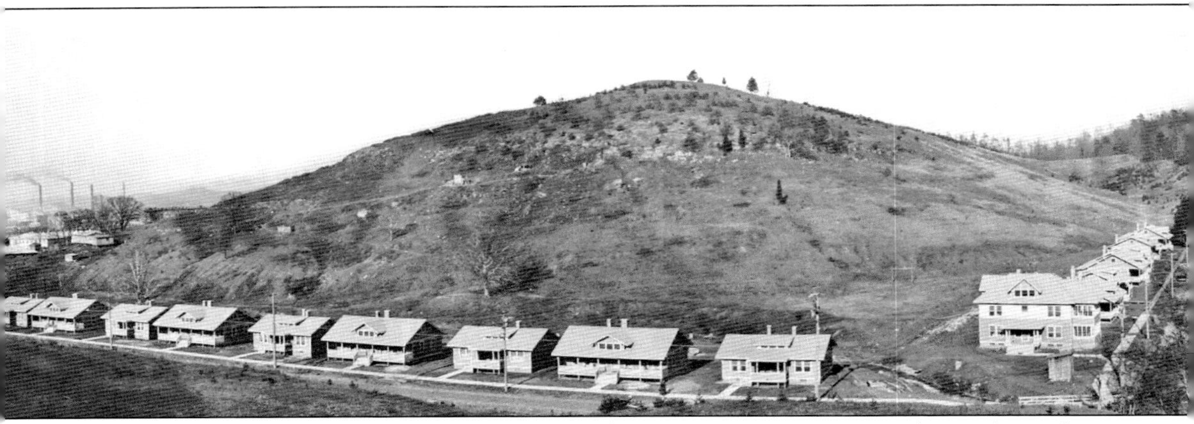

This panorama shows a long stretch of the large houses on Executive Row on the outskirts of town. Having the executive residences on the outer perimeter of the settlement afforded the quietest, cleanest, and safest locale for these community members. The large hill on the left-hand side of the image is the location of the Shelton family cemetery. The family had been the owners of a

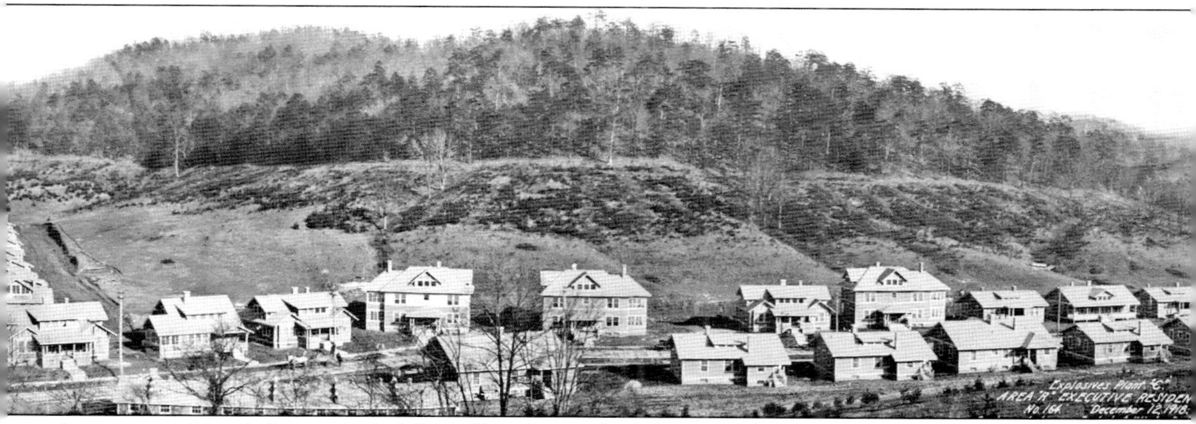

large tract of land that included the hill and stretched down to the edge of the Kanawha River. The Nitro water tower also stood on that hill in the middle of the 20th century. Today, thick woods cover the cemetery, which has unfortunately been subject to extensive vandalism and disrepair. (Courtesy of Rich Hively.)

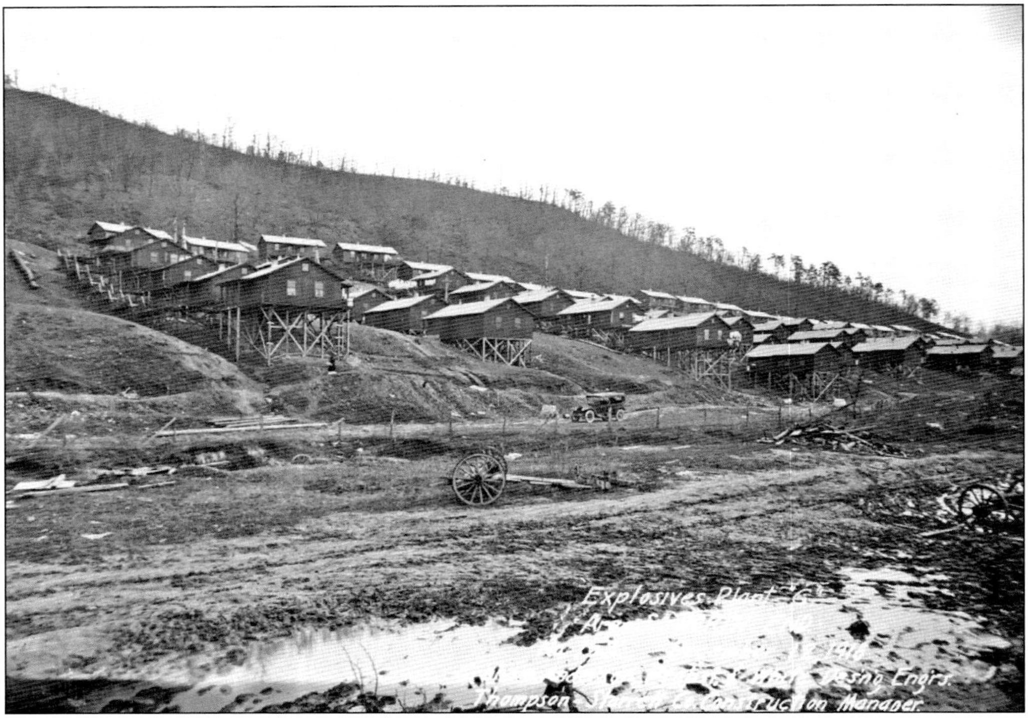

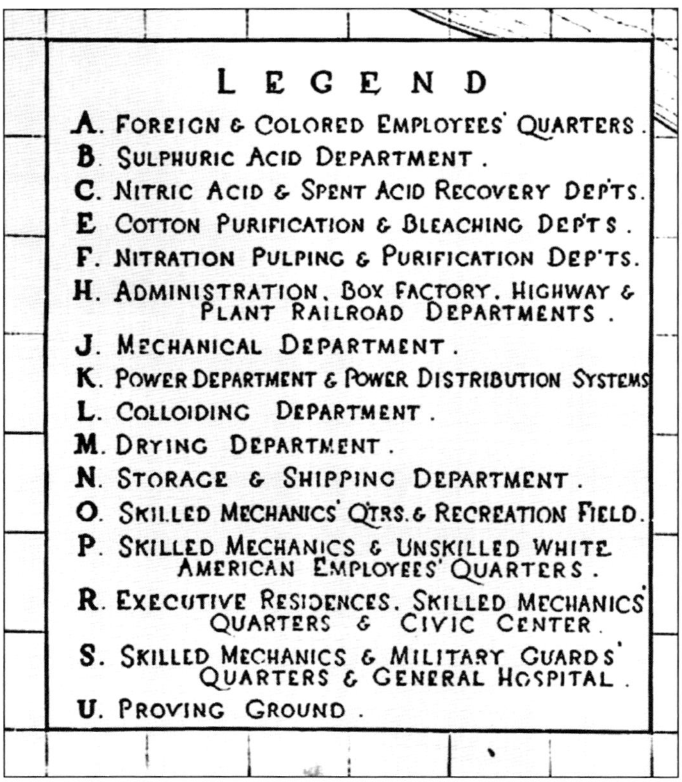

LEGEND

A. FOREIGN & COLORED EMPLOYEES' QUARTERS.
B. SULPHURIC ACID DEPARTMENT.
C. NITRIC ACID & SPENT ACID RECOVERY DEP'TS.
E. COTTON PURIFICATION & BLEACHING DEP'TS.
F. NITRATION PULPING & PURIFICATION DEP'TS.
H. ADMINISTRATION, BOX FACTORY, HIGHWAY & PLANT RAILROAD DEPARTMENTS.
J. MECHANICAL DEPARTMENT.
K. POWER DEPARTMENT & POWER DISTRIBUTION SYSTEMS
L. COLLOIDING DEPARTMENT.
M. DRYING DEPARTMENT.
N. STORAGE & SHIPPING DEPARTMENT.
O. SKILLED MECHANICS' QTRS. & RECREATION FIELD.
P. SKILLED MECHANICS & UNSKILLED WHITE AMERICAN EMPLOYEES' QUARTERS.
R. EXECUTIVE RESIDENCES, SKILLED MECHANICS' QUARTERS & CIVIC CENTER.
S. SKILLED MECHANICS & MILITARY GUARDS' QUARTERS & GENERAL HOSPITAL.
U. PROVING GROUND.

Much of Nitro was built on the naturally occurring flat ground found along that region of the Kanawha River; however, as the new powder plant and accompanying city were constructed, demands for buildings necessitated creative utilization of all kinds of differing landscapes and terrain features. Shown above are bungalows constructed in the north end of town that utilized varying foundation lengths made of lumber so that they could be located on the side of a rather steep hill. Today, this area of Nitro is where Interstate 64 runs from east to west, connecting Charleston and Huntington. Pictured at left is a powder plant–era legend listing the various sections into which Nitro was divided. (Both, courtesy of Rich Hively.)

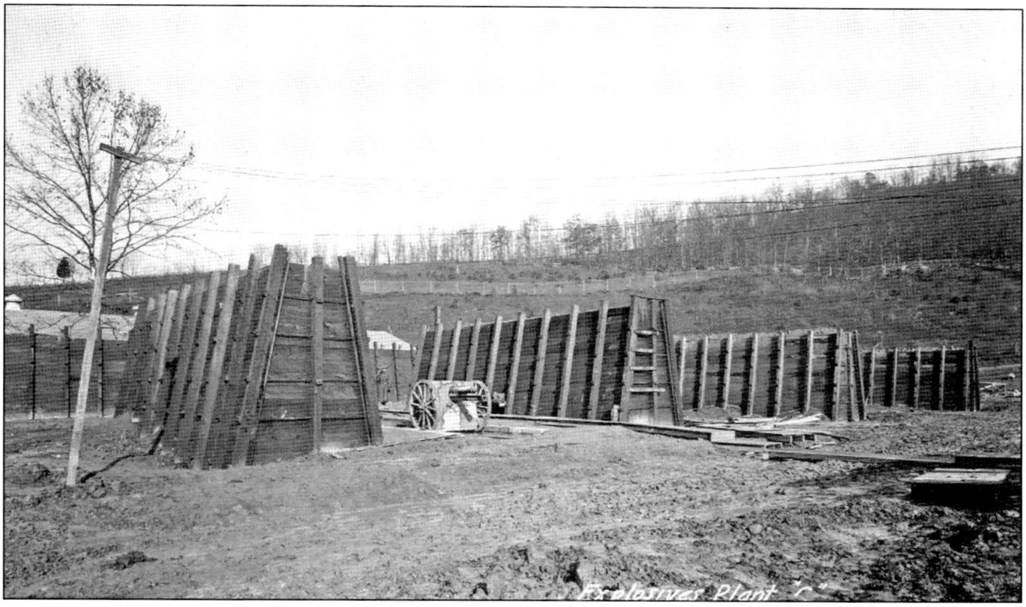

As loads of powder were completed in the blending towers, quantities were separated into airtight containers and transported into storage to await shipment over the rail lines and eventually be sent overseas. However, plant workers periodically tested the quality and reliability of the finished powder at a proving ground (above), located in nearby Rock Branch Hollow. At this location, artillery pieces were used to fire the powder. The safe storage of the finished powder was of great concern as well. Loads of ready-to-ship powder were sealed in magazine buildings (below) or, more often, in long trenches that were designed to protect against blast damage in case of accidental explosions. (Both, courtesy of Rich Hively.)

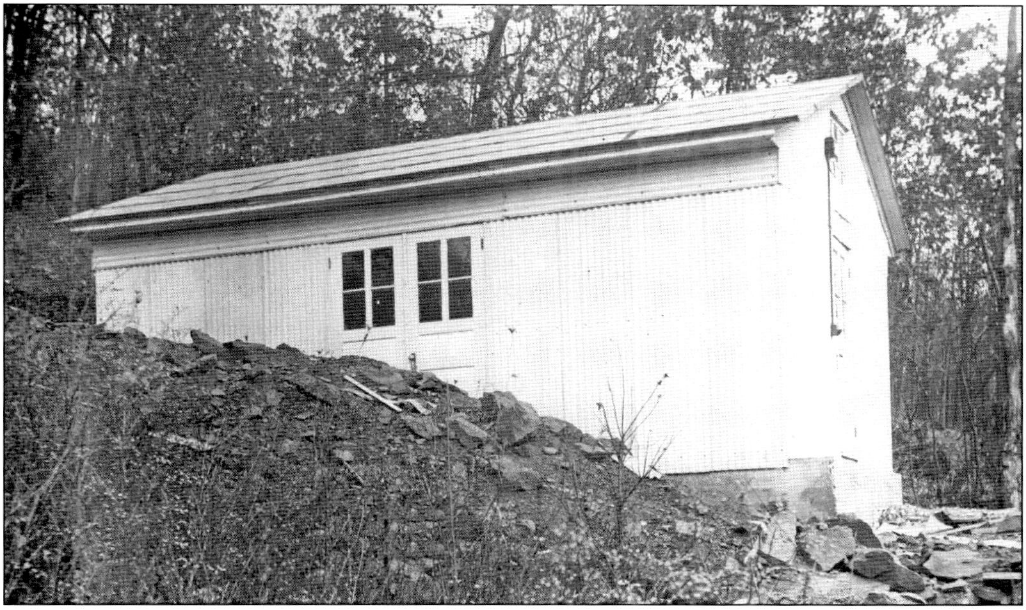

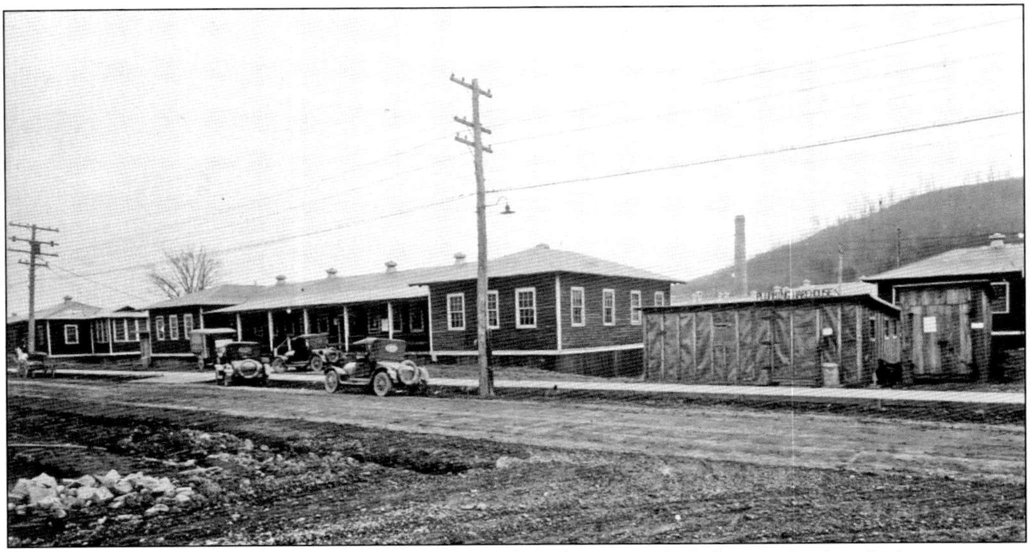

The general hospital was a large building complex that provided the vital role of administering heath care to the residents and workers of Nitro. The hospital had over 400 beds available for sick or injured patients as well as 50 doctors, 2 dentists, and 80 nurses and assistants. The US military did not operate and oversee the hospital by itself; instead, the United States Public Health Service agency was assigned to help administer the many functions of the site. Shown above is the officer in charge building on the left with several cars in front. Next door on the right is the superintendent of nurses office. Below is the community room of the nurses' quarters building, also located on the hospital grounds. (Both, courtesy of Rich Hively.)

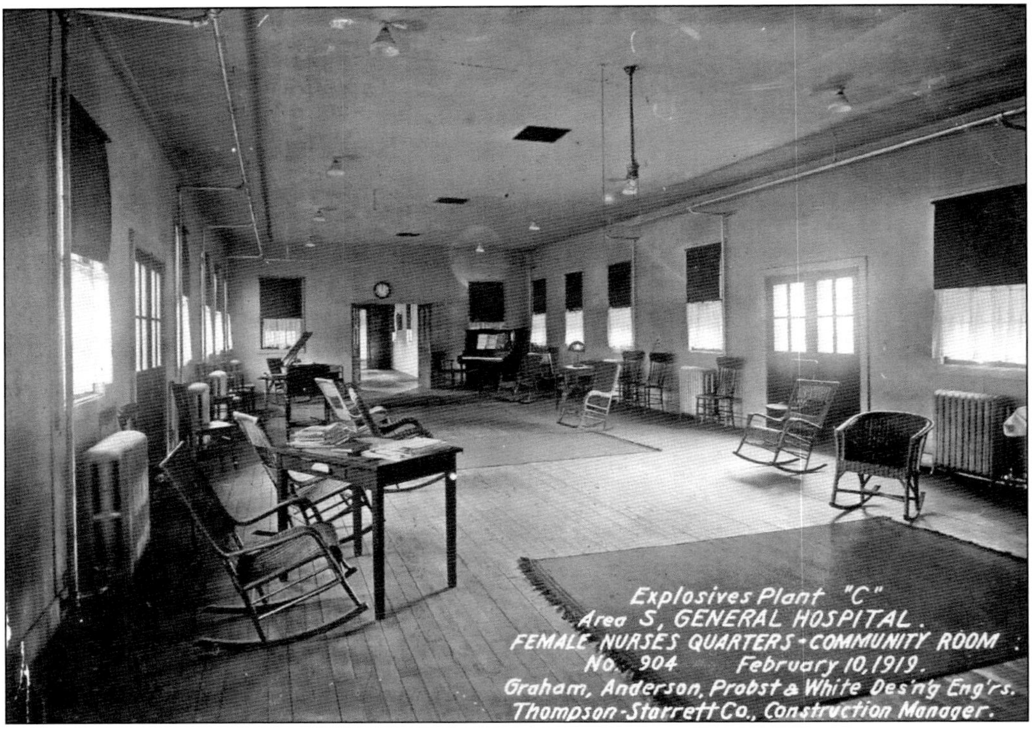

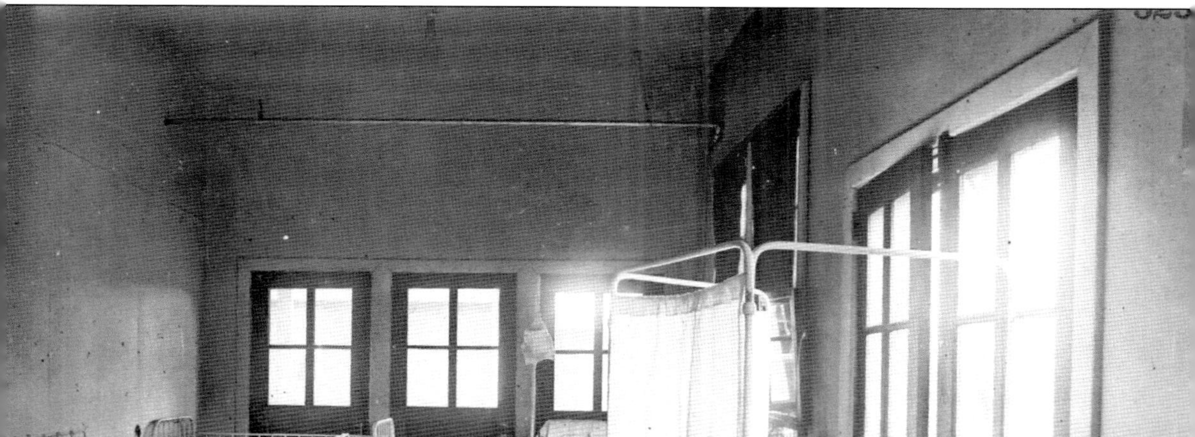

Photographed here is a young patient on the sun porch section of the children's infirmary, located in Nitro's general hospital. Though the exact nature of the child's illness is unknown, his presence in the hospital speaks to the countless people who became ill and required medical attention during the wartime operation of Nitro. Near the end of September 1918, the Spanish flu pandemic reached the workers of Nitro after spreading from Europe by way of returning American military personnel. As was the case elsewhere in the country, large numbers of men and women quickly caught the sickness. In the months to follow, nearly 10,000 residents of Nitro caught the illness, many of whom had to be hospitalized. Over 200 people in the community eventually died during the flu epidemic. (Courtesy of Rich Hively.)

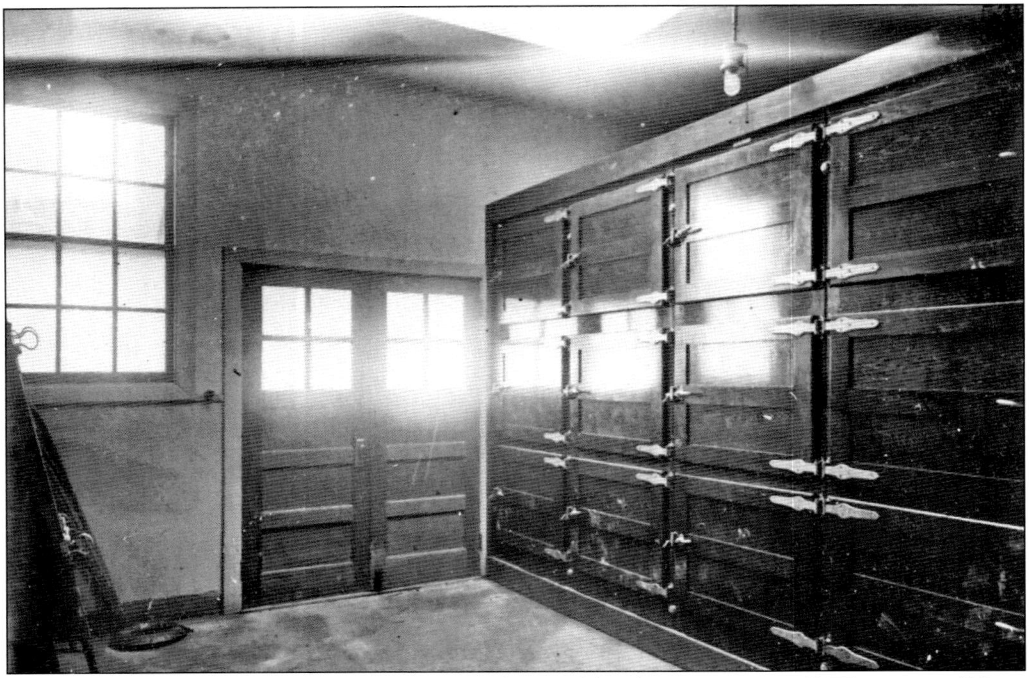

Shown here are the facilities used at the Nitro hospital by the mortuary staff. The town of Nitro presented a unique set of circumstances with which planners had to contend. With such large numbers of men and women traveling to the settlement for employment away from friends and family members, a sickness resulting in death or a fatal accident meant that the organizational structure of the town had to step in to care for the body. Many times, the remains of the deceased were kept in the cadaver room (above) until a relative could be contacted, during which time the mortician practiced embalming using the modern laboratory techniques of the time (below). Many of the deceased were sent by railroad back to families in cities located far away from the Kanawha Valley. (Both, courtesy of Rich Hively.)

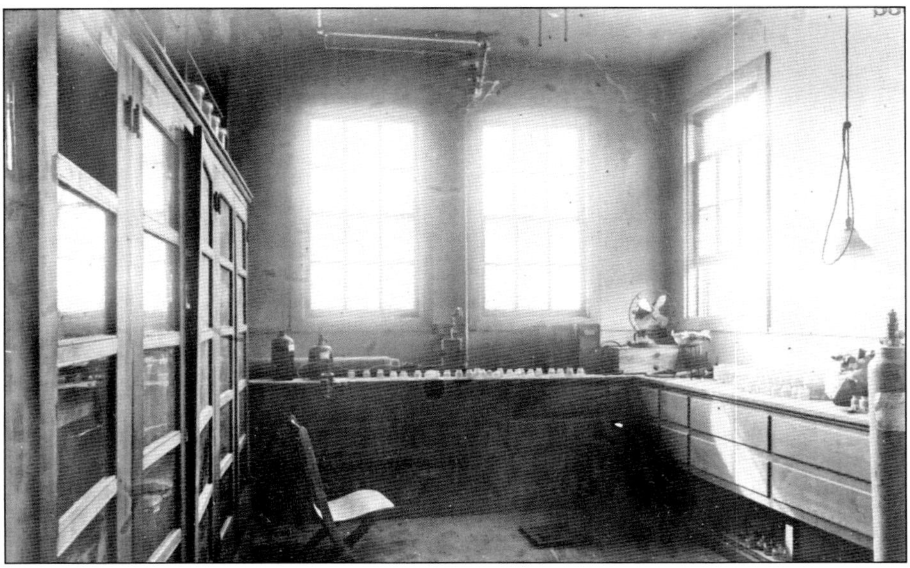

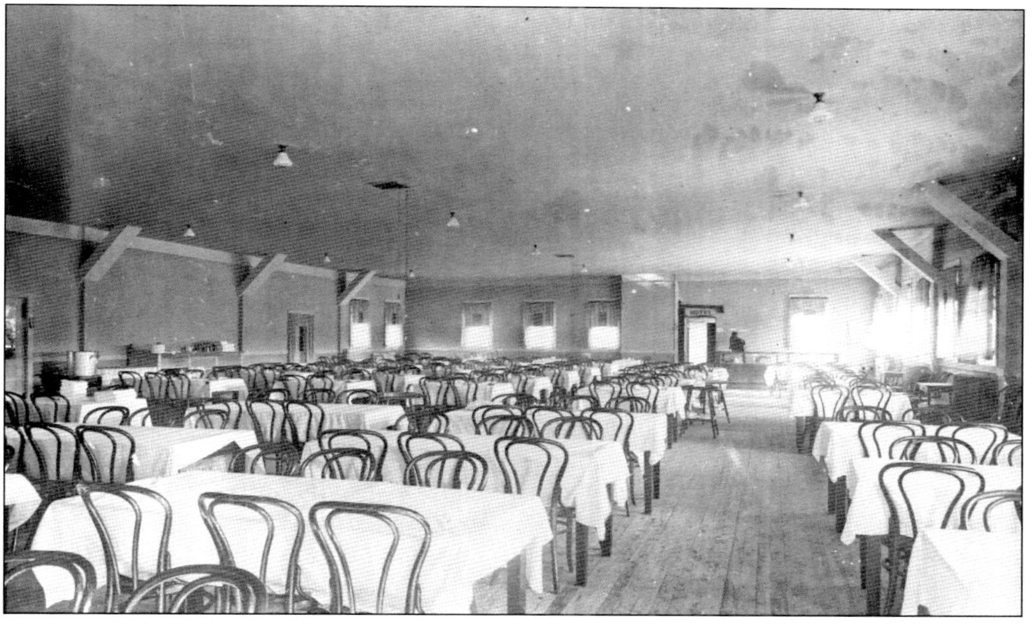

Shown above is the dining hall in the main hotel located in Nitro. Like other privately owned businesses at the time, this one was built and run by the US government. In the early stages of Nitro's existence, no such hotel facility existed within town. Temporary travelers to the town were put up overnight in the military barracks. Below is the kitchen in the room adjoining the dining hall. Between the kitchen located at the hotel, the kitchen at the base hospital, and the kitchen in the main mess hall, well over 6,000 men and women could be fed per hour in the city of Nitro. (Both, courtesy of Rich Hively.)

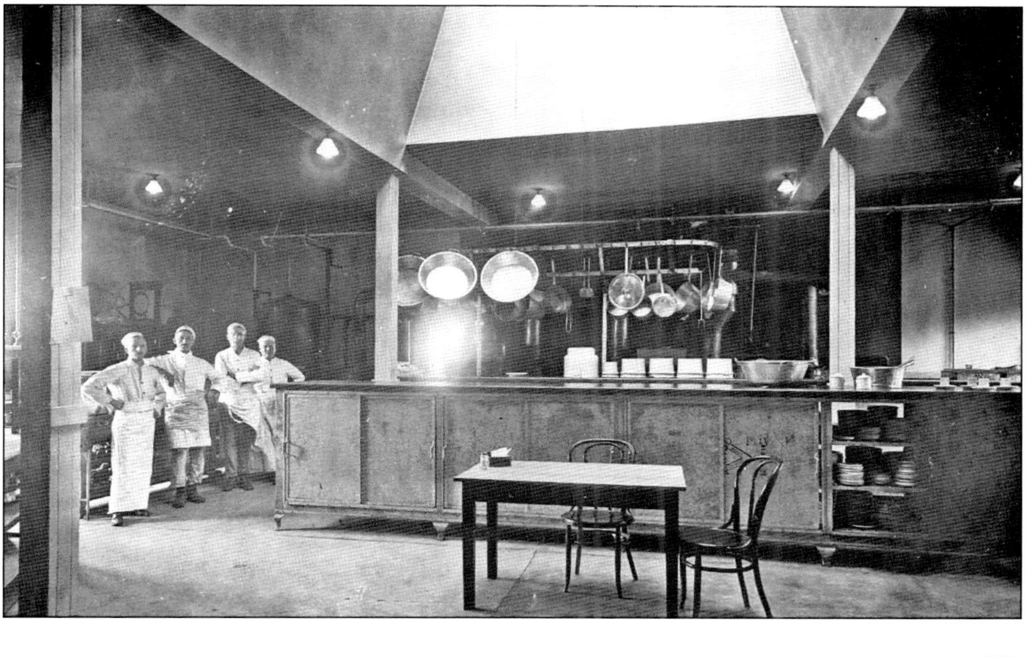

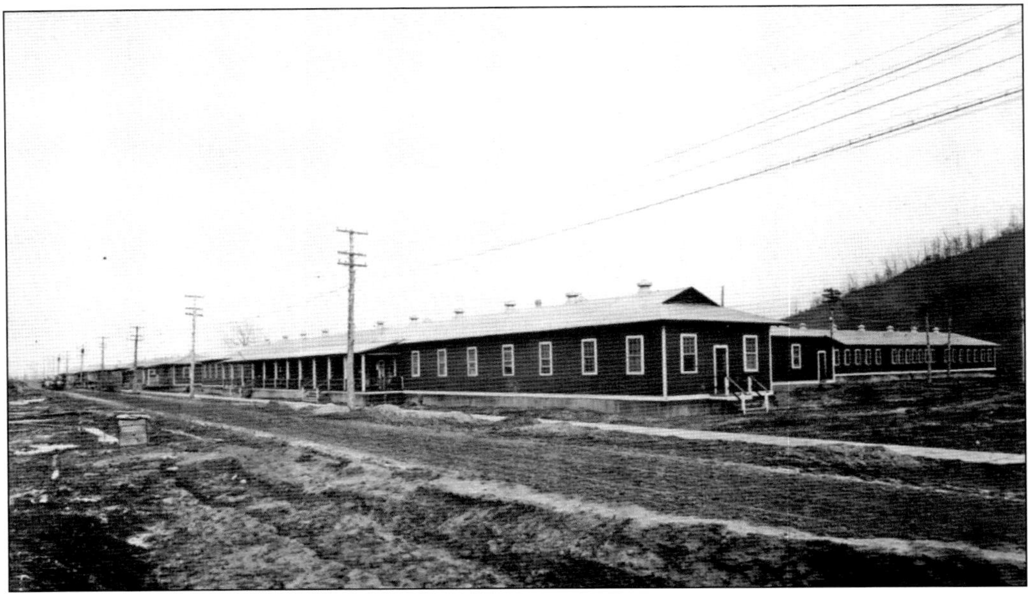

Historian William Wintz published a Charleston newspaper article that described the special celebrations that were held by residents of Nitro upon the completion of large buildings. For instance, when the base hospital (above) was completed in May 1918, a total of 15,000 people attended a large dance celebration at the site, during which over $1,000 was raised for the Red Cross. Located not too far from the hospital was a women's barracks house that provided living quarters for large numbers of nurses who worked at the hospital. Shown below are dozens of women in the tightly packed dining room within the structure. (Both, courtesy of Rich Hively.)

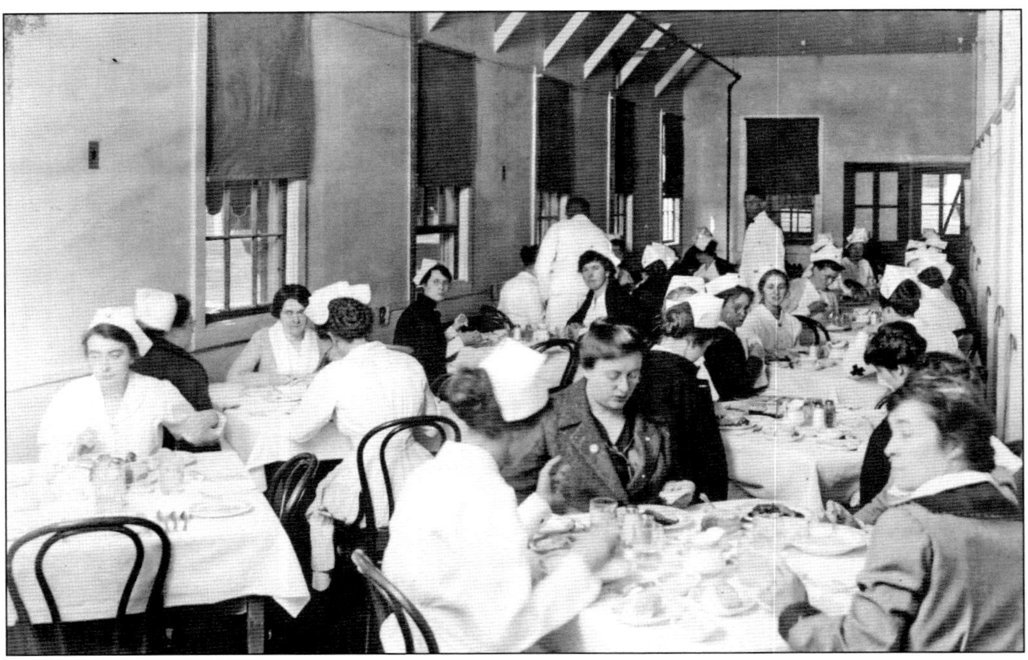

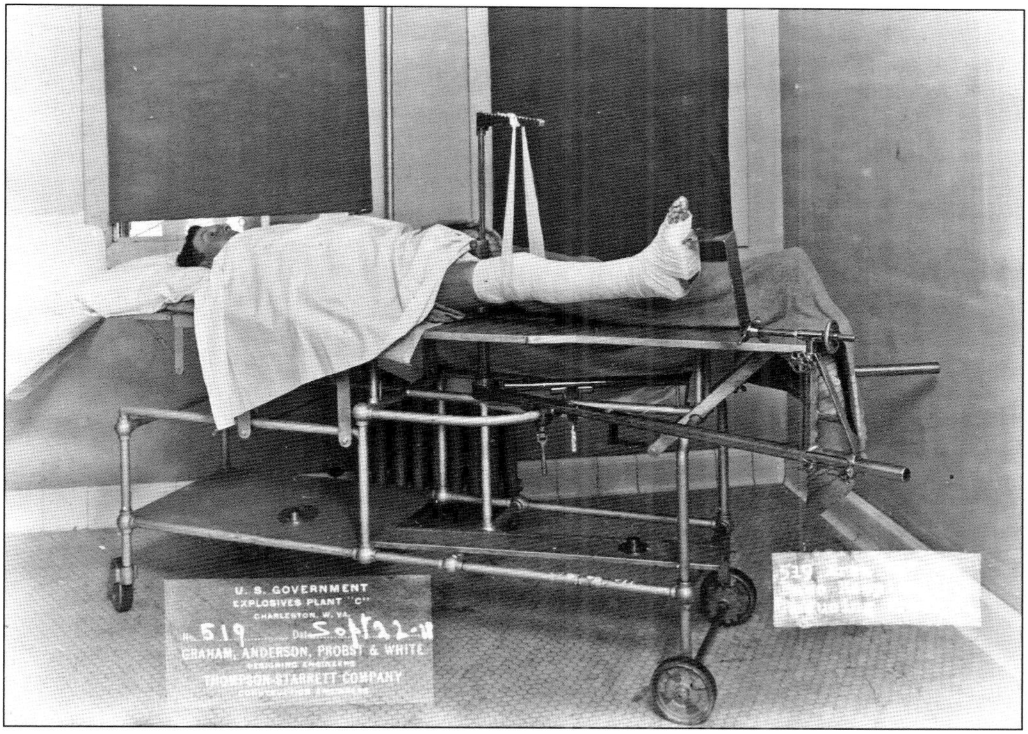

In addition to the dangers of disease always present in the high-density settlement of Nitro, work-related injuries were always a present concern and problem due to the inherent dangers of the factories and plants established at the site. Injuries resulting from fires, explosions, and workplace falls kept the hospital and its staff always busily attending to the latest patients. With a high turnover workforce that was always pressed for adequate supply, it was of the utmost importance that injured laborers be mended as quickly as possible and sent back to work. The Safety and Compensation Department at the Nitro military base kept records of injuries, reporting that in one year there were over 10,000 accidents, with 12 resulting in fatalities. (Both, courtesy of Rich Hively.)

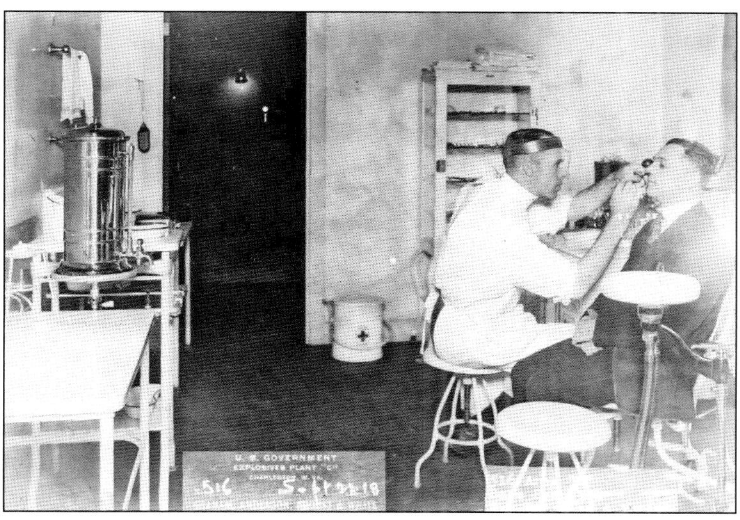

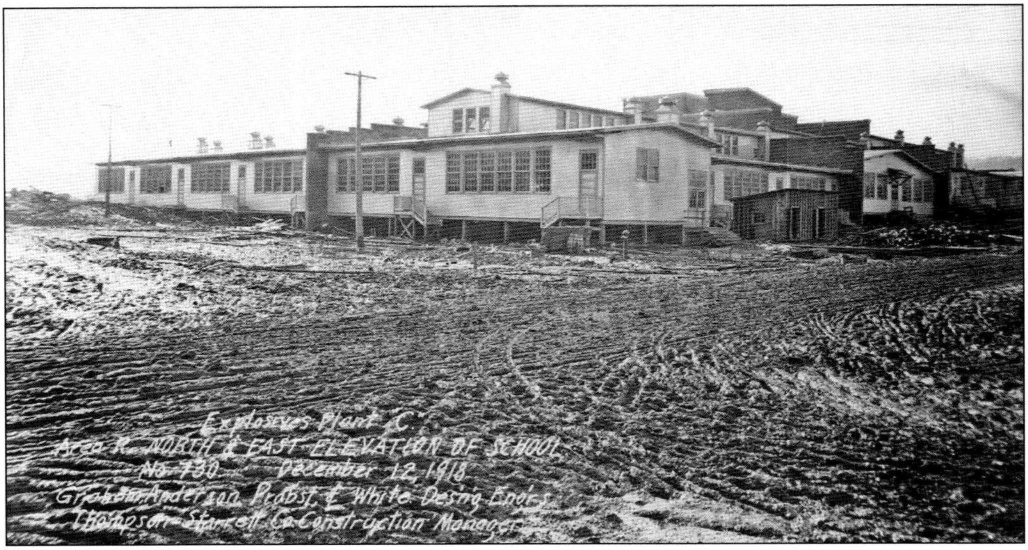

The plans for the construction of Nitro called for the establishment of an adequate school system for the education of children who came with working parents to the powder plant. Separate facilities were maintained for white and black children. The main school (above) was located on Twenty-first Street and was used until the late 1940s or early 1950s, when a new school was built that is today still partially occupied by the Nitro Police Department. The size of the original school's classrooms (below) were quite large in comparison to the one-room schoolhouses that had been the norm in the area around Nitro just years previously. (Both, courtesy of Rich Hively.)

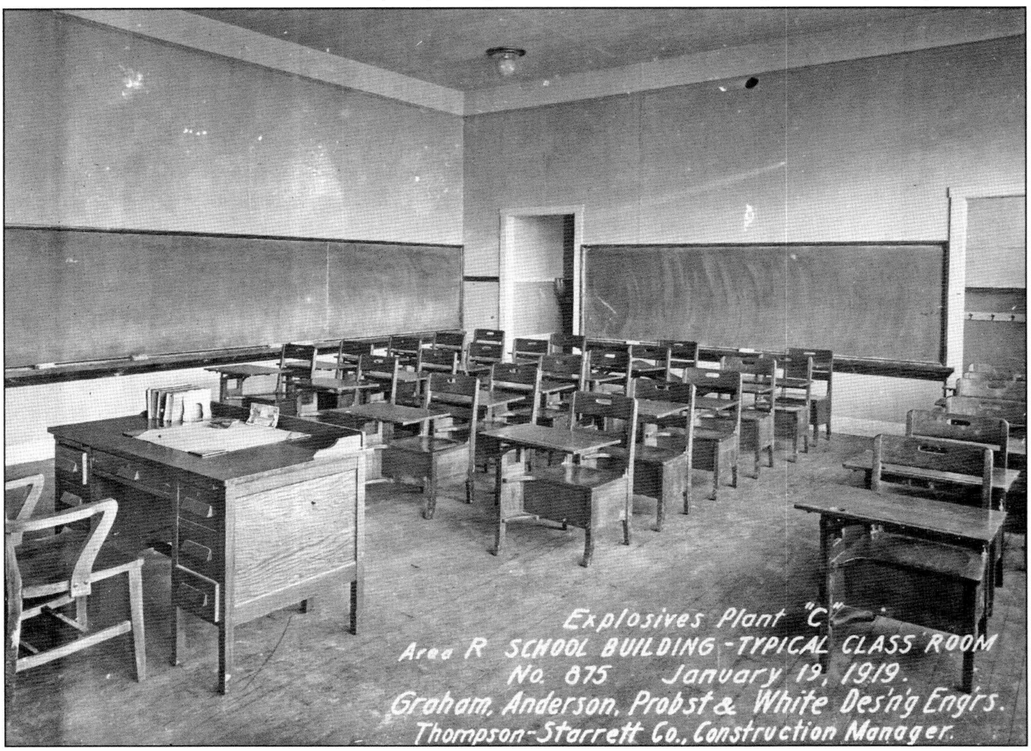

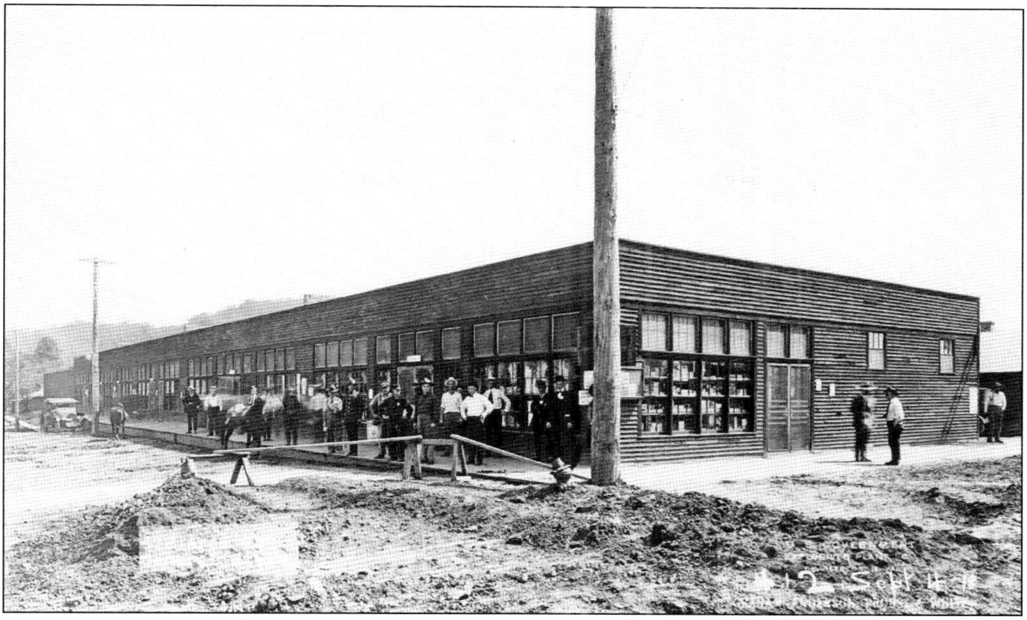

The General Store (above) was located on the corner of Forty-first Street and First Avenue and offered a rather new concept for the time of combining several businesses into a one-stop location. For instance, a large barbershop was located in the General Store, only steps away from a meat market, grocery store, clothing store, and other department store sections, such as items found in a hardware store today. Like the other stores in town, this location was managed by the commissary. Over 600 bungalow houses were located nearby, so this store was literally the Nitro community's first modern shopping center. (Both, courtesy of Rich Hively.)

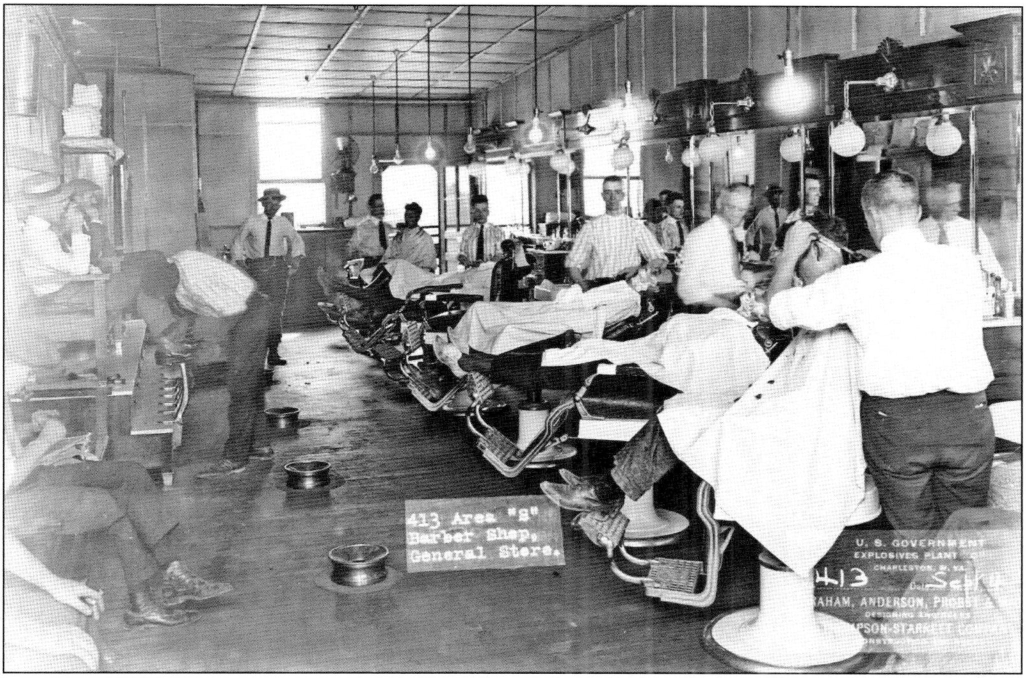

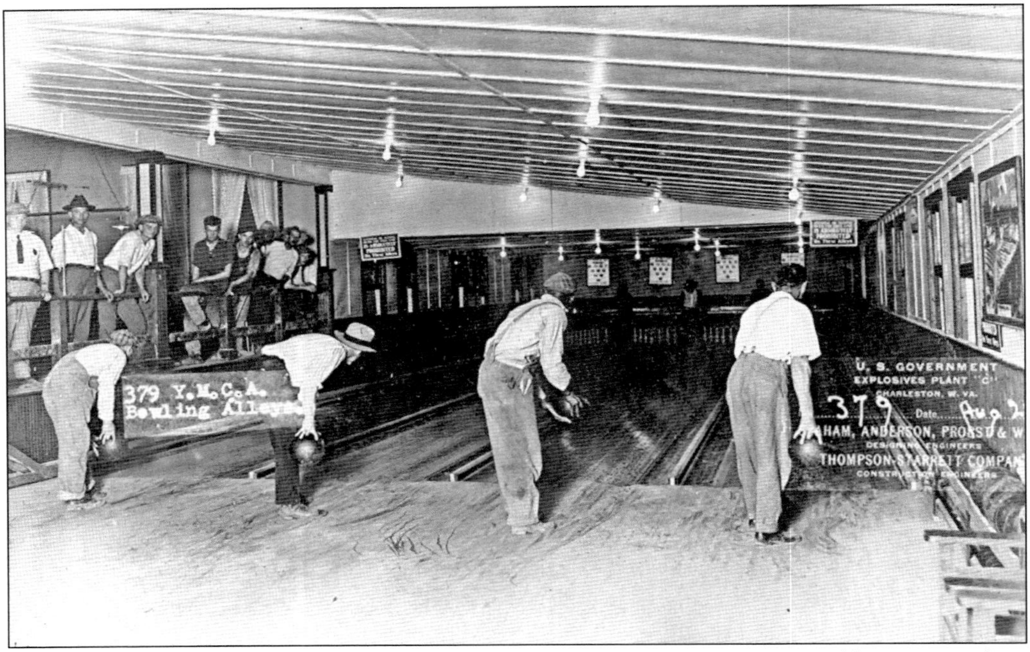

The YMCA was, in many ways, the social hub of the community in Nitro. In addition to outdoor sports that were highly popular among the young residents of town, the YMCA provided indoor sporting facilities, such as the bowling alley shown above. On certain dates throughout the year, boxing matches were publicized around town, with the event taking place in the large indoor auditorium at the whites-only YMCA facility. Boxing and wrestling matches in Nitro consisted primarily of contestants from the town; however, in the spirit of regional rivalry, there were several highly spirited matches between Nitro citizens and participants from nearby towns, such as Charleston. (Both, courtesy of Rich Hively.)

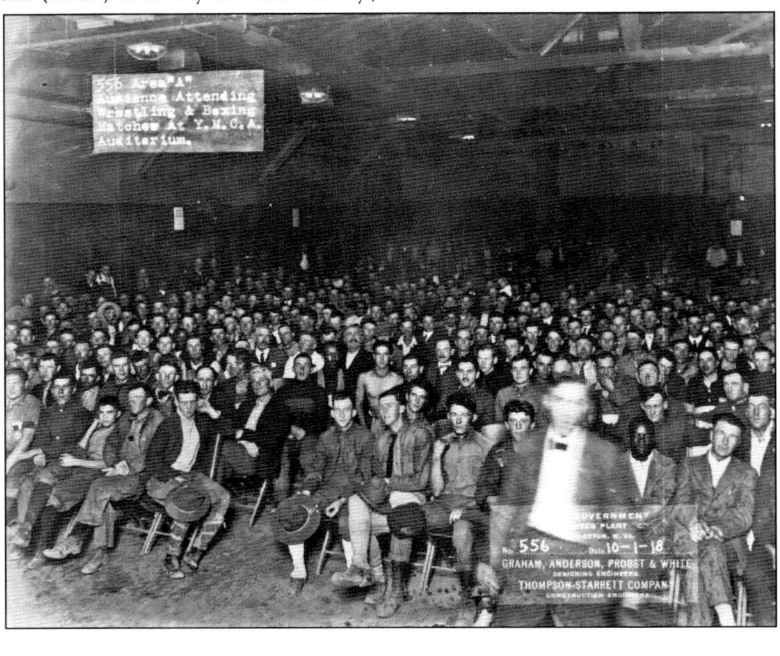

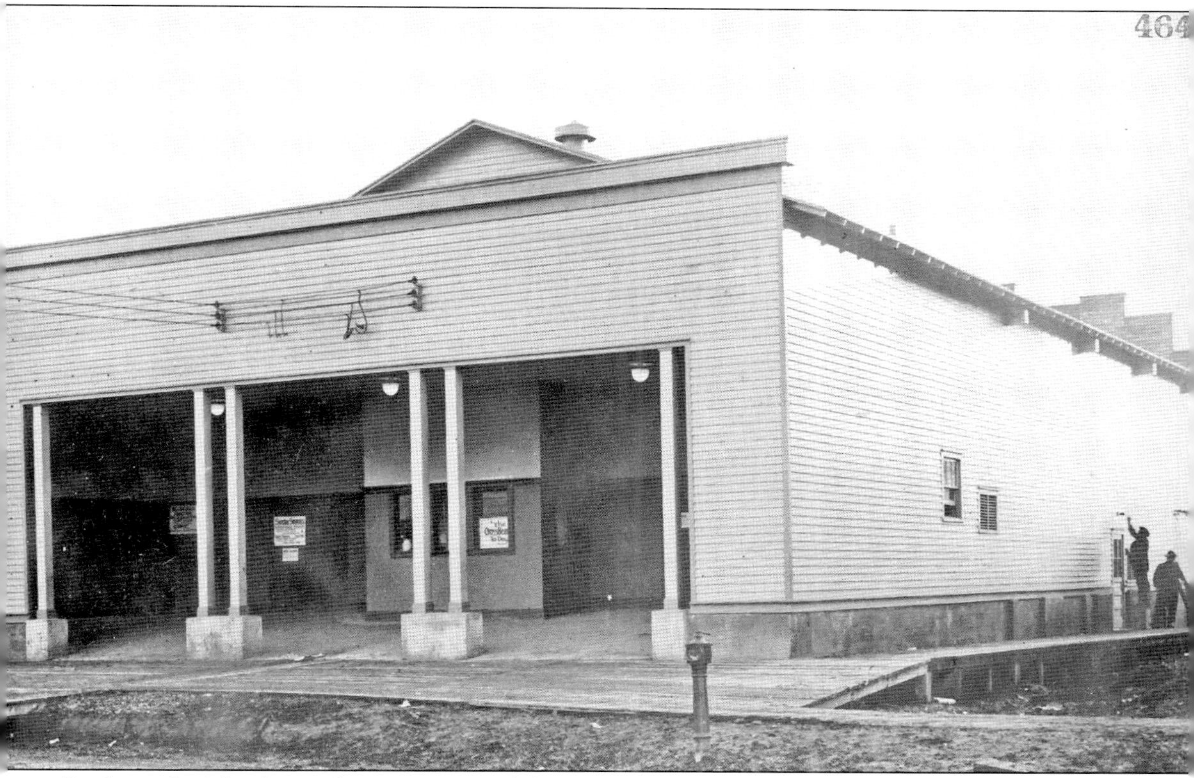

By the end of the frenzied construction of the town of Nitro, four movie theater buildings had been erected for the entertainment of the settlement's workers. The auditoriums were reportedly packed each night that they were open. The theater shown here continued in operation even after the government plants were shut down in Nitro following the conclusion of World War I. Sold to different owners, the structure bore witness to the early years of Hollywood films throughout the 1920s, 1930s, and 1940s. Eventually, however, the invention of television and the subsequent increasing affordability of the new device ultimately led to the theater's closure. (Courtesy of Rich Hively.)

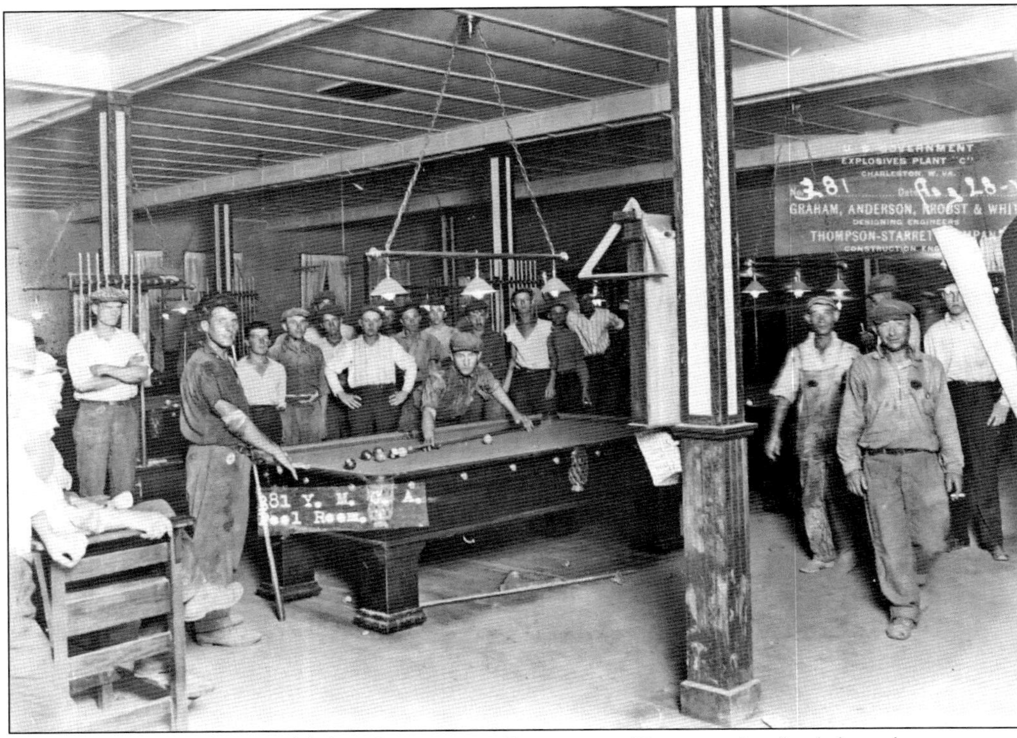

The YMCA helped to establish a Community Betterment Division that had the sole purpose of promoting community events and programs that were aimed at aiding educational, recreational, religious, and social prosperity in Nitro. The YMCA provided its own places for workers to socialize, such as rooms for billiards and libraries. To help promote morale in relation to residents' connections to family member and friends who lived far away, the YMCA established a writing room at their facilities so that workers had a place to write correspondence to those back home. The YMCA also oversaw the religious activities of the many religions and denominations in Nitro, including a sizable population of Judaism observers. (Both, courtesy of Rich Hively.)

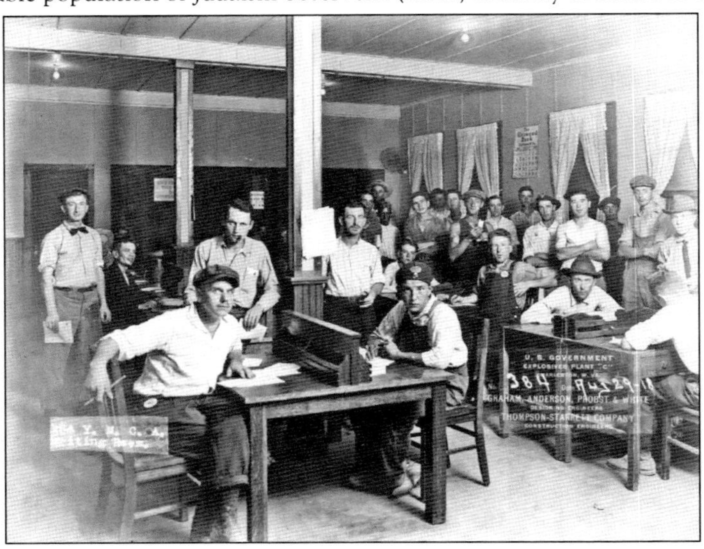

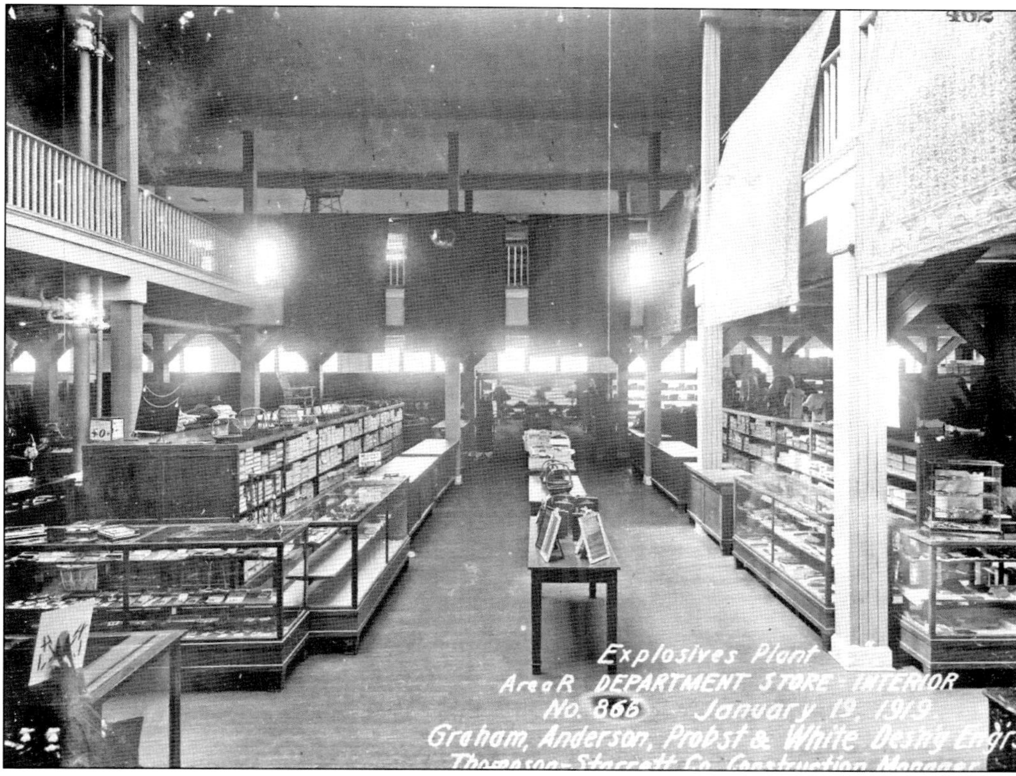

The store interiors shown here were stocked and operated entirely by Nitro's military commissary, which was seen as the best available entity to oversee the massive and potentially unwieldy process of establishing, constructing, and regulating the proper flow of necessary goods into the new town. The above photograph depicts the interior of the department store, while the photograph below shows a crowded scene of Nitro citizens shopping in the grocery market. Following the closure of the military's powder plant operations after World War I, these stores and markets were bought and, in many cases, run by private owners. (Both, courtesy of Rich Hively.)

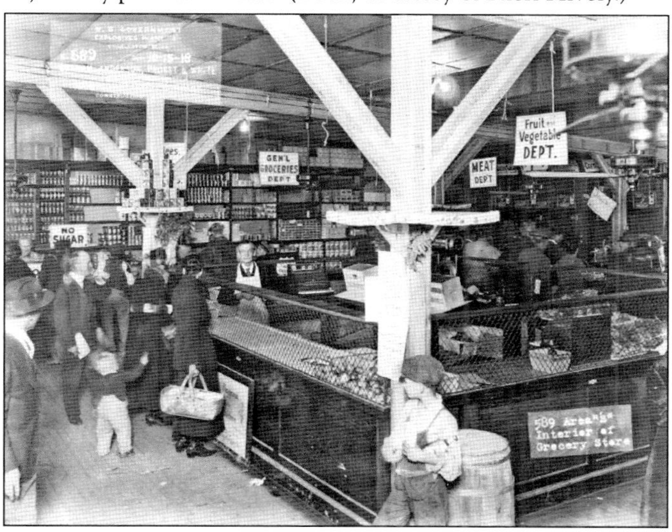

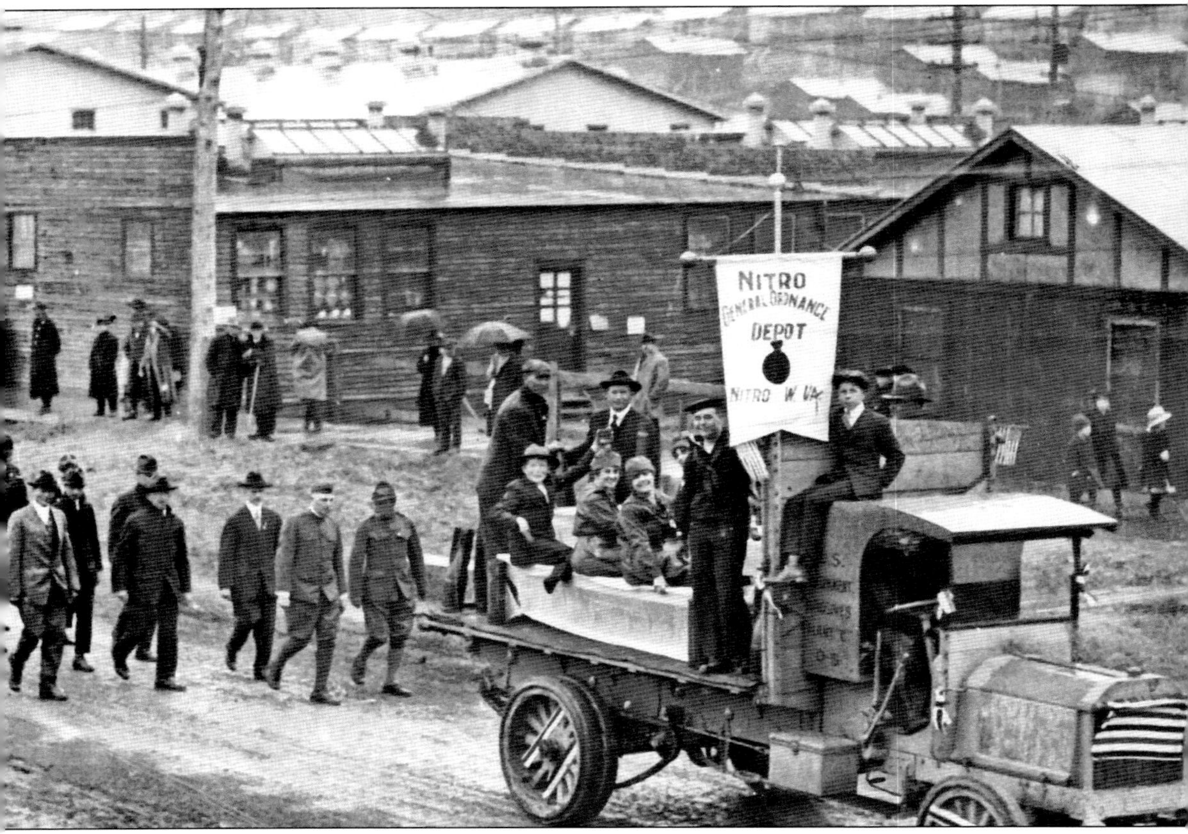

Social events meant to bolster morale for Nitro residents and workers were oftentimes coupled with more pragmatic goals of raising funds or accomplishing goals. Dances and music concerts were occasions for celebrating holidays or news from abroad but could also be used to raise money for the Red Cross. In April 1918, the Third Liberty Loan Drive was held in Nitro and was marked by a massive parade by the employees of Nitro, who amassed makeshift floats out of military and civilian vehicles, all with the express purpose of raising war funds. Photographed here are floats parading down Twenty-first Street in Nitro. Residents of Nitro and people from the surrounding countryside packed into the streets of the city to show their combined support for the war effort's loan drive. Similar scenes were witnessed months later in November 1918, when victory was declared in Europe. (Courtesy of Rich Hively.)

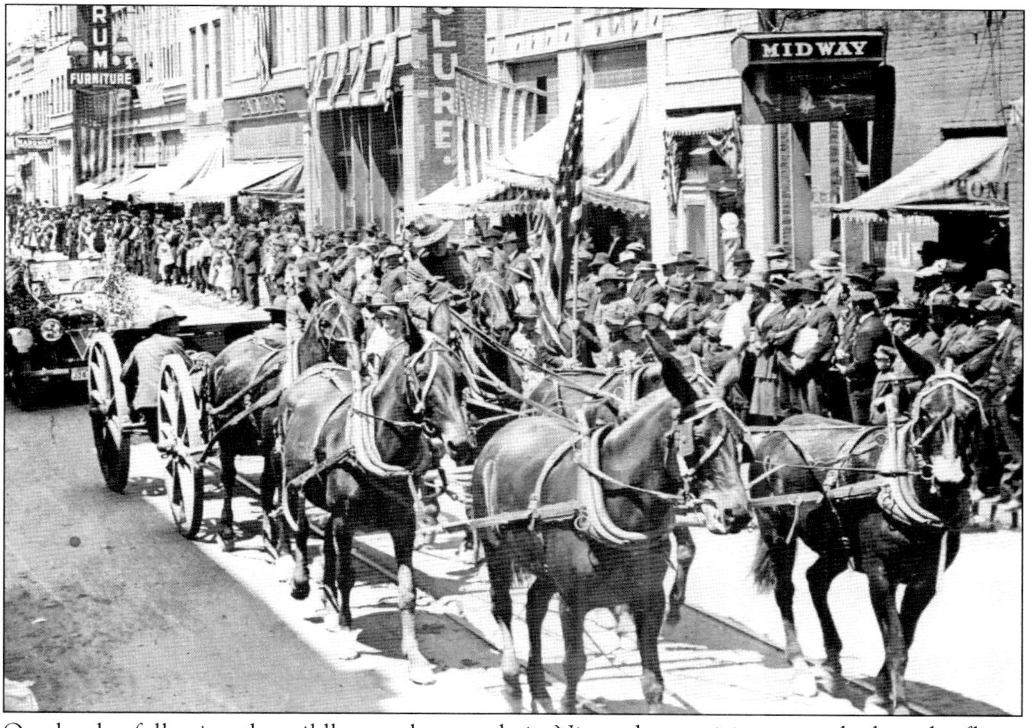

On the day following the wildly popular parade in Nitro, the participants packed up the floats and vehicles onto waiting train cars and traveled the 15 to 20 miles to Charleston, West Virginia, where a second parade was then staged. For this second-day extension of the Nitro parade, well over 10,000 people turned out on the packed streets of the state's capital city. (Courtesy of Rich Hively.)

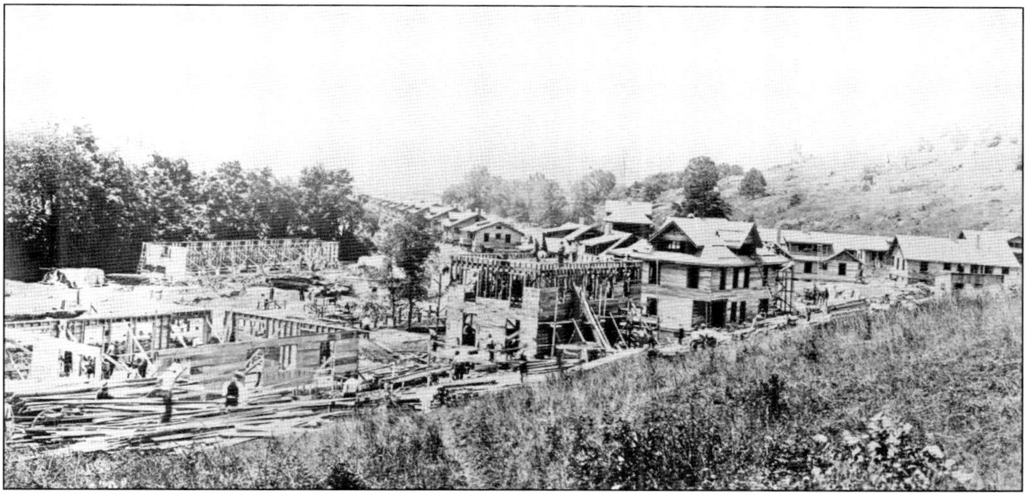

During the construction of housing in Nitro, construction laborers worked at an almost superhuman rate. In a span of four months, nearly 2,000 bungalows were constructed at a rate of nearly 20 per day. The frame houses shown here, constructed on Twenty-first Street, took longer to construct than bungalows but still rose from the ground at a rate of almost five per day. (Courtesy of Rich Hively.)

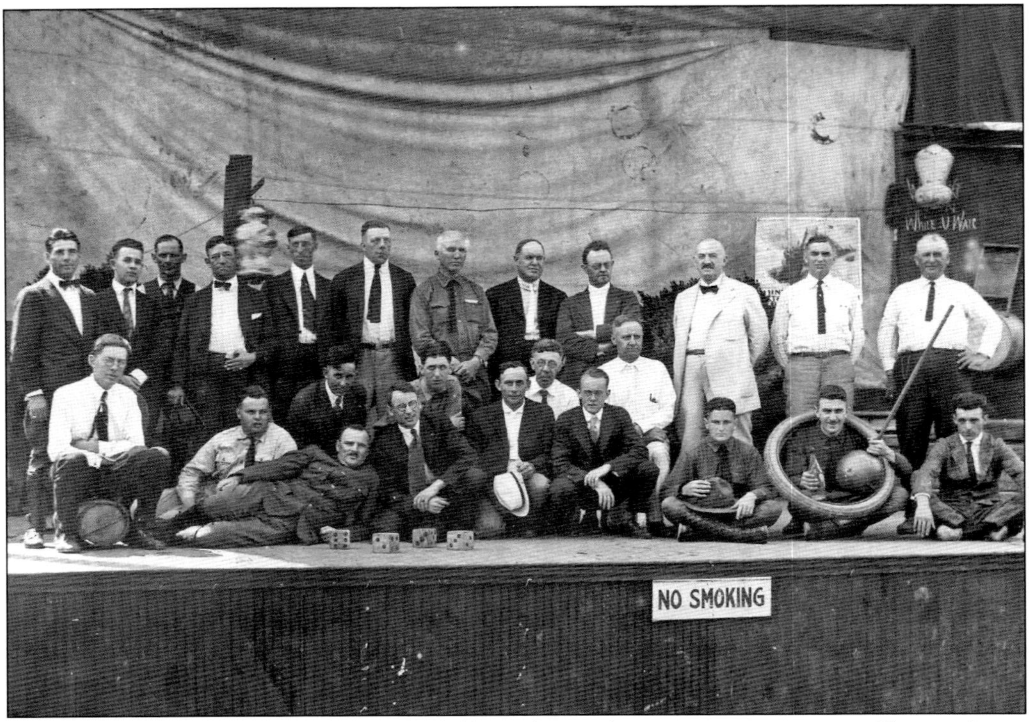

Entertainment in Nitro was widely available and very diverse in opportunities. Shown above, members of the Nitro band put on a play for the entertainment of the citizens of Nitro at the YMCA. Below, scores of workers assembled on the sloped hill bordering the athletic fields to watch a baseball or football game. Several months into the life of Nitro, numerous baseball teams had been established for residents, including teams for blacks, whites, and soldiers. Football's popularity also flourished in town, especially a semipro team that established rivalries with nearby towns. (Both, courtesy of Rich Hively.)

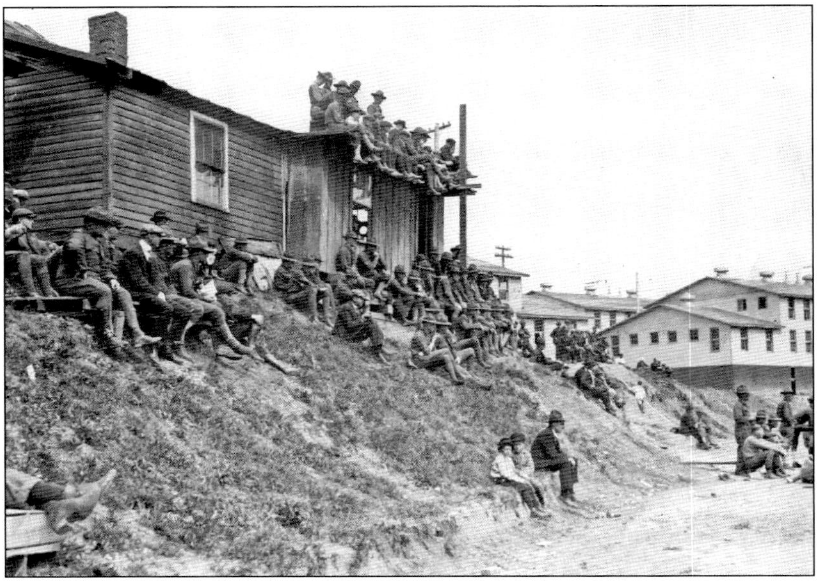

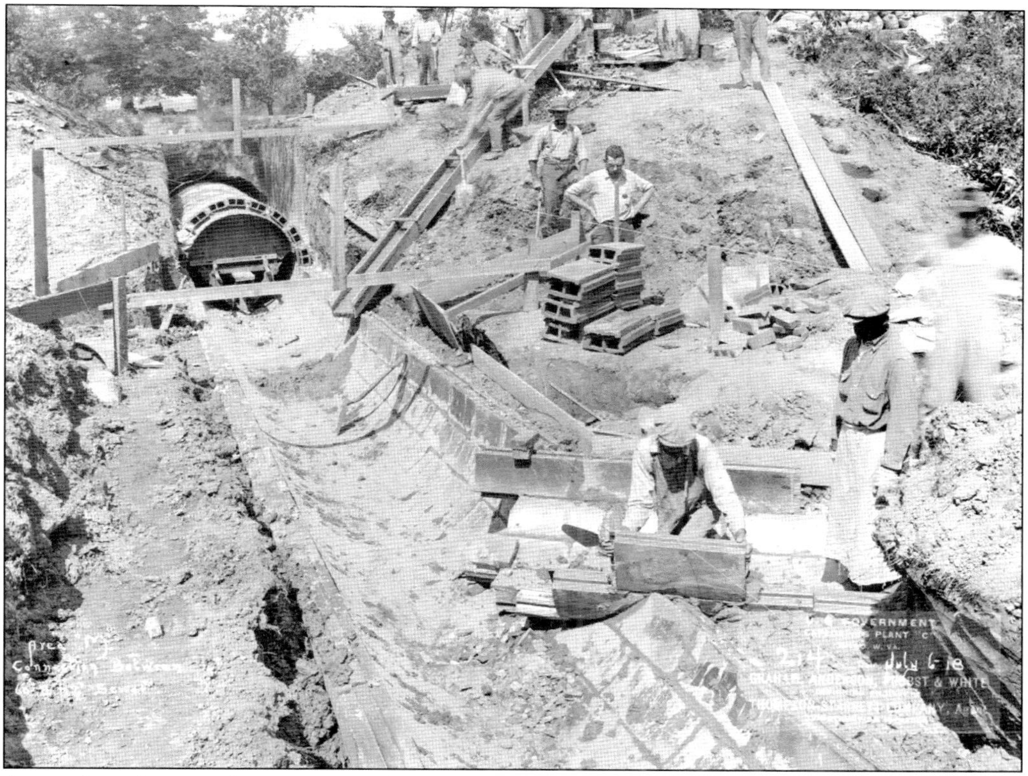

As is often the case during times of war, certain commodities and materials were rationed and restricted in use on the United States home front while the military mobilized overseas. Everyday infrastructure sometimes had to be improvised. Added to the rationing was the great speed with which Nitro was constructed, resulting in, as seen here, sewer and water pipes that were constructed out of wooden planks to conserve metal for other uses. The wooden planks used to make the segments of pipe absorbed enough moisture after installation to cause slight swelling, which pressed the pieces together to form a rather tight fit. (Both, courtesy of Rich Hively.)

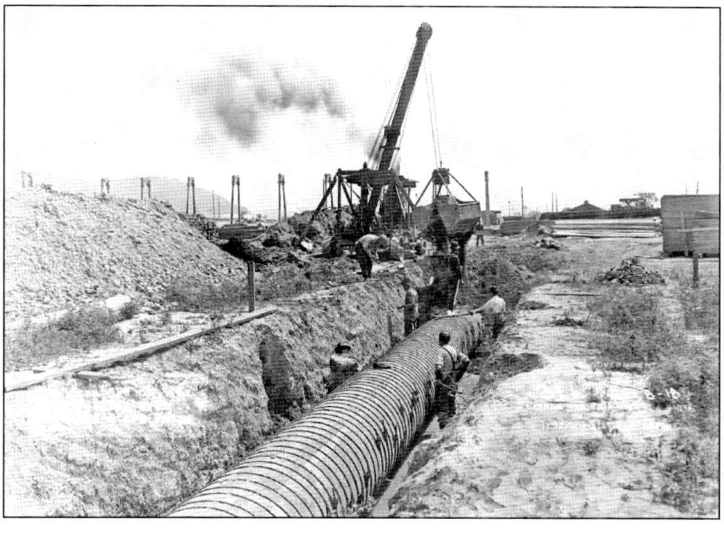

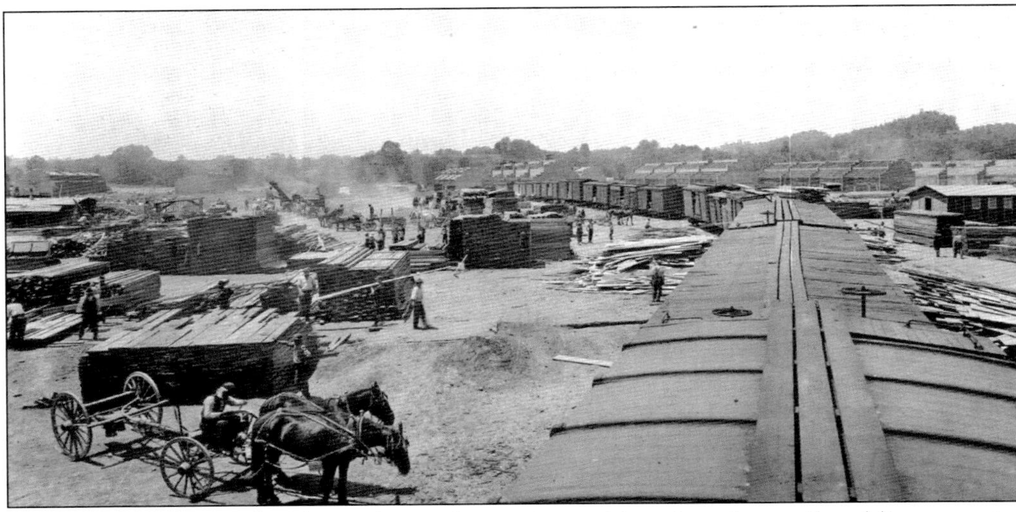

The location of Nitro had been chosen due to its good location along railroad lines running westward out of Charleston, which tied into the vast networks of the eastern seaboard as well as for the transportation afforded by riverboats and barges on the Kanawha River. Shown above is a photograph that captures the immense volume and activity of the railroad yard in Nitro during the chaotic and busy 11 months that it took to construct the city out of muddy fields. Below is one of many railroad cart lines that descended down to the Kanawha's edge where barges and boats could pick up or deliver supplies and finished products from the powder plant city. (Both, courtesy of Rich Hively.)

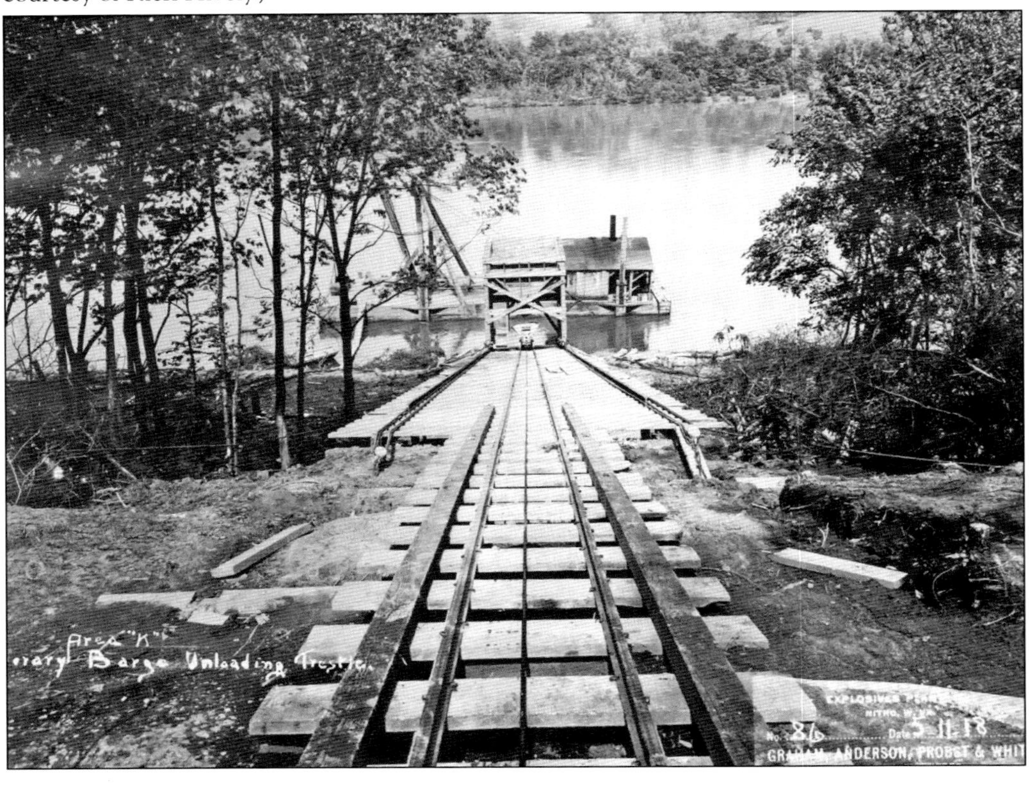

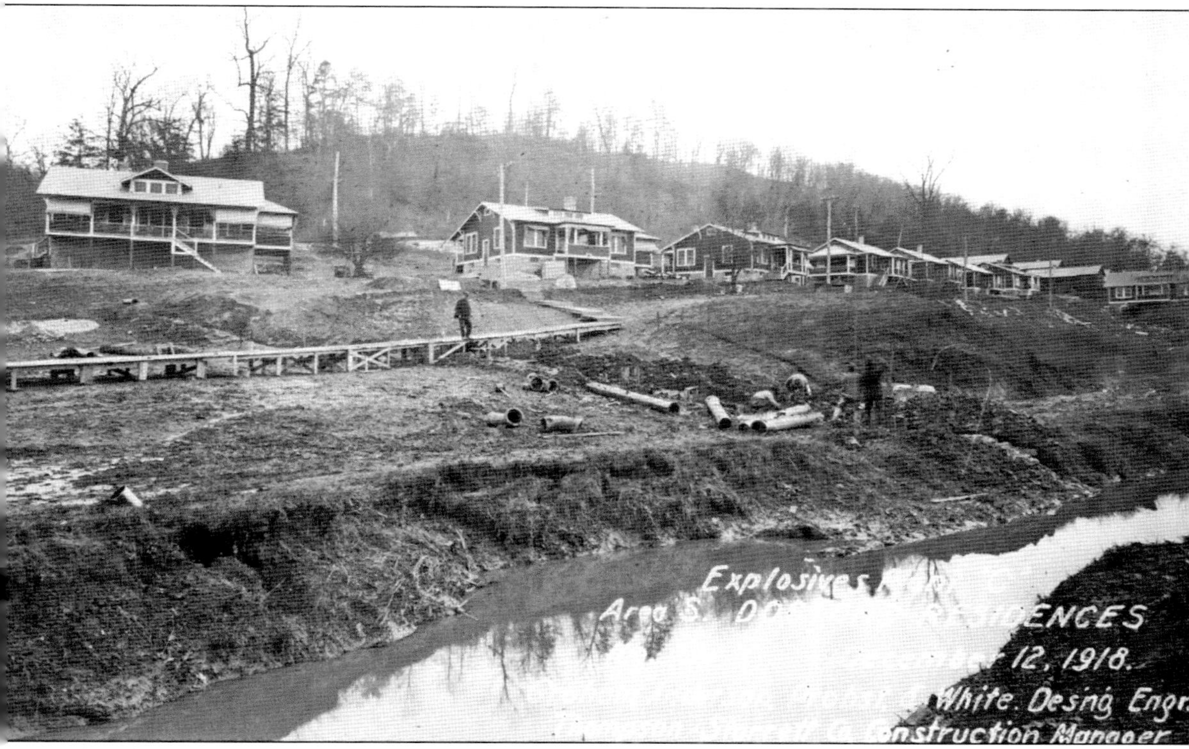

This photograph depicts a hillside bordering Blakes Creek with several medium-sized residences perched on the hill, all designated by the caption as doctors' residences, which would make sense given the location's proximity not too far from the base hospital. On the bank close to the water's edge can be seen a group of laborers working on installing a segment of the town's sanitation system of pipes. The layout of the system in Nitro had the sewage pipes run along the naturally sloping terrain of Blakes Creek and Armours Creek, after which the lines emptied directly into the water and down the Kanawha River. Original plans formulated by the military's engineers had called for sewage treatment facilities, but time restraints ended in abandonment of the ideas. William Wintz shares the quotation of officials who reassured that treatment "was not considered strictly necessary in view of the large volume of water always flowing in the Kanawha River and the consequent high dilution of the sewage." (Courtesy of Rich Hively.)

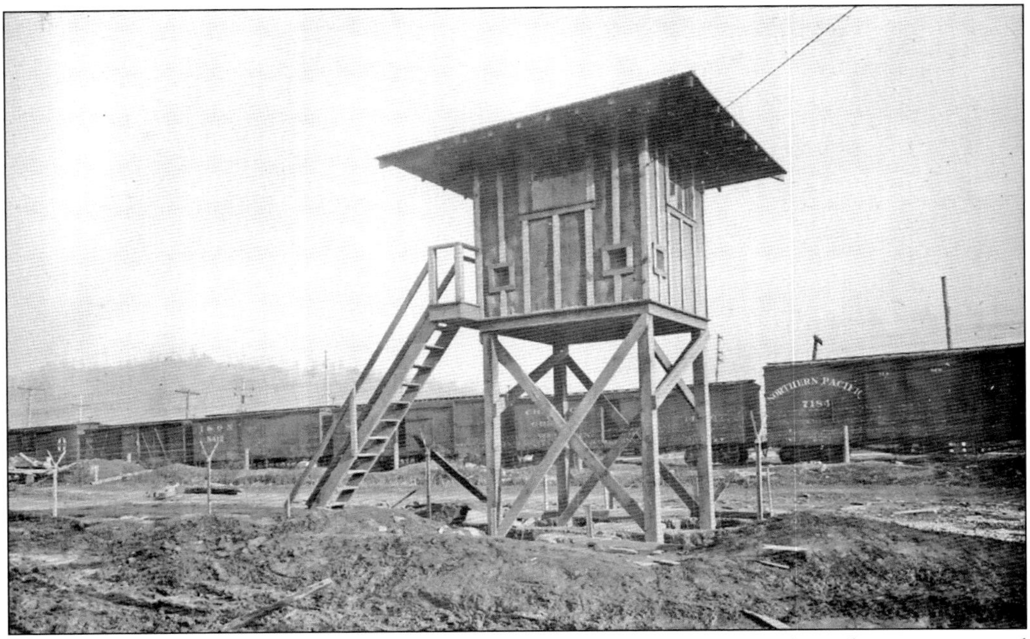

During World War I, US authorities on the home front were in constant fear of spy activity and sabotage plots, especially due to the large populations of German Americans living on the East Coast in the mid-Atlantic region. Worries over sabotage led the US military to implement various modes of security throughout the powder plant. Over 50 large wooden guard towers were placed at 1,000-foot intervals around the perimeter of the base (above). Additionally, mounted patrols, infantry guards, and secret agents kept a watchful eye on the town at all times. Below is one of two patrol boats that always operated on the Kanawha River to guard against an attack by water. The boats each had 30-caliber machine guns and searchlights. (Courtesy of Rich Hively.)

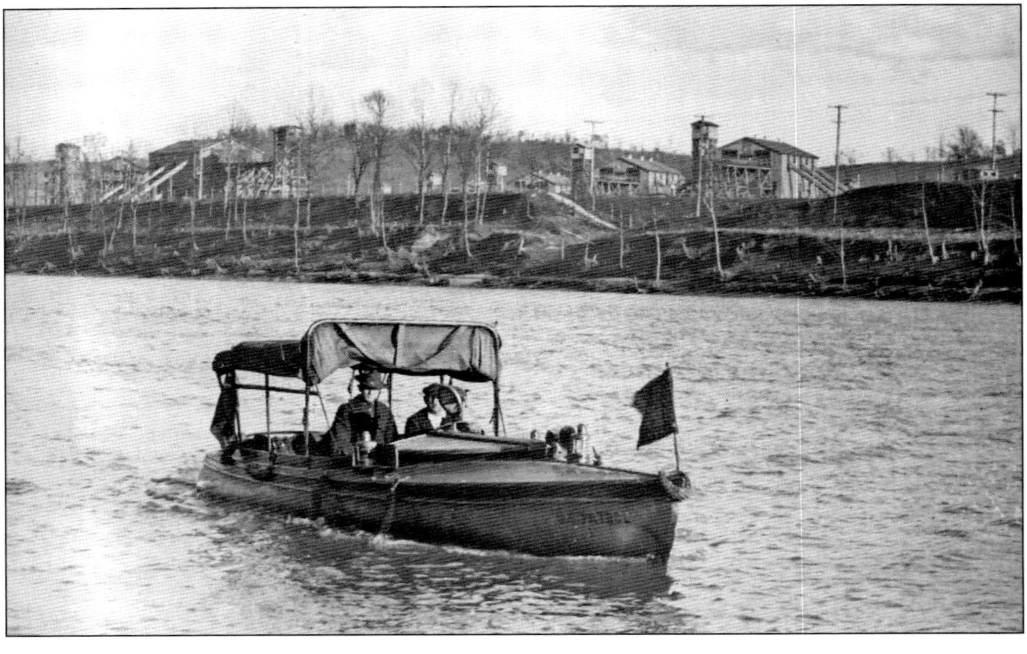

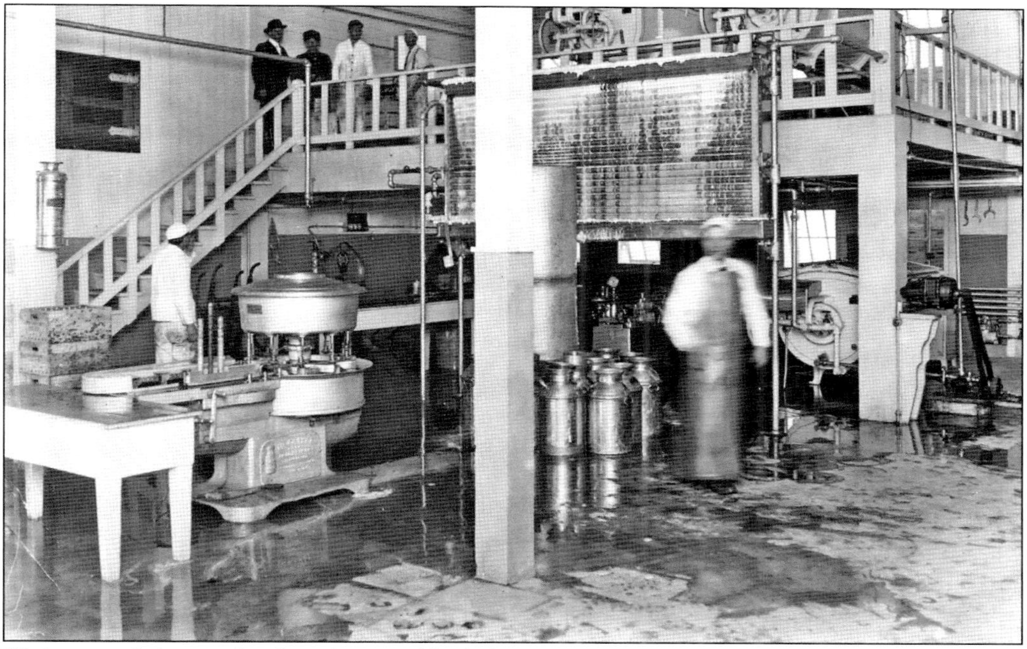

With tens of thousands of residents suddenly living in the newly created town of Nitro in 1918, demand skyrocketed for basic commodities that the already existing infrastructure simply could not support without new innovation. One example was the demand for milk. Early on in the project, the dairies around Charleston were simply unable to meet the increased demand for milk in addition to the capital city's already large demands. As a result, planners constructed the first large-scale reconstituted milk plant. Able to produce over 3,000 gallons of milk per day; the facility (the inside shown here) received powdered milk from other areas of the country by train at a fraction of the cost and space necessary for liquid whole milk. (Both, courtesy of Rich Hively.)

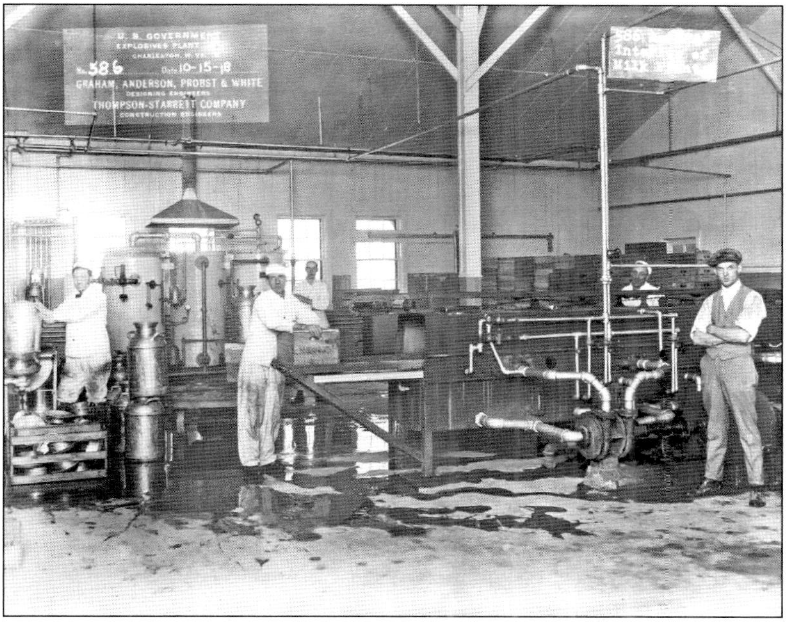

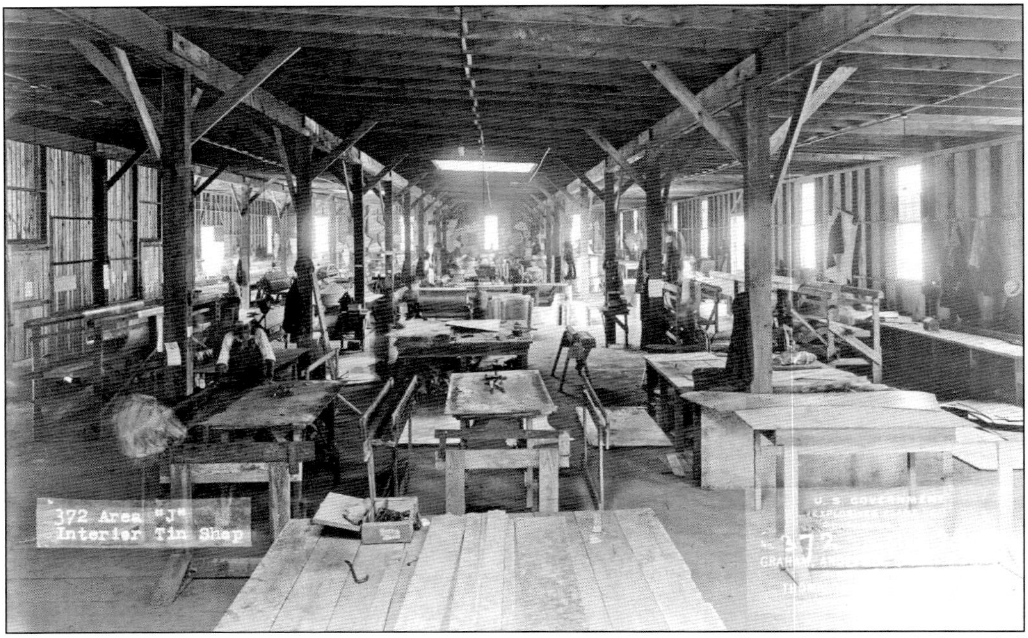

Nitro included a wide multitude of specialty workshops and factories, all of which provided needed output to help facilitate the ultimate goal of producing nitrocellulose-based explosives for the US military. Shown here are two views of the tin shop located in the industrial section of the city. The explosives produced at Nitro required a wide range of containers and packaging. Additionally, the blending towers used in the manufacture of nitrocellulose required metal parts that could be crafted on site in shops like these. Note the large skylight windows in the shop that allowed for natural light to flood the workspace. (Both, courtesy of Rich Hively.)

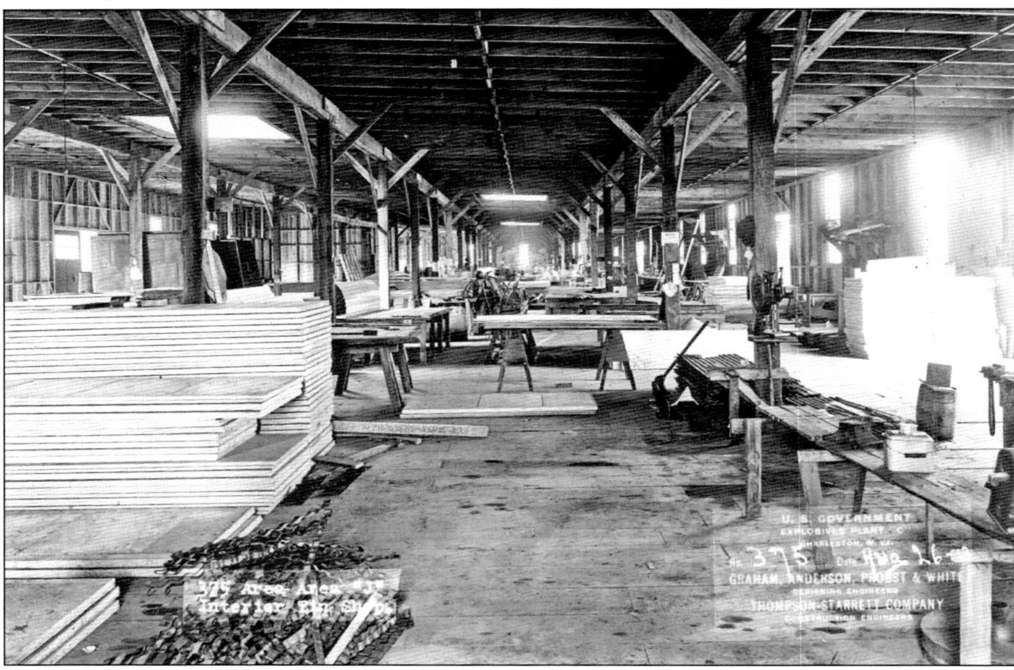

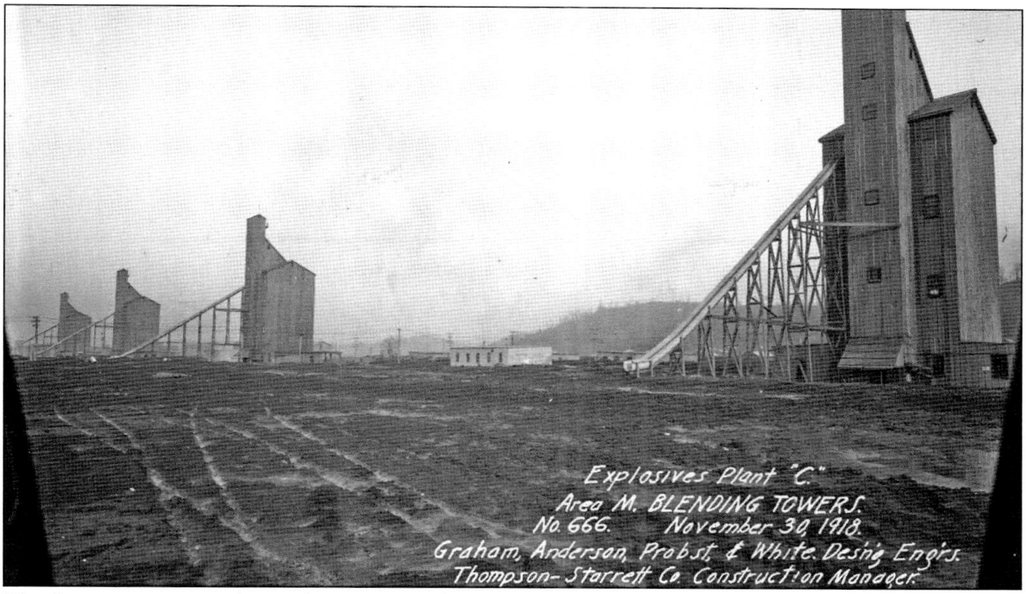

The large structures shown here were referred to simply as the blending towers. They played a crucial role in the processing of nitrocellulose powder—allowing powder batches of differing concentrations to blend together through long vertical chutes to produce variable mixes of explosives. Static electricity was always a present threat in these large towers, where any small spark could set off a massive explosion. As a result, giant sliding chutes were erected from the upper levels of the blending towers to allow workers to quickly escape during an emergency. Women were often employed in the blending towers, and a common anecdotal story says that during weekly emergency drills, nearby male laborers would gather around the chutes to watch the women, many in skirts, slide down to safety. (Both, courtesy of Rich Hively.)

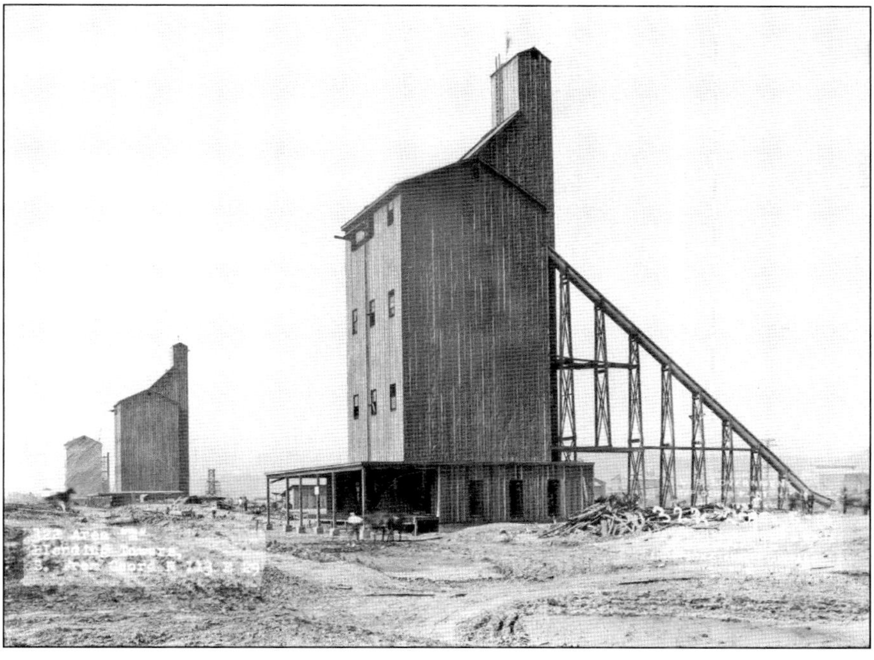

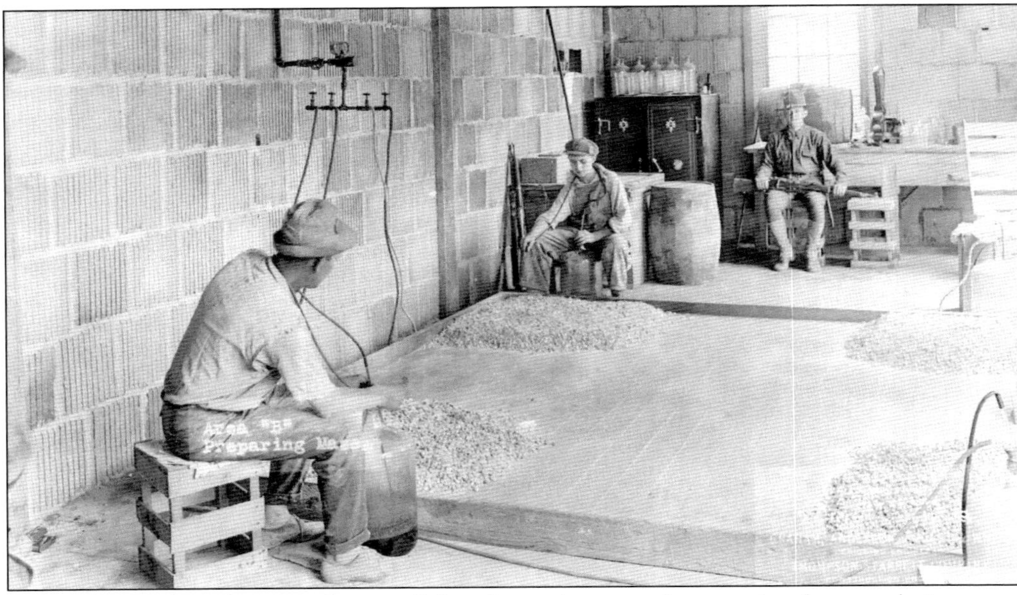

In the chemical production of nitrocellulose for explosives ordnance, the element platinum was used as a catalytic converter agent, just as it is often used today in the catalytic converter of an automobile. The element's rarity and subsequent expense meant that the supply of platinum in Nitro was kept under constant supervision to guard against theft, as seen in this photograph of Nitro workers preparing platinum for use, with an armed guard sitting in the background. (Courtesy of Rich Hively.)

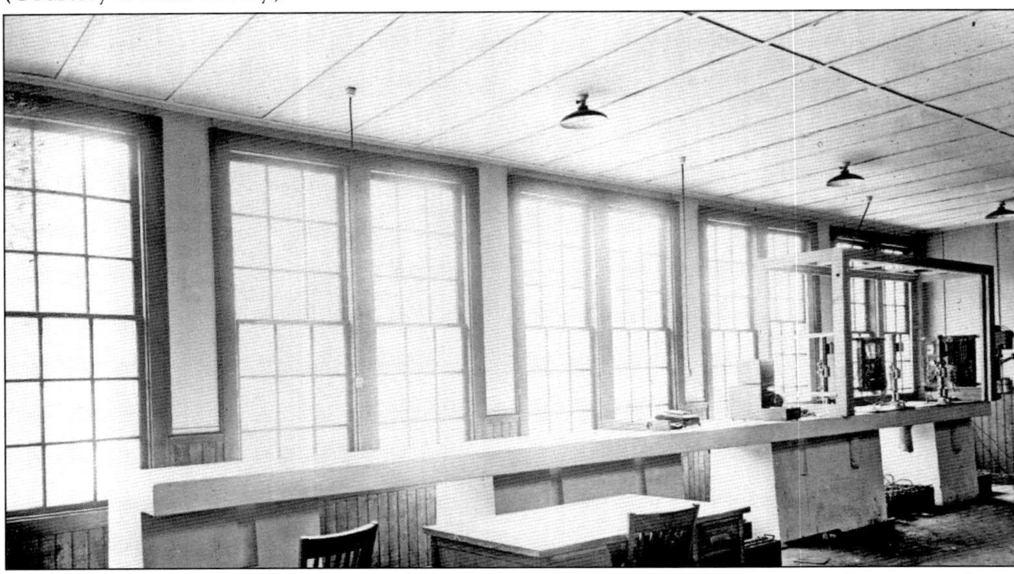

The production of nitrocellulose powder for ordnance use was an exact science that required very meticulous and exacting processes, which all ensured the uniformity and reliability of explosives powder that was shipped to the war's front lines. Photographed here is the laboratory of the rather small building known as the "chronograph house." On the lab equipment shown, workers tested the reaction velocities of burning nitrocellulose to make sure every batch that came out of the powder plant was of the same quality. (Courtesy of Rich Hively.)

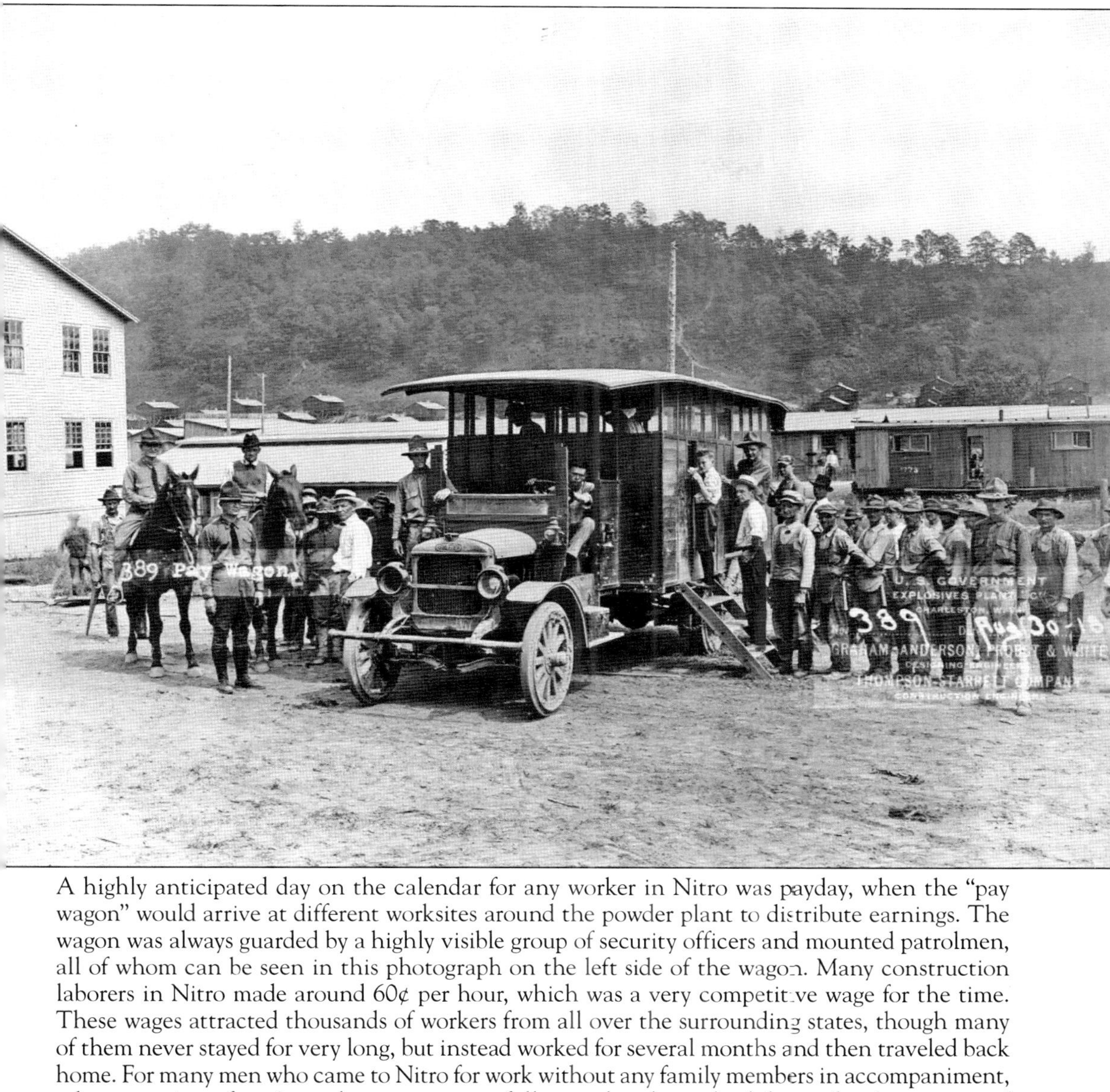

A highly anticipated day on the calendar for any worker in Nitro was payday, when the "pay wagon" would arrive at different worksites around the powder plant to distribute earnings. The wagon was always guarded by a highly visible group of security officers and mounted patrolmen, all of whom can be seen in this photograph on the left side of the wagon. Many construction laborers in Nitro made around 60¢ per hour, which was a very competitive wage for the time. These wages attracted thousands of workers from all over the surrounding states, though many of them never stayed for very long, but instead worked for several months and then traveled back home. For many men who came to Nitro for work without any family members in accompaniment, a large portion of one's total wages was carefully saved and sent back home for the support of loved ones. (Courtesy of Rich Hively.)

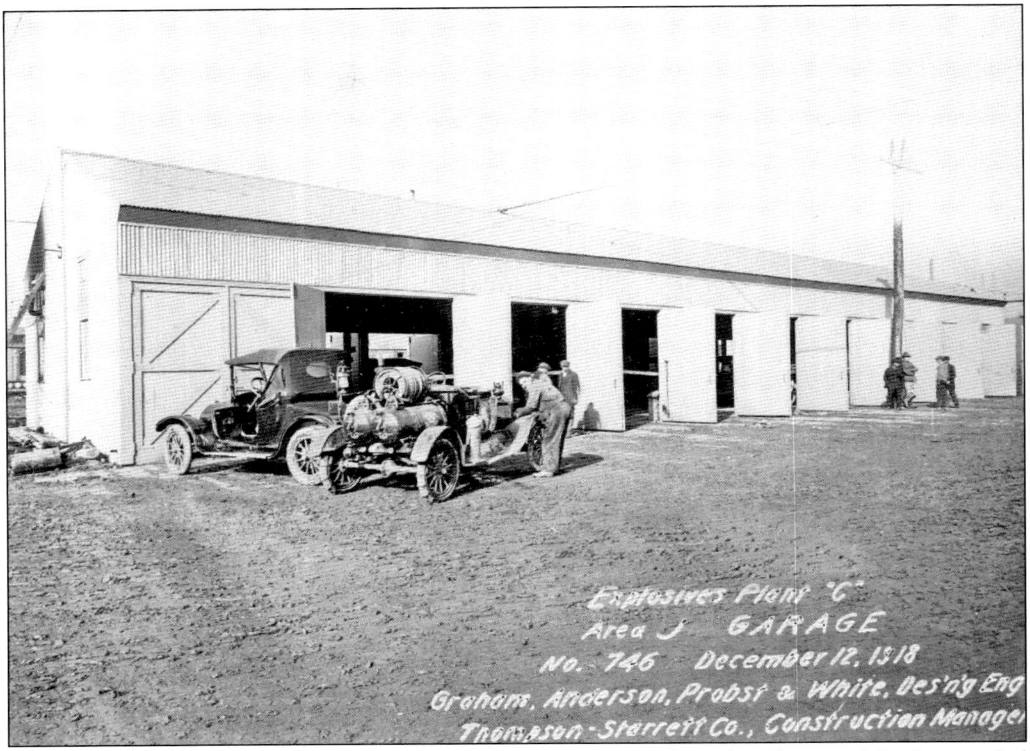

While river vessels on the Kanawha River and locomotives on the railroad network both provided valuable transportation in Nitro, the newer technology of automobiles allowed for additional means of moving supplies and finished powder in, out, and around town. Shown above is a mechanics' garage, where repairs and maintenance were carried out on factory vehicles. With railroad lines running the entire length of town, a stopped locomotive with hundreds of yards of boxcars could create a bottleneck for trucks and cars carrying equally important cargo. To remedy such an occurrence, an automobile bridge was constructed over the railroad tracks, like the one shown below. (Both, courtesy of Rich Hively.)

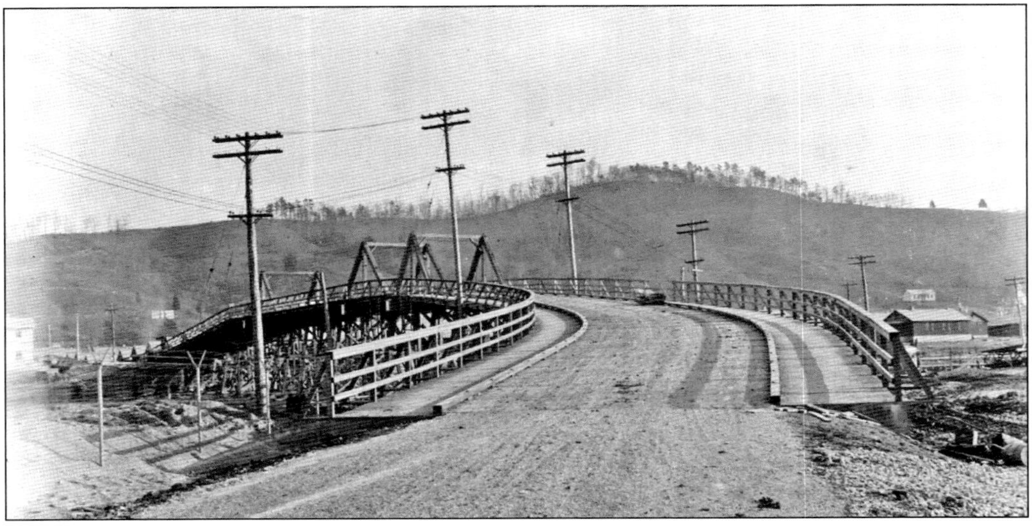

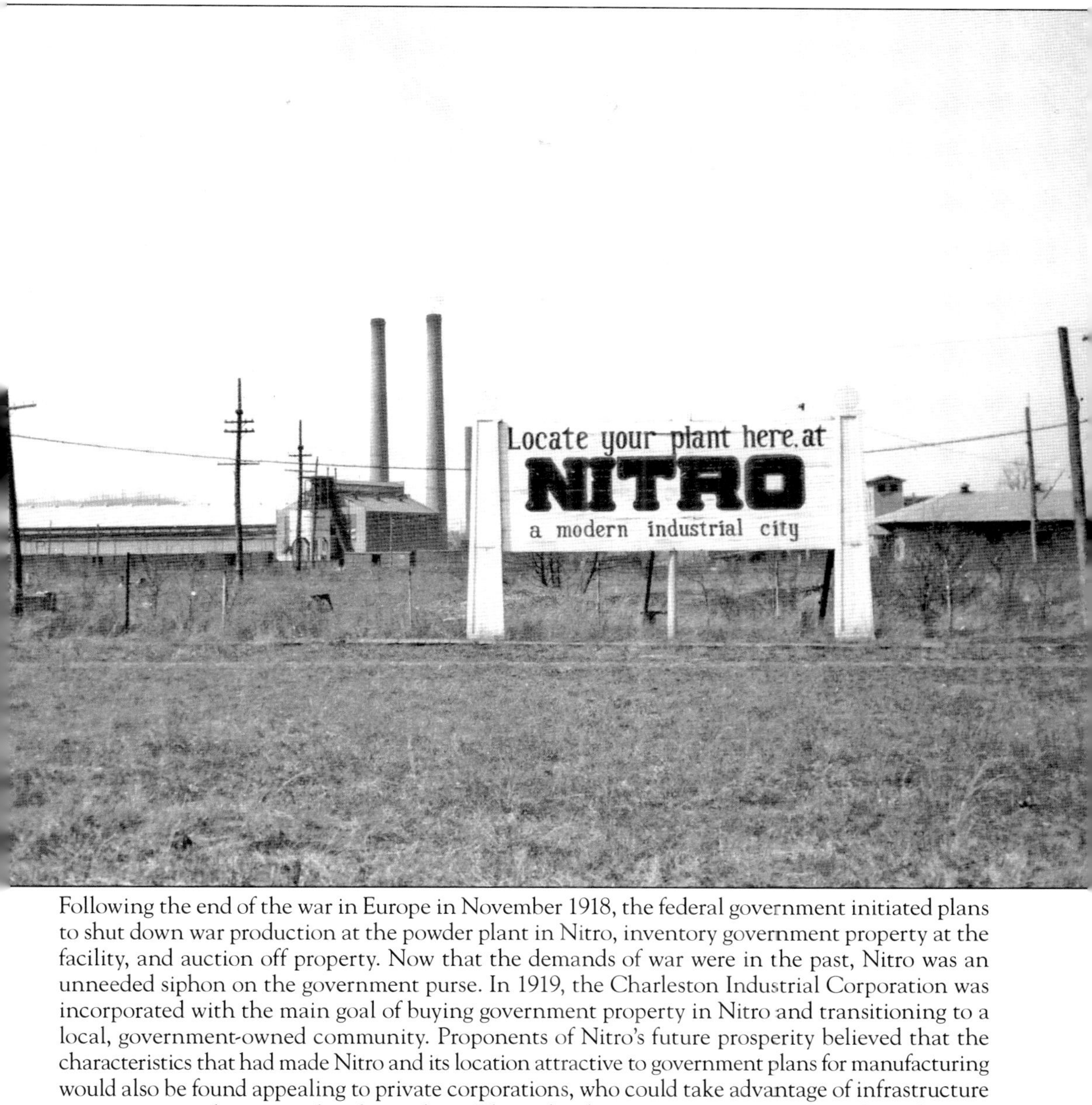

Following the end of the war in Europe in November 1918, the federal government initiated plans to shut down war production at the powder plant in Nitro, inventory government property at the facility, and auction off property. Now that the demands of war were in the past, Nitro was an unneeded siphon on the government purse. In 1919, the Charleston Industrial Corporation was incorporated with the main goal of buying government property in Nitro and transitioning to a local, government-owned community. Proponents of Nitro's future prosperity believed that the characteristics that had made Nitro and its location attractive to government plans for manufacturing would also be found appealing to private corporations, who could take advantage of infrastructure improvements that were already in place. Through advertisement campaigns, such as the sign shown here, advocates successfully brought large industrial plants to Nitro, which in the postwar years earned the region the nickname of "Chemical Valley." (Courtesy of Rich Hively.)

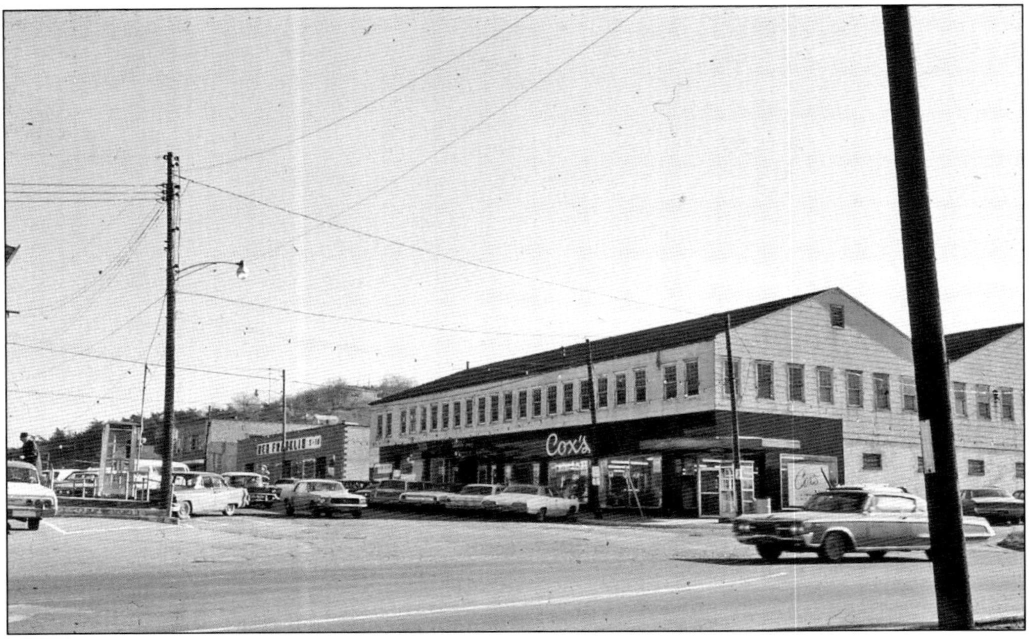

Photographed above is Cox's store on the corner of Twenty-first Street and First Avenue during the 1960s. Following the closure of the powder plant and the auctioning off of surplus property and goods in Nitro, the commissary stores and supplies were bought by A.W. Cox. Eventually, Cox consolidated several of the former commissary store locations into this one large store. The business remained in operation until the 1980s. The Ben Franklin store next to Cox's is now a Fruth Pharmacy. Shown below is the building that stood across Twenty-first Street from Cox's store and served as the town's civic center. The structure was torn down in the 1980s, and a new business was constructed at the site. (Both, courtesy of Rich Hively.)

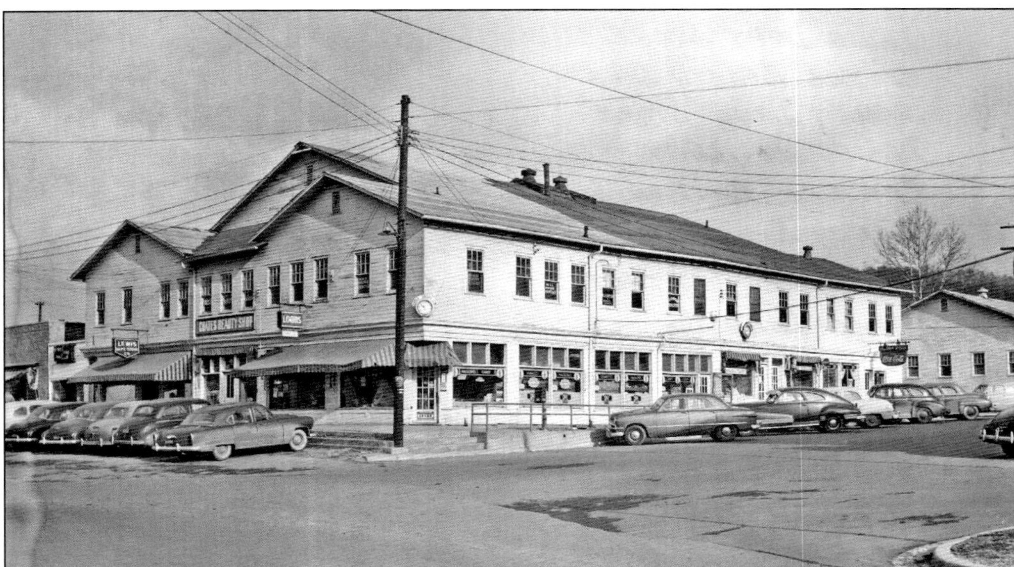

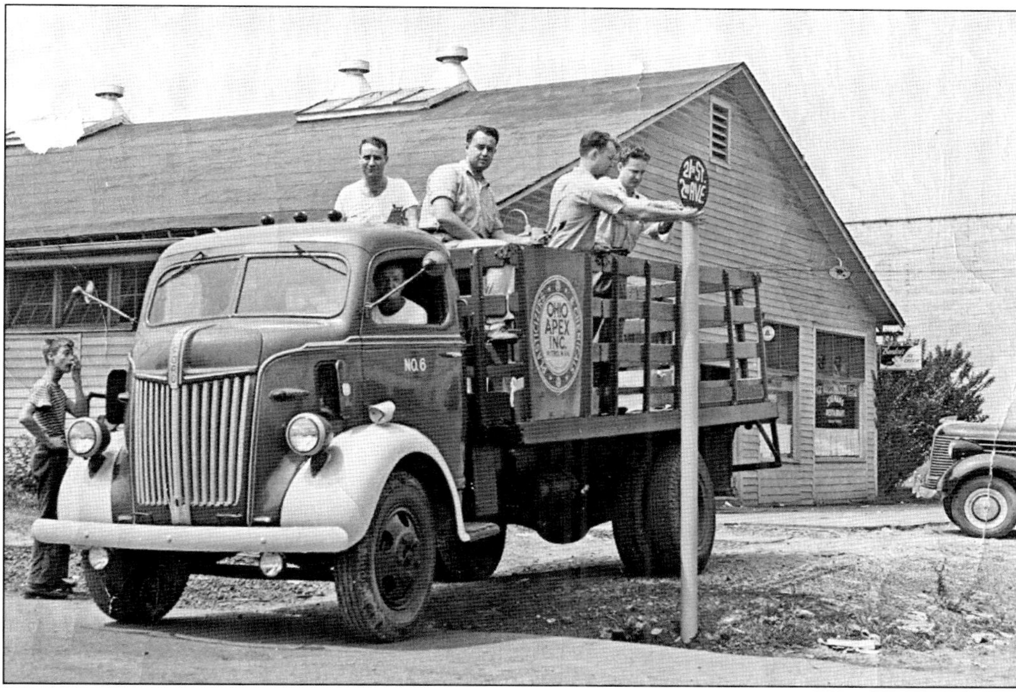

During the creation of Nitro and its operation during World War I and the next couple of decades, the streets of the town were signified with wooden or temporary signs, oftentimes affixed to the sides of buildings at the intersections of two streets. In the 1950s, the town finally got around to installing permanent, metal street signs, such as this one shown here at Twenty-first Street and Second Avenue. (Courtesy of Rich Hively.)

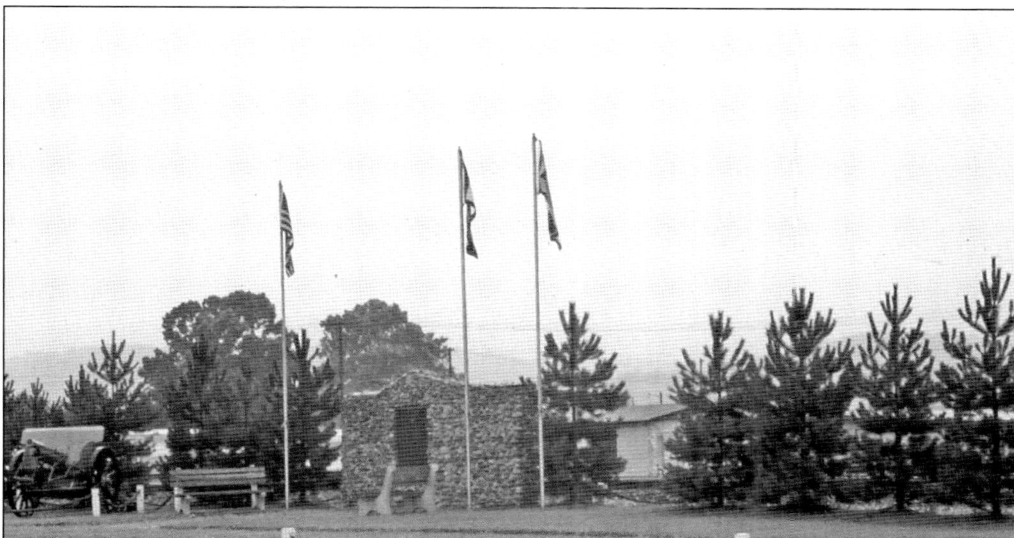

The town of Nitro and its citizens have always been proud of the community's military background—ranging from its creation as a powder plant city to the scores of residents who have gone off to fight in foreign wars. This war memorial stood on First Avenue before the bend in the street was smoothed and the memorial was removed in the late 20th century. (Courtesy of Rich Hively.)

BIBLIOGRAPHY

Charleston Gazette. Charleston, WV: 1953.
Kemp, Emory L. *The Great Kanawha Navigation*. Pittsburgh, PA: University of Pittsburgh Press, 2000.
Sutphin, Gerald. *Sternwheelers on the Great Kanawha River*. Charleston, WV: Pictorial Histories Publishing, 1991.
Upper Vandalia Historical Society, et al. *The Paradise Journals, 1884-1905, Putnam County, West Virginia*. West Virginia: Upper Vandalia Historical Society, 1981.
Wintz, William D. *History of Putnam County, West Virginia*. Charleston, WV: Pictorial Histories Publishing, 1999.
Wintz, William D. *Nitro: The World War I Boom Town*. Charleston, WV: Pictorial Histories Publishing, 1985.

About the Organization

Joseph M. Phillips writes on behalf of Rivers to Ridges Heritage Trail, a nonprofit organization founded in July 2006 through a coalition of interested regional entities and created to support projects that encourage heritage education and tourism throughout the communities of the lower Kanawha River Valley. The mission of the Rivers to Ridges Heritage Trail is to enhance and promote economic activities, through technical and financial assistance, and for the development of a tourism corridor that follows the Kanawha River from Nitro, West Virginia, to Point Pleasant, West Virginia. The intention is to preserve the physical and cultural remains of the region's unique heritage for the purpose of increasing and developing heritage tourism in Putnam and Mason County.